Pete Shelley

with Louie Shelley

the lost Buzzcocks tapes

T0332269

First published in Great Britain in 2021 by Cassell,
an imprint of Octopus Publishing Group Ltd,
Carmelite House, 50 Victoria Embankment,
London EC4Y 0DZ
www.octopusbooks.co.uk
www.octopusbooksusa.com

First published in paperback in 2024

An Hachette UK Company
www.hachette.co.uk

Distributed in the US by Hachette Book Group, 1290 Avenue of
the Americas, 4th and 5th Floors, New York, NY 10104

Distributed in Canada by Canadian Manda Group, 664
Annette St, Toronto, Ontario, Canada M6S 2C8

ISBN 978-1-78840-364-1

A CIP catalogue record for this book is available from the British Library.

Printed and bound in Great Britain.

10 9 8 7 6 5 4 3 2 1

Photos by Martin Phelps: v, xiv, 35, 51, 66, 97, 101, 107, 133, 136, 148, 166,
167, 180, 192, 233, 234, 240.

Publisher: Trevor Davies
Senior Editor: Leanne Bryan
Copyeditor: Monica Hope
Creative Director: Jonathan Christie
Designer: Jeremy Tilston
Senior Production Controller: Allison Gonsalves

This FSC® label means that materials used for
the product have been responsibly sourced

Dedicated to the memory of Pete, *lux vitae nostrae*
and all those who inhabit the Buzzcocks universe.

Extra special thanks to Malcolm Garrett, 'the fifth Buzzcock',
for graphic design concept and supervision, permission to
reproduce record sleeves, various introductions, miscellaneous
assistance and endless enthusiasm. Working with Malcolm
Garrett was a dream I didn't dare dream. This book is an *objet*
which, unlike other art, can be handled and admired closely,
without the need to stand behind a rope or don white cotton
gloves. I'm hugely grateful for Malcolm's 'vision' – it perfectly
commemorates Pete, his life and his works.

Contents

conclusion

Foreword by Henry Rollins

There are at least two great things at work with *Ever Fallen In Love*: Louie Shelley's bright idea to ask Pete Shelley hundreds of questions in a conversational interview format, do an enormous amount of research in order to lay out a timeline with carefully considered points of reference, establishing a chronologically smooth running progression of inquiry from past to present, allowing Pete to roll out a perfectly executed, highly detailed, incredibly interesting, readable story that answers so many questions a Buzzcocks fan would have about the songs they have loved for a large part of their lives. And then, of course, there's Pete, who we come to find out, had an astonishing memory. Stories from decades ago are rendered with keen exactitude as if it all happened moments before. Detail upon detail, perfectly placed, as if for decades, while writing songs and touring all over the world, he was preparing a thoroughly researched biography on someone who happened to be himself. Of course, this wasn't the case. He just happened to be an extraordinarily brilliant person with a sharp observer's eye, a natural talent for composition and melody and, as evidenced, an amazing ability to call up memories that many people would have either discarded or, more likely, simply been unable to retain.

As with any great biography, the reader is allowed to gain insight into the subject because the information is dispersed in a context-rich environment that shows why events played out as they did. Pete's descriptive narrative allows the reader not only to understand the time, and how different England is today, but also the sounds, the weary, rugged architecture and vigorous urban toughness of the Greater Manchester area. Narrow streets, black and white television, definitely not London. No doubt factors that went into the creation of Buzzcocks music.

How the band took off is an exciting story, and admirable as it was built on truly excellent songs and blazing performances that excused the band from the often grotesque contortions musicians are coerced into perpetrating in order to elicit sales, not that Buzzcocks would have engaged in these mundanities anyway. That the band had a steadfast value-for-money ethos when it came to their music being in the marketplace makes you see that it was only about the art and the work. Even after decades of great popularity, Shelley and Diggle still related to their fans as decent guys from a rough patch of a country that had seen quite a bit over the centuries.

Learning how the songs came to be is fascinating. Pete's utilitarian approach of not overthinking anything and getting the recording process done quickly, not to mention cost effectively, with such incredible results is, as we come to learn, his *modus operandi* in a nutshell. You can hear it in live recordings with the often casual way he counted in songs. The under promise of the almost bored 'One, two, three, four' and the resulting over delivery of the song, which hits the punter like a truck. It's almost funny.

Reading about these songs that we know from back to front, it's as if we fans had been unwittingly preparing for *Ever Fallen In Love* from the first moment we heard Buzzcocks music and knew, without a doubt, that we would be listening to the songs for the rest of our lives. Pete's ability to put names to dates to locations to everything else is incredible and allows so many dots to be connected. It's as if all the songs were one single uninterrupted exhalation.

The sheer amount of possibility Buzzcocks existed in during those years has no comparison in the present day. As an example, for several dates in October and November 1979, Buzzcocks had an opening band on the road with them. They were called Joy Division. Imagine that double bill. It doesn't seem possible.

Buzzcocks' United Artists period is one of the most memorable, multi-year floods of uncanny song-after-song greatness in the history of modern music. The band, along with Martin Rushent, who some might consider a fifth Buzzcock, released, seemingly without much trouble, music that didn't sound like anything happening at the time. Thanks to the vision of graphic artist Malcolm Garrett, the jackets, sleeves and adverts surrounding Buzzcocks music all had an exquisite, understated sophistication that allowed the music to do the talking. Coming back to the idea of context, the fact that Malcolm Garrett is interviewed for this book is so important. He was a Buzzcocks interpreter. The fact that Buzzcocks records had a 'look' without a doubt affected the listener's experience. This was the great talent of Malcolm Garrett. He found the right band to work with and Buzzcocks were fortunate to have him as a resource and liaison to the fan, as well as the label.

Not to overstate this but it's a fact that, without Louie Shelley's initial idea to steadily extract information from Pete, we would not have this book. Also, Louie's vast amount of meticulous research and dedication made what could have easily been a good book into a truly marvellous piece of work. Like all good interrogators and well-prepared biographers, it's obvious she knew many of the answers to the questions she was asking. *Ever Fallen In Love* is more than a biography; it is a fantastic collaborative effort. To read Pete so matter-of-factly respond seemingly instantaneously to every question Louie throws at him with such rich detail is to realise what a complete loss it would have been had his great mind not been so ably tapped. Oh, and something else that cannot go unmentioned, although you will no doubt pick up on it immediately: Pete had an incredible grip on the English language. He composes his thoughts beautifully. His humility and low-key humour are the through lines that make this book such a joy to read.

Just a fan's thoughts here but it is fascinating that Buzzcocks recorded with Martin Hannett, aka Martin Zero, to make *Spiral Scratch* before signing to United Artists and, at the very end of their UA period, reunited with him for some more recordings, all of which are really, really good. If you're a Buzzcocks fan, this book is a must. If you're not yet initiated, you probably will be within a few pages. Take it away, Pete...indeed.

Henry Rollins

Foreword by Kid Strange

It's extremely difficult for me to write about living with Pete. In my early days of getting to know him, of course, I knew Pete like everyone else had known Pete – through his music. In our shared later years, though, it was just Pete, my husband. A rather private affair.

This book is written by a very close friend of ours, who had both the pleasure and the sense to ask Pete these very important questions. Funnily enough, I never really talked that much about Pete's work; it would be brought up very seldom. I suppose someone like me should know all these things, especially since I did a few Buzzcocks tours as well!

I wish to extend my gratitude and thanks to Lou for not only asking the questions, but also taking the time to write this book about a particular period of Pete's career. It is a fitting tribute to someone so beloved and cherished, not just by me, his family, and friends, but by millions of fans worldwide too.

I think a common mistake many people made with Pete was in assuming he was a big, avid fan of music, of all music, because he wrote and created music. The reality is, quite shockingly, the opposite. Pete, as he always professed to me, wrote music 'for myself and people like me'. He always rejected the notion of liking music, or even the idea of being branded as 'punk' all the time. I suppose when you have a big industry such as music, there are bound to be a lot of fillers; something disposable.

But, truthfully, Pete and I always enjoyed a lot more pop songs at home than your typical punk or rock music. We were the kind of people who would gleefully sing Kylie Minogue's 'I Should Be So Lucky' to each other[1], he didn't mind my joyful excitement when I found Sylvester's 'You Make Me Feel' on vinyl, and put up with me singing Cher around the house. He even insisted that we watch Eurovision every year, something I never cared for but now I have to watch[2]. I suppose my fondest memories are of when he would sing me a very old-fashioned song from the Fifties or Sixties – of his childhood. Something I'd never heard of that would either be by a singer or from a movie that was popular at the time. I will always laugh if I hear Pat Boone's 'Johnny'. That no good Johnny[3]!

Pete made me realize that when you do something creatively, the number one rule is always to make sure you are doing it for yourself and never for someone else. There will be absolutely no pleasure or joy in doing something for someone else.

There were plenty of times when I asked about writing music – whether the lyrics came first or the instrumental parts. For Pete, certainly in his later years, it was more instrumental. Even on the last Buzzcocks album, *The Way*, I remember Pete having some trouble writing up lyrics for 'Virtually Real'. I am happy to say I helped out with the line, 'LolCats, confessions of Shiba'. The problem was that by this time a lot of the things he'd previously written about (mainly hardships in love) weren't things he was experiencing any more. Even when the opportunity came up again to write a 'classic' new Buzzcocks album, I was adamant that it would be hard on him as he was no longer going through the same heartache. We were both quite settled with each other. I should be so lucky/Lucky, lucky, lucky[4]!

Yes, the occasional joke did occur. I would threaten to have an affair, and then he would do something deliberately senile that made me not only laugh hysterically but also reject the idea because he 'clearly needed me more'. Or he'd jokingly threaten to have an affair to experience the emotions he needed to write about heartbreak, and I'd point out, 'But then I am the one who's hurt! How is that going to help?'

'I'll write it from your perspective...'

Eventually, he decided to scrap the idea of a new Buzzcocks album.

Sometimes, in the early days in our relationship, he would tell me how theme songs for TV shows reflected the title of the show, and would show me examples by singing the title throughout the instrumental theme songs – *Emmerdale* being one example. This was just a bit of fun, but it highlights Pete's inherent ability as a songwriter and his instinctive compulsion to formulate lyrics for even the most unlikely music.

There were many moments showing Pete's brilliance when it came to writing music. Being musically creative and talented came so naturally to him, it was something amazing to behold. It was always awe-inspiring to see his brilliance at work. Even learning a new instrument came naturally and easily to him. He just knew how everything worked, what notes were what; his brain could figure it out in seconds – especially if the instrument was something as basic as a rubber band over a tin box[5].

I could honestly go on and on about Pete and his absolute genius; I could tell you the stories he told me about being on tour over so many years. It is a bit strange when I think that at home, Pete was such a quiet, low-key, very private person, but when it came to his career, he was bigger than life itself.

I hope that you enjoy reading this book, and that it gives you some insight into my husband and what he was like during a specific period in his creativity. I hope this brings you joy and comfort in some way, as it brings me. I miss my husband so much; I miss all the joy that we shared together, and I am happy that people can share those joyful moments with me too.

Kid Strange
Widower to Pete Shelley

Notes

1   If you must know, Pete's favourite Kylie song was 'Wouldn't Change a Thing' from her second album, *Enjoy Yourself* (1989). We sang 'I Should Be So Lucky' because we were (obviously) lucky in love.

2   I always root for the stupid songs; I'm never serious.

3   I am reminded of Andy Stewart's 'Donald Where's Your Troosers?' too. Pete would sing this to me, copying his father's impression of bagpipes. Pete's father, John, was from Glasgow.

4   'I Should Be So Lucky' by Kylie Minogue, written by Stock Aitken Waterman (SAW).

5   Yes, really! He played me a well-tuned rubber band!

Preface

The seed for my love affair with Buzzcocks was planted with 'Harmony in My Head', in the summer that I left junior school.

I'd been aware of 'Ever Fallen in Love' – my mother and I had sat and watched it on *Top of the Pops* on Thursday evenings the previous autumn – but I was at an age where I was pretty contemptuous of love songs and everything that being in love entailed, so to some extent it passed me by. Steve Diggle's song, though, about fast-paced city living, with its 'clattering shoppers' and lines of buses, spoke to me in a way that love songs hadn't. It described sights and sounds with which I was enthralled, all delivered in Steve's cigarette-stained growl – which showcased his nasal northern-ness and was very different to the southern whine that was prevalent in punk – and accompanied by the buzz-saw guitars that my ears were quickly becoming attuned to. For me at that time it was the perfect song, and it kick-started both my interest in music and a lifelong devotion to Buzzcocks.

I collected anything about the band that I could get my hands on – although admittedly that was not a lot at that time, with a pre-teen's opportunities and early-Eighties pocket money. I devoured anything about the band that I could find to read. A particular treasure was a cache of *NME*s and *Melody Maker*s from 1977 to 1979 that I bought at a jumble sale, all of them packed with interviews with both Pete and Steve. I lived for their music; I drooled over their hard-candy-coloured record sleeves; I virtually inhaled their printed image. It was like I'd found God.

I was a teenage girl but I wasn't romantically interested in the band. I wanted to be their mate. I wanted to write songs with them. I wanted to be in the band. I wanted to be *them*.

At the time we lived across the road from M J of punk band The Drones (another member of the band lived next-door-but-one to him). We used to see him carrying musical equipment in and out of the house, dressed in black from head to toe – a tall, slender guy, he was the epitome of cool. I asked my mother whether she thought our neighbours across the road could in fact be two of the Buzzcocks. She said no, she didn't think that rock 'n' roll royalty would choose the dingy backwater that we inhabited as their abode. It was only five miles from Manchester, yet managed to combine the worst aspects of urban oikdom with the nasty cliquishness and nosy neighbours of a village; it was like the crossroads where *Coronation Street* meets *Deliverance*. My mother thought that the Buzzcocks would be living it up in Swinging London – though of course I now know that Pete Shelley was living in a similarly uninspiring hinterland to ours, only a few miles away in Gorton, to the east of the city; the band hadn't yet succumbed to the lure of the Smoke. When we found out who our neighbours were I was mildly disappointed that they weren't my idols but was comforted by the knowledge that they were part of our city's punk milieu – they probably *knew* Buzzcocks and may even have played on the same stage as them, and that was good enough for me.

I was devastated, then, when Buzzcocks split when I was 13. I was too young to go to gigs so I'd never seen them play live – and now I never would. I felt a sense of loss, almost of mourning, that my dreams of hanging out with the band – or at the very least of seeing one of their shows – would never be realized.

Fast forward to 1989. Buzzcocks have re-formed and I go to see them at the Manchester Apollo. I am no longer into punk at this time: I've become allergic to anything with guitars in it since taking my first E earlier in the summer (coincidentally, my first E experience was in a repurposed cinema in north Manchester that had in the late Seventies served briefly as Factory 2, an outpost of Tony Wilson's Factory club). I go to the show just for old times' sake – like meeting up with an old flame for a final, farewell fuck – but I don't wholly enjoy it. I just can't wait to get the bus into town so my clubbing buddy and I can go to our favourite haunt and take Es. The poignancy of the reunion is wasted on me. I devote the next three years to clubbing and drugging with a vengeance and waste the next seven years after that even more pointlessly on a career doing something I really don't want to do.

Fast forward again to 1999. I've just endured a difficult split with my partner of seven years and I need something to take my mind off it. I go with another friend to see Buzzcocks play at Manchester University. An acquaintance of my friend says that if we hang around after the show he can 'get us in to see the band'. My interest is piqued but I'm not entirely optimistic – it seems too good to be true, and I know how unhelpful the security staff at the university can be. We queue up with some other hopefuls outside the dressing room for what seems rather a long time. I'm close to giving up the ghost when the door to the inner sanctum is suddenly opened and we're welcomed in.

The band are friendly and hospitable. They offer champagne and food (although, somewhat bizarrely, their post-show buffet seems to consist mostly of raw onions). I notice Pete but am too in awe to go and speak to him. Instead Steve sits me down on a couch next to him and then we're chatting like old friends. It feels as though I've finally come home.

The band go and play some dates in the States, and by the time I next see them – only weeks after first meeting them – I've reinvented myself as a journalist. As I've started going out several times a week to get over my broken relationship I decide to write reviews, of both live shows and club nights; I've fallen back in love with guitar music but am two-timing it with clubbing. Buzzcocks are touring with their new album, *Modern*. I call their record company and ask if I can interview them when they next play in my area. The very amenable girl in the label's PR department gives me the phone number of the promoter who is putting on the shows in my region – Alan Wise, a larger-than-life character from Manchester's punk and Factory Records scene of the Seventies.

I call Alan and he very cordially invites me to accompany him to the five shows that he's putting on in the Northwest of England. I travel with him in his car to the first gig, in Liverpool, and when we get to the venue I find myself working as his unpaid runner – he seems pleased to have an enthusiastic young woman working for him for free. He sends me to Lidl to buy the alcohol for the band's rider and the food for their buffet (which this time consists of white finger rolls – no butter – and a block of cheap Cheddar with nothing but a plastic knife to cut it with). And he sends me into the dressing room to get the titles of the songs so he can print out the setlist. I'm mortified. I suppose I'm there in a professional capacity, but I'm painfully shy and also concerned that the band will recognize me as the avid fan from a few weeks back and worry that I've successfully managed to stalk them. And yet they don't appear to think anything of the sort; they're friendly and open – and I reward this good-natured approach by being tongue-tied and flustered.

I accompany Alan Wise to those five shows and have the time of my life. My career as a journalist commentating on Manchester's creative scene takes off and within a few short months I'm writing for a number of regional and national titles. I have a ball – out every night, sometimes going to three events in one evening, while also running a business. Something has to give, though, and that 'something' is my physical and mental health. I become severely ill with ME. I'm too sick to work, my personal life falls down around my ears and I 'don't know what to do with my life'. I limp through the next few years like a tragic Victorian heroine before a change has to be made.

I end up living in Spain, in a vain attempt to improve my health. Years pass, then in December 2004, feeling nostalgic for the soundtrack of my youth and my more recent escapades as a journalist, I travel to the UK to see three Buzzcocks shows. It is five years since I first met the band, and I haven't seen them in all that time, yet when I bump into Pete backstage he beams as he says, 'Oh, it's you!' He hasn't forgotten who I am, which I find disquieting as well as comforting. Steve is just as welcoming as he was the first time I met him and I strike up an easy conversation with bassist Tony Barber too. I am welcomed back into the fold and – just briefly – it's like old times.

Back in my rented apartment on southern Spain's Costa del Sol on Christmas morning I wake with a start from a vivid dream. I had dreamed of the band and their music, and my dream ended with Steve performing the spoken ad-lib from the end of 'Mad Mad Judy' in its entirety: 'There were these three fellas and one says to the other. So I said to them, I said – I told them straight. I made me point. Do you understand now? I understand. *I've got all the answers.*' Alone in my 'half-empty bed' on Christmas morning I see this as a sign – a call to go back to the UK to do the one thing that's made me happiest in recent years. I decide to follow the band as they tour – perhaps they *have* got all the answers. It turns out to be the best decision I'll ever make.

A number of exciting years with the band ensues. I drive all over England to see them with my gigging buddy, Elsa. I make myself costumes – fabric-painting the band's lyrics on to a nurse's tunic, among other things. I make a 'What Do I Get?' shirt for Pete, similar to the ones that the band wore in the Seventies. The floodgates are opened and I then can't stop painting. My health is still an issue, but these Buzzcocks-inspired art projects are something I can offload my nervous energy into along with my passion for and obsession with the band. It feels good to be able to give something back and I'm thrilled whenever I see Pete onstage or on TV wearing my creations.

Eventually I find myself managing the band's merchandise, travelling with them to all of their shows around the UK. It's the realization of my teenage dream, touring with them in the 'bus' (a less-than-glamorous converted Transit van), sharing meals, chatting easily with them, seeing the show night after night. How my 12-year-old self would have envied me...

And that's how I came to write this book – as a fan of the band. I suggested to Pete that we conduct a series of interviews about Buzzcocks' early years, his exploits in the beating heart of the punk scene and the whirlwind adventure of becoming a world-renowned musician and writer of some of the most memorable, iconic songs of the punk era – as well as getting under the skin of his creative process, the stories and meanings behind those famous songs. I was thrilled when he agreed.

We recorded everything during web chats, with me sitting up in bed while Pete talked from his home in Estonia. The interviews were really just conversations. I asked the questions that any fan would like to ask and Pete responded with anecdotes that any fan would like to hear – how the band got together; the inspiration for the songs; where they played gigs; the minutiae of recording and rehearsals and anecdotes about life on the road – all delivered with Pete's characteristic wit, warmth, razor-sharp memory and occasional lubricious aside. To me, that's the real beauty of these interviews – that some of the easiness and intimacy of our friendly conversations shines through. This book is a chance for a music icon to tell his Buzzcocks story, in his own words. But behind the anecdotes, in his humour and his openness, there's also a snapshot of the real Pete that I, his family and close friends knew.

It had been my intention to quiz Pete about his solo career and Buzzcocks' later exploits too; but time ran out on us, as it so often does. Pete passed away on 6 December 2018. In the world of rock 'n' roll, life can be all too short – and 'After all,' as Pete sings, 'life's only death's recompense.'

The band are extraordinarily good to their fans. I suspect for some devotees they take the place of family – and for some the idolization of the band is perhaps even a substitute for traditional spiritual beliefs. Pete had been a fan himself so, although modest, he understood the way people felt about him. He was always kind, patient, gracious and generous – something that comes across in abundance in the conversations that follow. He gave of himself, and for his fans this was the greatest gift.

After Pete's passing, our interviews sat unused for some time. At first the emotions and memories they evoked were too painful to uncover in too much detail. But, as time has passed, I have come to see the true value that they hold. Pete never wrote his memoirs, never committed his story to the page, and so the story that he tells in our recordings – not just the story of Buzzcocks, but also his own memories, his inspirations, and the emotions he drew upon to write the songs that are so loved by so many – offers a chance for people to hear him tell things his way, at least in part. And so, with the blessing of Pete's widower, this book allows Pete to speak with his fans.

To preface the interviews, which pick up the story when the band signed their first record deal with United Artists, I wanted to offer a more complete view of both Pete's and the band's early years. By speaking with his family, bandmates, friends and contemporaries, I have pieced together what I hope is a fascinating backstory, for those who don't know it, as well as a way of better understanding both the man himself and the place in which he grew up.

In particular, I feel that my familiarity with and love for Manchester have perhaps helped me to understand the band in a way that a writer from another town couldn't. Like Joy Division, Buzzcocks developed as a product of their environment: the gritty, grimy wasteland that was post-industrial Manchester, before it became aware of its own charm and reinvented itself as a city-break destination and site of musical pilgrimage.

And now, in a peculiar twist of fate, I find myself living in the town next to Leigh, where Pete grew up. These days Leigh town centre consists mostly of pound stores, charity shops and pawnbrokers; it has none of the record or music shops that it boasted when Pete was young. But I think of Pete every time I go shopping there and I am comforted to know that I'm close to the place where he wrote some of those timeless songs.

Louie Shelley

introduction

Reality's a Dream: The Buzzcocks Story

Britain, third week of April, 1955. It's not quite ten years since the end of the Second World War. Meat rationing ended only last year, in 1954, and cheese is still scarce. Petrol will be rationed in the next year because of the Suez Crisis. Despite this austerity, the gramophone-record industry is flourishing and, in 1952, a UK Singles Chart was devised to track the sales and thus the popularity of newly released discs. Britain is still using the old, pre-decimalization currency at this time, with 12 pennies to a shilling, which is likely why the nation is still thinking in dozens rather than tens – for a Top 12 is compiled by the *New Musical Express* (the *NME*) from information gathered in phone calls to around 20 stores, very probably all based in London. These 'charts' are seen as being a valuable marketing tool and soon several competing publications, including *Melody Maker* and *Record Mirror*, start publishing their own.

It's common in the Fifties for American artists to occupy as many as half or more of the slots in the UK charts, and so it is no surprise that the No. 1 spot in the week beginning 15 April 1955 is 'Give Me Your Word', sung by Tennessee Ernie Ford, an American TV and radio personality and devotee of country and western and gospel music.

The liveliest song in the UK charts this week is 'Mambo Rock' by Bill Haley and His Comets, who already had a hit last year with 'Rock Around the Clock'. Although it will soon be eclipsed by rock 'n' roll, in 1955 skiffle is the predominant teen 'craze' in the UK. Lonnie Donegan's 'Rock Island Line', a pacy rendition of an American folk song accompanied by homemade instruments such as washboard and tea-chest bass, reaches No. 8 and is certified gold (unusual for a debut single). It will be skiffle, and not rock 'n' roll, that inspires the young John Lennon to form his first band, The Quarrymen – which, after a fateful meeting with Paul McCartney at a church fête in 1957, evolved into The Beatles.

It is into this musical landscape that Peter Campbell McNeish, a much-wanted first child for Margaret and John McNeish, is born in Leigh, on 17 April 1955.

The town of Leigh is situated in the borough of Wigan, the most westerly and far-flung of Greater Manchester's sub-divisions. Prior to being subsumed by the city's wider area, Wigan and Leigh were in Lancashire, as evidenced in the accent of many of the locals – including, eventually, a young Pete.

Leigh had been powered by the Industrial Revolution into a hub of cotton mills and coal mining, and in 1955 was thriving. It boasted a bustling town centre, the heart of a community populated by traditional businesses such as butchers, bakers, greengrocers, fishmongers and haberdashers. It also had the benefit of daily markets. The traditional market, with either outdoor stalls covered with awnings or individual booths housed in a red-brick market hall, is a particularly northern phenomenon.

In the Seventies, when Pete was a teenager, there was still a good selection of family-owned retailers in the town centre, with the record and music shops that Pete mentions in his interviews, as well as the Woolworths that graced almost every town centre in the land. By this time many of the coalmines in the area had closed, but the few that remained employed many hundreds of people, as did other major manufacturers of the pre-Thatcher era, such as Sutcliffe Speakman, a group involved in both engineering and specialist chemicals, and BICC, a maker of electrical cables.

Leigh's fortunes, however, have been mixed since then, and the town in which a young Pete took his first steps in life became rather less vibrant than it had previously been. All the biggest businesses, the mills and the mines closed down during the Seventies and Eighties, leaving the retail and hospitality industries as the largest employers in the town today. Some

Bradshawgate, Leigh, looking towards Railway Road, 1980.

of the mill buildings still survive: grand Victorian temples to industry built in Accrington brick and terracotta, many of them on attractive canal-side sites. As the town's population gradually shrank from its Fifties heyday, the Leigh in which Pete came of age would have been increasingly dotted with large empty buildings, slowly turning from industrial hubs into imposing but crumbling shells.

A pervading air of faded grandeur was characteristic of many northern towns in the shift from the middle to the latter decades of the 20th century, as major industrial employers closed and work became scarce for many. Inevitably, it was a quality that had an impact on those who grow up there, giving them a different experience to those based in London, which was the progenitor of so many social and cultural movements.

It's worth noting that Leigh is on the up today. Many new housing estates and retail developments have been built – one of the largest 'strip malls' is on the site of the old Parsonage mine[1]. The site of another coalmine, at Bickershaw, is being redeveloped as a country park and upmarket housing. Although the railway line closed in 1969, a 'guided busway' to Manchester opened in 2016: this is where a double-decker bus drives

Pageboy Pete at his Auntie Pat's wedding, Astley Methodist Church, 1960.

along part of what used to be the railway line before joining a specially designated bus lane on the main thoroughfare into the city. The town will further benefit from the physical memorial to Pete Shelley that is planned, and in the longer run the Pete Shelley Memorial Campaign intends to establish a trust that will benefit aspiring young musicians in the area – and what better memorial to Pete could there be than this?

But the experience of the young soon-to-be Pete Shelley was of Leigh in its earlier state. Howard Lycett was Pete's younger cousin and close friend, and sheds some light on the early experiences of young Peter McNeish.

'My grandma, Alice, was Pete's mum's sister – his mum, Margaret, was the youngest of the siblings. They came from Astley, a mining village halfway between Manchester and Wigan. You can still see an old mine there, the pithead. My grandma's family actually lived in Pit Yard, in the grounds surrounding the mine. The miners' cottages are still there.

'The Industrial Revolution started around Astley. Astley's an ideal site as it's got the mine and it's right near the Bridgewater Canal, which would have been used for transporting the coal. There was a big cotton mill there as well and on the Moss the

'Our Gary', cousin Howard and Pete, c.1963/4.

COURTESY OF HOWARD LYCETT

first ever railway line was built – Stephenson's *Rocket* was actually trialled on there. The railway line was laid on bales of cotton from the mill so you've got all the components of the Industrial Revolution there. Our family had been involved in coal mining for generations so that's where Pete got his work ethic from – he was from a long line of grafters.

'When Pete was born, Margaret and John were living in a little terraced house just off Railway Road, right near Leigh town centre. Pete was born in the kitchen, after a long, difficult labour.

'Before she got married, Auntie Margaret worked in a cotton mill in Factory Yard, Astley, with her two sisters: Alice, my grandma, and Annie, my auntie. She also worked at Ward & Goldstone in Leigh, at their Butts Mill, making electrical equipment for cars and buses. Uncle Johnny was from Glasgow and he had been in the Navy. Auntie Margaret was in the Land Army during the war and I think she met Uncle Johnny then[2]. So Uncle Johnny moved from Scotland so they could get married. He was a fitter, an engineer, repairing and maintaining mining machinery at Astley Green Colliery – the mining equipment needed constant maintenance, to ensure health and safety; but also there are pumps running all the time, otherwise the mines would fill up with water.

'Their second house was the bungalow in Pennington, not as close to town, where Pete's blue plaque is now. Pete was proud to be from Leigh but he never made a big deal about it as he didn't want fans finding out where he lived and mithering[3] his mum.

'In the Sixties, Leigh was grey and depressing, full of smog from factory chimneys and coal fires, but it had a sense of community – the constant threat of danger for the men working down the mines meant that everyone was looking out for each other. The factories and pits would shut down for two weeks in the summer – "the wakes", we used to call it – and everyone would go off to Rhyl or Blackpool on a charabanc[4] or on the train for a seaside holiday. Most of the shops in the town would be closed during that time, even the newsagents – you'd have to buy your paper from a little mobile stall that was put there for the wakes. Everyone went away together, not just families but all the people who worked together. They were happy times, despite some of the hardships.

'Pete did well at school and he passed the eleven-plus, meaning he could go to the grammar school. Pete excelled at English from the earliest age. All his writing skills came from his mum, Margaret. She was so talented at literature, particularly poetry, that the headmaster at her school wanted to send her to university – unusual for young women in those days – but her dad wouldn't allow it. It was a shame. Auntie Margaret still wrote poems even when she was older. I remember Pete saying, "I wish I could write like my mother." She was very eloquent – like Pete, she was a wordsmith.

'He was brilliant at English but he wasn't so good at maths. In fact, he went to Bolton Institute a year late because he had a bit of catching up to do with the maths before he could get on the course that he wanted to do.

'Pete and I were very close. My school and Leigh Grammar were separated by a fence. We'd meet at lunchtime on either side of the fence and have a chat but then, when it was winter, we'd have snowball fights instead!

'There hadn't been any musicians in our family before Pete. He got his first guitar as a young teenager – I remember him playing The Beatles, T.Rex and then Bowie on his acoustic – but he'd never had music lessons or anything like that. He'd never even played the recorder at school, or been in the school choir. He was a born performer, though, from the earliest age. Every year on the Marsh playing fields that's at the back of where the Sainsbury's is now – on the old Parsonage site – there'd be the

Miners' Gala. Everyone in Leigh was involved with the mines in some way or other so it was a huge event where the entire community got together. There'd be a big fair, clog dancing, games for the kids; and there'd be thousands of people there. You can guarantee that at some point in the day Pete'd go missing – then 20 minutes later you'd hear over the tannoy, "Can Mr and Mrs McNeish come to the stage and pick up their son Peter?" That's how determined to be famous he was!

'My mum is always saying that Pete's first gig was her wedding – that would have been when he was five. He was a pageboy – he looked a picture in his little outfit – and at the reception he got up on the stage and was singing the pop songs of the day (it'd be all that Fifties stuff – Elvis and rock 'n' roll and Doris Day songs). They said they didn't need any other entertainment. He'd do the same thing when they took him to Blackpool on the charabanc – on the way back he'd be singing for all the other mums. He loved music and he loved to please people.

'He was in a few shows when he was at the grammar school as well, mostly plays. When he was thirteen they put on *The Mikado*. Pete was a member of the chorus, playing the part of a Japanese maiden – they were all dressed as geishas, complete with wigs and fans (of course it was a boys' school, so there were no girls to play those parts). He didn't object to it as much as some of the other lads did!

'When I was about 12 or 13 my mum hired him so he could help me with my homework on a Saturday morning. Pete'd come to ours on the bus and he'd have this long denim jacket on, long hair and a flared collar – he looked really cool (it was 1973). After about 20 minutes he'd ask if I was bored and of course I'd say yes. So then we'd talk about the universe, cosmology and music. It was like having a friendly big brother – you could talk about anything with him. He was very advanced for his age.

When the other kids were playing football or chasing girls he'd be reading, researching the subjects he was interested in. I mean it's easy now, when you can just read about anything you want on the internet, but in those days you had to go out of your way to find that kind of stuff. He'd try to explain about concepts like time and eternity – it was the kind of thing that Brian Cox talks about in his programmes now but at that time there was nothing like that on the telly. There was the BBC's *The Sky at Night*, which was about stargazing, but there was nothing beyond that until those Carl Sagan programmes[5], which weren't broadcast until the early Eighties. Pete said that in space there's probably no-one out there but there may have been, or maybe there will be, only they're on a different timeline to us – or maybe even in a different dimension. I don't know where he was getting his books from – he might have been going to the Central Library in town [Manchester] because I don't know whether they'd have those kinds of books at our local library here in Leigh. It was beyond astronomy – he was talking about things like the theory of relativity and quantum physics. But he explained it to me, who was so much younger than him, in a way that I could understand.

'Pete used to talk to me about music as well in our Saturday-morning sessions. He'd talk about Bowie and how the persona he'd invented was a "product", or he'd tell me how to listen to certain songs, what to watch out for in them. You could tell how deeply he understood pop music, even then.'

By all accounts, Pete was popular at the grammar school and had friends there – although he took his studies seriously. One of those school friends was Garth Davies. He had been taking guitar lessons for some years and was already a keen and competent musician. A rock 'n' roll aficionado, he had harboured ambitions to be a pop star from pre-puberty. Pete and Garth were introduced when they worked together on one of those school plays. They formed Jets of Air, with Pete on guitar and Garth on bass, and played locally many times, staging and promoting their own shows in church halls and anywhere else that would accommodate them. Their set included Bowie, Beatles and Velvets covers, as well as some of Pete's earlier compositions – some of which he would rework in later years for Buzzcocks and for his own Eighties solo act. His careful analysis of the works of musicians he admired and his study of the craft of songwriting were evidently paying off.

Second week of September, 1974. This is the year in which there will be two General Elections in the UK – and the Watergate scandal in the US. The Three-Day Week is imposed in Britain to conserve power, which is in short supply due to the continuing oil crisis (caused by unrest between countries in the Middle East). Germany win the World Cup on their home turf and Muhammad Ali beats George Foreman in the Rumble in the Jungle. Abba win the Eurovision Song Contest and the first McDonald's opens in London.

In the UK Singles Chart 'Love Me for a Reason' by The Osmonds occupies the top spot, 'Kung Fu Fighting' by Carl Douglas is at No. 2, cashing in on the Bruce Lee craze (he died in 1973 in circumstances that some believed to be mysterious), and there are a couple of Motown songs in the charts (The Three Degrees' 'When Will I See You Again' at No. 7 and 'Baby Love' by Diana Ross and The Supremes at No. 14). There is a surprising dearth of glam-rock records in the charts this week; but disco is just beginning to emerge, with 'Rock the Boat' by The Hues Corporation and 'Rock Your Baby' by George McCrae both charting.

Last year, Tony Wilson started work as a young reporter on ITV's regional news programme for the Northwest of England, *Granada Reports*. This year, prison-based BBC sitcom *Porridge* is broadcast for the first time, as is *Tiswas*, the Saturday-morning children's variety show that soon becomes a diverting hair-of-the-dog for adults recovering from 'the morning after the night before'. Meanwhile, the revolutionary surrealist sketch show *Monty Python's Flying Circus* is aired for the last time.

Films released in 1974 include the disaster movie *The Towering Inferno* and the low-budget (but highly influential) slasher horror *The Texas Chainsaw Massacre*. There's also *Confessions of a Window Cleaner*, the first of a handful of films in the 'Confessions' series, rated by some as a wonderfully nostalgic example of typical British 'seaside postcard' saucy fun, yet slated by others as a 'Carry On' clone with more nudity, more scenes of depressing Seventies' sitting-rooms and considerably less wit.

And it is at this time, against this cultural backdrop, that Peter McNeish starts studying for his Higher National Diploma in electronics and computer science at the Bolton Institute of Technology.

The early to mid-Seventies in Britain was a grim time for the youngsters of Generation X – and it can be difficult for the more fortunate individuals of Generations Y and Z to imagine just *how* grim. Unemployment was on the rise after the boom times of the Fifties and Sixties. There were fuel shortages and frequent power cuts. There were nylon underpants, nylon sheets, noisome sterilized milk and hard toilet paper. The shops were closed on Sundays, and in many towns for half a day midweek as well, and the TV shut down for the night before midnight. At this time the UK only had two and a half TV channels – BBC1, ITV and the part-time BBC2, which seemed to be dominated by Open University programming delivered by socially awkward geeks wearing heavy NHS specs and tweed jackets with leather elbow patches.

Few people had central heating, a surprising number of homes had only a black-and-white telly, and many terraced houses up and down the country – but mainly in the north – still had outside toilets and no indoor plumbing apart from the Ascot heater above the Belfast sink in the scullery. Somehow the sunshine and flowers that the Sixties had promised had passed us by. The Summer of Love had erupted in balmy California and may have touched the more with-it parts of London, but the rest of the UK was still mired firmly in the monochrome post-war years.

Britain was considerably less homogenized than it is now and in the early Seventies there were stark differences between the north and south. Southerners and northerners were equally suspicious of each other. Those from the south thought northerners were brusque and unsophisticated, while those from the north viewed their southern counterparts as effete and insincere. These were the days of regional brands of foodstuffs and even household commodities such as washing-up liquid. The localized nature of beers was a source of enmity between north and south: southerners found the Northwest's Boddingtons to be soupy and unrefreshing, while northerners slated Watneys as anaemic and urinous. Even the London water provided cause for complaint for Mancunians who visited the capital – you couldn't make a decent brew with it, it produced no lather when you went to wash your hands and some even griped that it made you constipated.

Fashion had taken a wrong turn since the Sixties. The nation's couturiers seemed to be suffering some sort of nightmarish comedown in the wake of their psychedelic-inspired confections of the preceding decade. By 1975 the variety of styles available in mainstream shops was surprisingly limited – women wore A-line or maxi skirts with American Tan tights and clumpy shoes, while men sported tit-tickler collars and kipper ties. Sideburns were de rigueur for those able to grow them and the only trousers you could buy were flares; the wider they were the more stylish. In fact some Northern Soul fans wanted their Oxford bags so voluminous they had to have them especially tailored.

Man-made fibres abounded and all clothing, it seemed, was available only in beige, bottle-green and shades of sludge. The man (and even teenager) in the street seemed satisfied with this state of sartorial affairs and any diversion from the norm was noticed and goggled at. There may have been libertines having Sex[6] and Grannies Taking Trips[7] on the King's Road but there was none of that outside the capital. Vivienne Westwood and Malcolm McLaren were selling their bondage gear and fetish wear by the bucket-load in swanky Chelsea but, in the nation's Market Streets at that time, the most outré item of clothing you could hope to buy was a nylon nightie from Littlewoods.

Popular music, too, after showing so much promise in the preceding decade, had hit a brick wall. Prog rock, with its outlandish costumes and stage sets, virtuosic yet interminable solos and bizarre lyrical subjects, dominated the music press, while the charts were teeming with studio-manufactured bubblegum pop, novelty records and one-hit wonders – The Wombles were one of the biggest-selling acts of the first half of the Seventies, earning the *Music Week* award for Top Singles Band of 1974. *Top of the Pops*, with its ersatz 'party' atmosphere and overly tactile hosts, was the flagship popular-music programme for teenagers, although there were short-lived outliers such as the Bay City Rollers' 'Shang-A-Lang' (bafflingly, it couldn't make up its mind whether it wanted to be a music programme or a comedy sketch show and the recordings at Granada's Manchester studios suffered frequent stage invasions by tartan-crazed zealots who had to be hauled off, swooning and sometimes screaming, by security). In 1977 there was also Bolan's *Marc* show, another Granada production, which ended after one season with the diminutive corkscrew-haired singer's death.

Meanwhile, for musos and fans of AOR (both the album and adult-oriented varieties) there was the more sophisticated *Old Grey Whistle Test*. Any youngster in the early Seventies might have been forgiven for thinking it was so-called because you had to be old and grey to want to watch it, but it was actually named in reference to a music-business adage: if a new song could be hummed or whistled after just a couple of listens by the grey-suited, usually older, commissionaires who manned the doors in the music-industry offices in New York's Tin Pan Alley, then it had passed the Old Grey Whistle Test.

Punk, then, when it came thrashing and kicking into the world, was like a breath of fresh air.

At that time, though, the scene that would evolve into Punk was small and London-centric: it was the Sex Pistols and the coterie of admirers who followed them, the Bromley Contingent (hailing from the small suburban town in Kent), who religiously attended the sporadic and chaotic gigs that the band played in and around the capital. Punk didn't truly find its feet as a genre until the Pistols' notorious foul-mouthed exchange with the allegedly alcohol-addled Bill Grundy on prime-time, teatime television on 1 December 1976. The tabloid press had a field day with the incident and it was then that 'punk' became a household word, shorthand for an attitude and a way of life as much as it was the name for a phenomenon of popular music.

Punk caught the imagination of the nation's more rebellious youngsters while simultaneously disgusting and outraging their parents and grandparents, some of whom may even have been born in the latter years of the Victorian era. It's easy to forget what a danger to the country's youth punk was deemed to be at the time, when today the F-bomb and even the C-bomb are dropped regularly on TV and when you can buy Ramones T-shirts in Primark and green hair dye in Poundland. When they first hit the headlines, even the name Sex (*sex!*) Pistols was shocking. We lived in different times[8].

Imagine, then, Greater Manchester in 1974. (The region itself, an amalgamation of parts of Lancashire and Cheshire, was only named such on 1 April that year.) In an industrial town to the northwest of the region, Peter McNeish is a sensitive and intellectually curious student, eagerly reading as much as he can and listening to bands to which few of the more conservative pop-pickers of Lancashire would give elbow room: The Velvet Underground with their opiate-enamoured panegyrics, the flamboyant and flouncy Roxy Music (*men wearing make-up!*) and the brazenly bisexual Bowie, as well as the more staid Bolan and The Beatles. He is enjoying student life, although he still lives at home with his parents, and is taking advantage of as many social opportunities as he can in his freshers' year.

On the other side of the city a young Stephen Diggle is also learning the guitar after being inspired by The Beatles and the Small Faces. His other interests are modern art and literature – including poetry. He has had a job, briefly, but discovers that the world of work isn't for him. When he's not recording his own self-penned songs on a reel-to-reel tape recorder in the bedroom he shares with his brother, he spends a lot of time lying on the couch in his parents' parlour reading D H Lawrence. He has ambitions to be the Pete Townshend figure in his own band, but when he asks his dad to get him an electric six-string guitar, Mr Diggle senior mistakenly procures a bass guitar – it had an unlucky tumble from the back of a lorry at Mr Diggle's place of work. Steve accepts it and begins to learn how to play.

Meanwhile, in genteel Prestwich, a suburb north of Manchester, an equally restive Steve Garvey has tried a number of jobs, including working in a petrol station, while he too is developing into a very able bassist and guitarist. And a teenage John Maher is still only studying for his O levels at an old-fashioned Catholic boys' school in south Manchester's leafy Whalley Range. He, too, is attempting to teach himself to play guitar and has as yet never picked up a drumstick (apart from, perhaps, a turkey one at Christmas).

In his second year at Bolton Institute, Pete meets Howard Trafford, an alumnus of Leeds Grammar School who is studying humanities after making a false start on a psychology course. He is an ardent fan of The Velvet Underground and places an advert on the college notice board appealing for others who would like to do 'a version of "Sister Ray"' – perhaps one of the Velvets' most lyrically challenging songs, with its themes of murder, fellatio, cross-dressing sailors and intravenous drug use ('I'm searching for my mainline'). It is also a song that would test the staying power of the audience, as the studio version clocks in at 17 minutes 29 seconds and some of the live versions last for over half an hour[9]. The Stooges may be mentioned in Trafford's advert too.

It's worth noting in the timeline of punk that this ad was placed in October 1975, some weeks before the Sex Pistols played their first gig with the 'classic' Rotten, Matlock, Jones and Cook lineup at Saint Martins in London – the art school where Glen Matlock was studying – on 6 November of that year, so it seems likely that Pete and Howard had their first rehearsals before they had even heard the London band.

Howard says later in an interview[10] that his inspiration for starting a band was 'seeing bands in college and really getting... bored of it...Nobody was interested in being, or at least pretending convincingly to be, a bit dangerous.' Pete and Howard, though, were committed to 'pretending convincingly'. In the same interview Pete says: 'We used to scare people when we walked down the street...particularly when me and Howard hennaed our hair.'

At around this time Howard also had a pair of trousers taken in to form drainpipes, which couldn't be got for love nor money in Manchester, and Pete says the non-standard strides made 'people...stop and stare'. This may sound like a hyperbolic flight of fancy but remember that this was not in London or even

the metropolis of Manchester, but in Bolton, which at that time (like Leigh) was an L S Lowry painting brought to life, whose inhabitants still ate tripe.

Pete and Howard hit it off, both musically and personally; a few months later they find that they have a mutual curiosity about the Pistols as the southern oiks start to gain coverage in the music press with their pugilistic performances and their even more confrontational off-stage behaviour (which at one early gig included trashing the equipment of the headlining band who'd been kind enough to offer them the support slot). The article that really piques Pete's and Howard's interest, though, is a review of a show where the Pistols supported pub-rock mainstays Eddie and the Hot Rods. Not only had this performance ended with Rotten's by now trademark hooliganism, but it had also included a semi-striptease by the female Bromley Contingent pin-up Jordan. Again, in an age where there is a lap-dancing club on the high street of every respectably sized town, and when music videos can look like three-minute soft-porn films, it's difficult to comprehend how shocking a woman appearing topless at a pop concert would have been in the Seventies.

Determined to witness the debauched spectacle for themselves, one grey weekend in February McNeish and Trafford borrow a car and travel to London to see the Pistols play. They don't actually know whether the band are performing that weekend; they call Neil Spencer at the *NME*, who had written the review that captured their attention, to ask if he knows where to find them. He informs them that the Pistols' manager, Malcolm McLaren, runs the clothing outlet Sex at World's End, the less felicitous western end of the King's Road, where the niche boutiques peter out and are replaced by social housing and, at this time, surprisingly down-at-heel terraced homes.

The pair go to see Malcolm in Sex and he tells them that the Pistols are playing two gigs over the weekend: a support slot for musical eccentric and political chancer Screaming Lord Sutch that night, at the Buckinghamshire College of Further Education in High Wycombe; and at the Hertfordshire College of Art in St Albans the following night. Colleges and art schools were among the only venues that would host the musical renegades at that time, such was their burgeoning notoriety.

The two shows don't disappoint. As the Pistols are finding it increasingly difficult to source venues that will let them play, Howard asks Malcolm if – hypothetically – the band would come to play in Manchester, if it proves possible to organize such a show (Pete already has valuable experience as an amateur impresario from his Jets of Air days). Of course McLaren agrees and the two wannabe promoters set about staging the gig that will catalyze a whole series of events, transforming not just pop music, or the Manchester music scene, but popular culture in the wider world too, for good.

Pete and Howard return from their foray to London not only formulating a plan to host a gig, but also determined to form their own Pistols-esque group. They call themselves Buzzcocks after an item they read in the London listings magazine *Time Out*, a copy of which they'd picked up in the capital. It's headlined 'It's the Buzz, Cock!' and concerns a TV drama, *Rock Follies*, which is all the rage at the time and charts the adventures of a fictitious all-female rock band. The group features the *Evita* songbird Julie Covington and the Senior Service-and-vodka-voiced Rula Lenska as ambitious yet struggling musicians.

As an aside, while it was produced on a budget and with some quirky styling borrowed from fringe theatre, *Rock Follies* nonetheless spawned some surprisingly good music. The songs were written by Andy Mackay, Roxy Music's woodwind wizard, and the three female protagonists demonstrated that they weren't just pretty faces and tight jeans – they really could sing. The show's soundtrack went straight into the UK charts at No. 1 – a rare enough feat for a debut album, and particularly so for one by female artistes. Each episode featured the band performing several songs in a new, challenging situation, and the drama–music crossover was a groundbreaking format. Some of the storylines would have been quite controversial at the time: there is much bed-hopping, some minor drug-taking and in one episode the three girls are enticed into starring in a blue movie – yet the heroines always stick to their principles and a strong feminist thread runs through the narrative. *Rock Follies* looks unexpectedly fresh even today and is worth finding on YouTube as it provides a charming historical document of those few years in the mid-Seventies when the cultural and moral landscape really began to shift.

With its overtones of sex and noise, the Buzzcocks appellative is extremely fitting for a punk group, yet its suggested sauciness is so subtle that it will cause no offence when it appears on the band's homemade posters and flyers – nor (although they certainly aren't thinking that far ahead) will it preclude them from appearing on national TV in the future or prevent their records from being stocked by Woolworths.

Buzzcocks plan to play their first gig at their college in Bolton on 1 April with Howard (now with the adopted surname Devoto, reportedly after a character from a case history he studied in his philosophy class) on vocals and Pete (now re-branded Shelley – reportedly the name he would have been given had he been a girl, though it's difficult not to see some association with the Romantic poet) playing guitar.

They recruit Pete's old school friend Garth to play bass and borrow a drummer from another local band just for the night. They have a short set, comprising a smattering of their own songs accompanied by some interesting covers of Sixties and glam-rock numbers. They haven't rehearsed as much as they could have done and on the night they don't even get to debut their own songs as they're hauled off stage prematurely by the show's promoters before they've even finished the warm-up numbers. Garth – who at this time aspires to play in working men's clubs and at weddings – feels that the punk delivery and some of the racy lyrics in Pete's songs won't help the band to progress and tells Pete that the band is 'not for him' (although further down the line he'll change his mind).

The proto-Buzzcocks, then, find themselves without a rhythm section. They advertise for a drummer and bassist in the city's listings paper, the *Manchester Review*.

Meanwhile Devoto and Shelley are preparing to put on the Pistols show they discussed with Malcolm McLaren. The venue they choose is Manchester's Lesser Free Trade Hall, an upper room to the resplendent Free Trade Hall, which was the home ground of the city's Hallé Orchestra[11]. They persuade Malcolm to pay for the hire of the venue and set about printing up and selling the tickets themselves for the grand sum of 50p. They'd approached the Student Union reps at their own college, Bolton Institute, with a view to staging the show there but the Pistols' reputation must have preceded them, as the Bolton bods refused – thus depriving the establishment of the musical kudos that it might have otherwise earned for staging the first Pistols show outside the Southeast.

The show is scheduled for 4 June. Malcolm produces some A3 posters – this is where his art-school training comes in handy – and Pete and Howard paste them up around the city. On the night of the show McLaren is equally determined to publicize his band: he loiters outside the venue in his black leather trousers[12], attempting to lure people in off the street to see the show. One of those he accosts is Steve Diggle, who – in an unlikely instance of synchronicity and serendipity – has arranged a rendezvous with a guitarist whose ad in the *Manchester Review* he has answered. The two had arranged to meet outside the Free

Trade Hall with a view to going for a drink and a chat in the nearby Cox's Bar. When Malcolm learns that Steve has come to meet the guy who wants to start a band he ushers him in, saying, 'Yes, he's in the box office selling tickets. Go in and talk to him, he's expecting you.'

As it happened, Howard had just that afternoon received a call in response to the ad *he* had placed in the regional paper, from a bassist who agreed to meet him and Pete at the Pistols show. So, when Diggle introduces himself to them, they presume he's the guy who answered their ad.

It takes some minutes of rather confused conversation before Shelley and Diggle realize the error they have both made; however, they seem to have similar musical aspirations and are happy to sound each other out. Diggle – who has not yet been tuned in or turned on to the Pistols – has an almost Damascene experience at the show. Punk, he realizes, is the way forward, and he abandons his dreams of forming the new Who for the altogether grittier, spittier musical revolution that is just beginning. The next day, Devoto, Diggle and Shelley meet to play together for the first time at Howard's flat in Lower Broughton Road. They find they have an instant chemistry – each apparently being able to read the others' minds, in a musical sense – and Buzzcocks as we know them are born. As they say, there's no such thing as coincidence.

It's not clear how many people were at the first Pistols show in that modest upper room – some say as few as 40 were there; others estimate as many as 100. (Howard Devoto errs on the more generous side and he should know, as he held the purse strings and the ticket stubs on the night.) Whatever the case, at least the cost of the hire of the hall was covered; and McLaren, Devoto and Shelley plan a second outing for the Pistols in Manchester at the same venue. The show is scheduled for 20 July and the newly formed Buzzcocks offer themselves as the support act. The only trouble is, they don't have a drummer.

The young John Maher has by this time realized that there are too many guitarists in the world ('Five guitar players, one guitar', as it says in The Clash's 'Garageland') and has switched his focus instead to the drums, hoping he will be more in demand from nascent bands as a percussionist. It becomes apparent all too quickly that his new choice of instrument pleases neither his parents nor their suburban neighbours and so Maher desperately searches for a band to join who have a dedicated rehearsal space where he can make as much noise as he wants. He answers an ad in *Melody Maker* appealing for novice musicians. The young female drummer who placed the ad has been contacted by Howard and, in another fortuitous turn of events, she is unable to make the meeting and instead puts Maher in touch with Devoto. Howard turns up on John's doorstep just before the fifth-former is about to leave to sit his chemistry O level (20-plus years before the dawn of the mobile phone, many households didn't even feel the need for a landline and the Maher residence was one of them). He invites the young drummer for a jam with the band that weekend, without having heard him play; when they do hook up, however, Maher's style fits the band's like a glove and they are happy to have him.

Buzzcocks rehearse weekly from thereon and within not much more than a month are ready for their debut, supporting at the next Pistols show. Maher proves to be an innovative and creative drummer, and exceptionally skilled after his meagre six weeks of self-tuition. After his O levels he is offered a job with a Christian financial institution but turns it down.

The second Pistols show at the Lesser Free Trade Hall attracts a far bigger crowd than the first – many newcomers to punk have heard about the first show by word of mouth and want to see what all the fuss is about (strangely the entrance fee has doubled from 50p to £1 in just six weeks, but that doesn't deter them).

Malcolm McLaren has invited a gaggle of music journalists

to see his stars shine and the regional TV news anchorman, Tony Wilson, is also present. He has a music show of his own on Granada, the Northwest's regional TV station, and Howard has piqued his interest in Buzzcocks by sending him a demo tape.

Buzzcocks are playing their first real gig together but they decide they don't have time to be nervous. They just get out there and do it. On stage, Pete smashes up the cheap guitar he has bought especially for the occasion and they far outperform the other support, the over-confident, overly ambitious Slaughter and the Dogs (a troupe of glam-inspired teenage tearaways from Wythenshawe[13]). Buzzcocks attract the attention of the visiting London journalists and a review of their performance appears in *Sounds* – it's not particularly favourable but still helps get their very memorable name known nationwide.

The band rehearse and gig doggedly over the next few weeks and at the end of August are invited by the Pistols for a 'gig swap' – the two bands play at the Screen on the Green in Islington, accompanied by The Clash. By now punk is fully fledged and this is one of the seminal gigs of the genre. Buzzcocks have honed their set and they sound confident and authoritative. They garner another dubious review in *Sounds* – perhaps due to their sub-standard equipment – but they're nevertheless grateful for the media coverage.

Three weeks later they play at the celebrated Punk Festival at Oxford Street's 100 Club. By the time they go on stage on the second night much of the audience has left, presumably to catch the last bus home. (If Lambrettas and Vespas were the chosen mode of transport for mods, and Hondas and Suzukis were favoured by rockers and metallers, the tube and the Routemaster were the preferred ride of the punk.) The northerners are nevertheless reviewed favourably in *Melody Maker* by Caroline Coon, who must have stayed the course (maybe she, unlike a lot of the punk attendees, could afford a taxi).

A month after this the band records a demo tape of their set at Revolution Studio in Stockport and, by December, they're supporting the Sex Pistols on their 'Anarchy' tour, taking the place of The Damned. It was felt that Sensible and Vanian had blotted their copybooks by submitting to an obscenity test by the local council officials in Derby who wanted to hear what the bands were like before they gave the go-ahead for the booking, and they are slung off the tour. When it came down to it they just weren't punk enough.

Shelley, Devoto, Diggle and Maher have decided to put out their debut EP themselves. The DIY method proved itself highly serviceable for the staging of the two Pistols' shows and, they surmise, there's no reason why it can't be applied to releasing a record. By a suitably democratic process they have chosen the four tracks that will appear on the 7-inch and have borrowed money from friends and family to fund the venture ('crowdfunding', as we would call it today). They buy 'dead time' at Manchester's Indigo Studios: it's the period between Christmas and New Year when everyone else is too hungover and turkeyed-out to be bothered recording, so they get it cheap.

Buzzcocks' choice of producer is Martin Hannett, a mythical and multitalented figure on the periphery of the Manchester music scene who has a degree in chemistry and an interest in electronics. Hannett himself is a bassist, having played in the early Seventies in a band alongside Paul Young, later of supergroup Mike + The Mechanics (not to be confused with the teen heart-throb Paul Young). His production experience was initially gained by sound engineering at pub gigs and he had worked as part of Manchester's 'socialist music agency' Music Force with his partner Susanne O'Hara. Music Force was a 'one-stop shop' for promoters and performers: it provided sound and equipment hire, fly-posting and publicity, and could even source and hire out musicians.

Hannett will go on to produce Joy Division's two studio albums and become a director at Factory Records, brainchild of Tony Wilson. For Factory he will produce Happy Mondays' album *Bummed* (even the forward-looking Wilson, famed for his audacious commercial risk-taking, would concede that the sales potential of a disc called *Fucked* – which is allegedly what the Mondays wanted to call their second album – could be limited). This will be as a freelance producer, though, not as a member of the Factory board, as he'll forfeit his directorship with the label in 1982 over a lawsuit concerning 'financial matters', which will be settled out of court in Hannett's favour.

Hannett was an enthusiastic user of substances and the Mondays allegedly kept him generously supplied with ecstasy for the six weeks it took to record their seminal 1988 album to prevent him from getting drunk during the sessions (and if the Happy Mondays think you drink too much, it's probably safe to assume that you drink too much). It seems likely now that at least some of Hannett's substance and mental-health problems were sparked by the suicide of Joy Division's Ian Curtis in May 1980. Although a taskmaster and even perhaps a tyrant as the band's producer, Hannett had been something of a mentor to the younger men. Shortly after Curtis's death, Hannett turned down the opportunity to produce U2's debut album, *Boy*, as he was too grief-stricken to commit to working. His career, and maybe his life, could have panned out very differently had he taken this opportunity but at the time U2 were just another young post-punk band: their ascendance as one of the biggest and longest-lived names in pop was yet to play out.

Pete's father is also at Indigo Studios as overseer, to ensure that the 'crowdfunding' is not squandered (he was the most bounteous of the crowd-funders, after all). The band works exceptionally efficiently and the four tracks are recorded in a day: 1,000 copies of the 7-inch are pressed and the band spends many hours painstakingly quality-controlling each one under an angle-poise lamp before packaging it in the black-and-white paper sleeve that they have designed with the help of their manager, Richard Boon, who also took the Polaroid photo for the front cover. The four-track EP is sold for £1 in the Virgin store in Manchester and in Rough Trade in London, and is also available via mail order (Rough Trade also helped with the distribution).

The EP attracts the attention of both the music press and alternative BBC DJ John Peel, and in total the original 1977 release will sell 16,000 copies. It will be reissued in 1979 on the New Hormones label, remaining in the UK Singles Chart for six weeks and peaking at No. 31; it will be reissued as a CD by the eminent independent label Mute in 1999; then, in 2017, it will be reissued *again* on vinyl by another notable independent, Domino, to mark the 40th anniversary of the original recording, deservedly entering the UK Physical Singles Chart at No. 1.

Pete's cousin Howard says: 'I remember when they recorded *Spiral Scratch* – they recorded it in under four hours. Pete's dad was there, keeping an eye on things; and being Scottish he was a bit worried about the cost of the studio time. Pete kept cocking up the two-note guitar solo in "Boredom" – I mean, how could you cock it up? It's just two notes! Time was ticking and Uncle Johnny was going mad because he was worried about the money. Pete played that solo time and again and, just on the last minute, he got it right. They made enough money from the sale of the record to be able to pay Uncle Johnny back and also to pay for the second pressing.

'Pete was very astute when it came to business. He encouraged other bands to see that they, too, could go down the independent route – and, because he'd had the experience of putting out his own record, when Buzzcocks did get signed to a major label he was determined to make use of the music industry, rather than letting it use him.

'Something else he did a bit later, in about 1980, was to invest in £10,000 worth of equipment from Australia – all electronic gear: drum machines and synths and that. He had a place in Manchester where he stored the stuff. The Human League found out about it and asked if they could hire the equipment to record one of their albums[14]. In those three weeks of leasing them the equipment Pete earned back all the cash he'd forked out. So he was no fool when it came to money.'

After the success of their debut recording, though, Devoto feels that being in a band has, for him, run its course. He's realized all his creative ambitions in those six short months and now wants to apply himself to his college course. At the time, being a pop star seems nothing more than a precarious and short-lived distraction so he considers it best to hedge his bets and apply himself to forging a career. However, he will be tempted back to the music industry less than 12 months after resigning from Buzzcocks (and when his diploma is safely in the bag) with his band Magazine.

Shelley, Diggle and Maher are only temporarily wrong-footed by Devoto's resignation; they quickly decide to continue along their auspicious trajectory with a re-shuffling of the lineup. Shelley remains on guitar but also assumes the role of vocalist and Diggle is promoted to second guitar (he did, after all, always see himself as a frontman rather than as a lynchpin of the rhythm section), so now all they have to do is find a bassist – and of course Shelley is still in touch with his schoolmate and fellow Jet of Air, Garth, who is welcomed back into the fold.

The new lineup of Buzzcocks continues to gig throughout 1977 and they are now stalwarts of the punk scene. They are invited to take part in the genre-defining 'White Riot' tour – the only non-London presence in the roadshow and, as such, proud representatives of the North. They are approached by several record labels but hold out until they find the right one – and the 'right one' turns out to be the co-operative and encouraging United Artists, already home to The Stranglers, who signed to the label at the end of 1976.

In October 1977, though, only a couple of months after Buzzcocks sign to United Artists, bassist Garth leaves the band (not necessarily voluntarily). Barry Adamson, who had recently joined Devoto's Magazine, was recruited to fill the Garth-shaped gap on a handful of gigs until a permanent bassist could be found. Barry recalls that time:

'I'd already been playing with Magazine for a few months but we were between projects so I had a little time. I'd already met Pete a few times because of my association with Buzzcocks (through Howard) and they were kind enough to let us use their equipment every now and again; I'd run in to Pete or see him out and so we'd chat a bit.

'Buzzcocks had already been an entry into the world of musicianship for me, having stood next to Pete at the bar and watching him walk away, just walk on to the stage and pick up the Woolworths Starway guitar and start it. I was absolutely blown away, because not long before that I'd seen massive gigs, like Led Zeppelin playing at Earl's Court with all the PA hanging from the roof – but the ideology of punk was that you could just "do it". That really instilled something in me; it was an occasion I'd never forget. With Buzzcocks there was no staying backstage, having to be kept away from the crowds and all that kind of carry on. Pete just literally walked from the bar to the stage. It was really inspiring to see that that's how you did things.

'It is pretty much true that I taught myself bass the night before my audition with Magazine. I'd played a bit of guitar here and there, a bit of strumming, all quite basic, but not played bass before. I bumped into an old friend and he took me to his house in Withington[15]. He had this room that was full of guitars and basses and drums and he said, "See that bass over there?

You can have it if you want." It had two strings on it so I went into town to buy the other two strings and there was the advert placed by Howard, asking for other musicians to join him. I rang him and he said, "Come tomorrow" – so I literally had to just put the new strings on and stay up all night to practise, playing with the neck of the bass leaning against the wooden bedpost so it would reverberate. My main method was to just play the lowest note, the E, in a sort of rhythm – then, the next day, Howard showed me "The Light Pours Out of Me", and playing that bottom note repetitively suited it perfectly – and so I was in.

'It was a few months after that that I started playing live with Magazine. We did three songs at the Electric Circus and then we played at Rafters but we were rehearsing every day so I was quickly gathering momentum, trying to fit in in a way that suited me but also trying to make myself stand out in a certain way at the same time. We'd just come out of the Seventies prog-rock era of the bass player standing in the shadows and not really expressing themselves; and at the other end of the scale you had people like Bootsy Collins playing on James Brown's "Sex Machine" – I was a huge fan of his playing on that record – and Larry Graham in Sly Stone's group and Dennis Dunaway in Alice Cooper's band. I thought they were just tremendous musicians so I'd listen to them and take them as kind of "food" to the rehearsal the next day.

'I was familiar with Steve's basslines on *Spiral Scratch*, which were relatively basic, and I'd seen the band play live a few times so I knew what was in their set. I picked up a bit from Garth but also threw in a bit of my own stuff as well. I remember keeping it quite simple, because of the speed at which they were playing. I mean, why play ten notes when one series of the same note will do!

'I did learn stuff from playing with Buzzcocks, yes...For one thing, they had a 16-song set, which blew me away because we only played about 9 with Magazine and a lot of those songs were mid-tempo. 'Shot by Both Sides' was probably the fastest song that Magazine played but Buzzcocks' songs were incredibly fast. Their tempos fly out the window so I was trying my hardest to keep up. From the band's point of view they saw that I could keep up, I could do the job and I fitted in; but at the end of the set, I looked down at my arm and the muscle in my forearm, just behind the wrist, had swollen up to probably three times its normal size! And my fingers were these little chubby mitts that were clinging on to the plectrum for dear life, especially during "Fast Cars". I'd make it through each night, but I'd have to "fake it to make it", you know, keep smiling. Playing those dates with Buzzcocks was a trial by fire. It felt a lot more chaotic than playing with Magazine – there was a slightly shambolic feel to it.

'The thing that stood out for me on *Spiral Scratch* was Howard's incredible lyricism and the way he approached the song and the singing, but also this teenage tour de force on drums that gave them an identity. John Maher...I've got to be honest, I'm a fan, because his playing is unlike that of anyone I've ever played with in my life – it's a blur of sticks but at the same time it's a technical feat, because it's beyond what you should be able to do at that speed. It's staggering.'

On their return from this tour Buzzcocks advertise for a new bassist. As the *NME* has reported Garth's decamping from the band there is no shortage of 'hopefuls' who turn up for the auditions in Manchester's Drum Studios. Like the Ugly Sisters trying to force their size-8 trotters into Cinderella's glass slipper, none of them fits. There were 'musos' who just didn't sit well with Buzzcocks' punk vibe; there were candidates with oddball personalities and eccentric stage personae who just didn't 'look right'; there were ones who wanted Buzzcocks to learn *their* songs. When the band had almost given up hope, along came Steve Garvey and Mog, from quirky Manchester new-wave band The Smirks – perhaps best remembered for northern reggae anthem 'Up Eh Up (Lancashire Dub)' and their peculiar, high-stepping dance routine. After days spent auditioning dozens of duds, the band now found themselves having to choose between two equally promising aspirants – but it's Steve Garvey who ends up getting the gig. As Barry Adamson says: 'Steve Garvey had everything: he was good-looking, he had a punkiness about him, he was bright and he could play – he fitted in beautifully.' He was in.

A stream of hit singles ensues over the next four years, accompanied by three albums and many media appearances. Some of the most sublime pop songs in history are created during this era. Yet in hindsight – and maybe even at the time – it was a puzzle how Buzzcocks fitted into the chaos and clamour that was punk...

The Clash were singing about 'Hate and War', bemoaning the lack of 'Career Opportunities' ('the ones that never knock') and, apparently, inciting young white men to start 'a riot of their own'. The Stranglers' catalogue included songs about domestic violence ('Sometimes' and 'Ugly'), interbreeding with sewer rats and some supremely comedic blasphemy (the lyric of 'Hanging Around' suggests that Christ is quite content to remain hanging on the cross and doesn't want his mother to intervene as he's got a panoramic view of Jerusalem from his elevated vantage point). The Damned, never known for their subtlety, were vocalizing about 'Problem Children' and their desire to 'Stab Yor Back' (complete with punk spelling), as well as boasting that they were 'Born to Kill' – and that's when they weren't exhorting the record-buying public to 'Smash It Up'. The Sex Pistols' 'God Save the Queen' proclaimed that 'all crimes are paid' and suggested that Elizabeth, the British monarch and Defender of the Faith, didn't even qualify as a human being; the song was considered so shocking in the year that the Queen celebrated

25 years on the throne that it was banned not just by the BBC but also by Independent Local Radio, the umbrella organization of commercial radio stations. Figures for the UK Singles Chart were massaged that week in June of 1977 so that a double A-side ('I Don't Want to Talk About It'/'The First Cut is the Deepest') by rotten Rod Stewart appeared to be No. 1., although The Pistols' previous single, 'Anarchy in the UK' – which likened what was once the proud head of the largest empire in history to a failed social-housing project and compared it to a list of organizations that, in the early to mid-Seventies, were combatants in violent civil wars – was arguably even more inflammatory.

The Slits – who, unlike the Sex Pistols, had a genuinely tendentious moniker – wrote lyrics critiquing (or maybe mourning) the rise of rampant consumerism: 'Spend, Spend, Spend', after a phrase famously uttered by (then later made the title of the autobiography of) Sixties football-pools-winner Viv Nicholson, who married five times and became a penniless drunk and, after that, a penniless Jehovah's Witness; and 'Shoplifting', a petty thief's how-to manual set to music. X Ray Spex were also lamenting the avidity for consumer goods, particularly those aimed at young women, in 'Art-I-Ficial' and 'Plastic Bag', as well as exploring themes of mental health problems, culminating in self-harm, caused by intrusive scrutiny by the media ('Identity' – now more pertinent than ever in the age of the 'celebrity'). Their 'The Day the World Turned Dayglo' is a heartfelt tirade against the proliferation of man-made fibres and other non-biodegradable substances (frontwoman Poly Styrene seemed to have foreseen the dangers of plastics to the environment 25 years before the first 'carrier-bag tax' was imposed). And then, of course, there is 'Oh Bondage Up Yours!', the title of which was contentious enough without even considering the lurid imagery in the lyric (although it could have made an appropriate anthem for the suffragette movement, had it been written 60 years earlier, what with all those middle-class ladies chaining themselves to railings and throwing themselves under horses).

Meanwhile Buzzcocks were singing...love songs. Not anti-love songs, like ATV's 'Love Lies Limp', or love songs with a punk twist, like The Damned's appositely titled sixth single, which says, 'I'll be the rubbish, you'll be the bin' (surely the most romantic metaphor for sexual intercourse ever devised), or The Stranglers' 'Princess of the Streets' in which Hugh Cornwell likens the object of his affections to a 'piece of meat'. No, Buzzcocks were singing heartfelt, melodious tributes to Eros that had more in common with those of their Mancunian forebears The Hollies and fellow northerners The Beatles than with the experimental Velvet Underground or the avant-garde, Eno-era Roxy Music that had inspired Devoto and Shelley to form the band.

The United Artists-years Buzzcocks slotted into the punk milieu because they'd gained a strong fan base when Devoto was at the helm. *Spiral Scratch* endeared them to the punk community, with the frantic vocals, abrasive guitars, crude recording and lyrics contemplating terminal ennui, chain-smoking and the urinary excretion of stress hormones, not to mention the obligatory four-

letter words. Although a few fans may have fallen by the wayside when Howard left the band shortly after the release of the self-funded debut ('Devoto was the Buzzcocks!' the occasional bloody-minded unregenerate exclaims), the revised lineup garnered far more followers than they lost with their galvanic live shows and perfectly crafted pop masterpieces. Although many of Buzzcocks' songs in their 'classic' period are not about punk themes, the band – with their dedication to the DIY ethic, their fizzing, fervent energy and their commitment to exposing the workings of the record-making process – exuded punk sensibility.

Buzzcocks were a punk band because they originated at a certain time, at the dawn of a certain 'scene'. Howard and Pete were attracted to the perversity of punk, the iconoclasm and the democratic spirit: the feeling that 'anyone could do it'. And yet the bulk of Pete Shelley's songs that were recorded in this period (with the exception of 'Oh Shit' and maybe some of the tracks from the latter stages of the United Artists period that deal with depression, philosophical anxieties and feelings of alienation) are not punk songs. They're delivered in a punk style – short, pithy compositions, played frenetically fast with yelped vocals, a driving beat and buzz-saw guitars – but the songs themselves, the lyrical content and the melodies, defy genre. Had Buzzcocks formed five years earlier, they may have been a glam-rock band – and if they'd evolved four years later, maybe they'd have been New Romantics. Had Pete been born ten years earlier, he could have been the mainstay of a very respectable beat band. Who knows?

Take a classic Shelley composition such as 'What Do I Get?'. Add some brass, a walking bassline and a guitar chop on the off-beat and you'd have a ska tune. Slow the tempo down a little, add some 'swing', maybe a little improvisation and a handful of blue notes (slightly flattened notes that are different from the expected note and give a more 'minor' feel), exchange the bass guitar for double bass and the guitar solo for a sax solo and you'd have a very acceptable jazz standard. Or, replace the four-piece rock-band lineup with a nylon-strung acoustic guitar – plucked with the fingers instead of a plectrum – and a surdo (Brazilian bass drum) playing a repetitive rhythm with the emphasis on the second beat, add a breathy, slightly nasal Portuguese female vocal and you've got a bossa nova number. There are very few genres in which Pete's pure, no-nonsense pop songs couldn't be sung and this is testament to his ability as a lyricist and tunesmith.

Buzzcocks also broke the mould by not pandering to punk fashion. They never wore so much as a semblance of a Westwood-prescribed outfit, generally favouring the 'Man at C&A' look over bondage trousers, cheesecloth Destroy shirts and 'tits' T-shirts. What's more, unlike some of their contemporaries, they were well-groomed and well-mannered: no vomiting in the business-class lounges at the airport for the clean-cut northern lads!

Their record sleeves, too, bucked the punk trend. The cover of The Clash's first album was – appropriately – in conflicting colours of brilliant orange and a NATO green, hinting at a militaristic style. The front of the cover showed a bleached-out photo of the band, which looked as though it may have been produced on a photocopier. The photo appeared to have been torn round the edges and the band's logo was in 'stamped'-style lettering, adding to the DIY look. The reverse was formed from a similarly high-contrast photo of police charging at revellers during a riot at the Notting Hill Carnival in 1976, the year before the record's release. The slapdash styling was completed by the song titles appearing in typed (rather than typeset) lettering, and was intensified by random puffs of red spray paint. This record sleeve, conceived by eminent commercial artist Rosław Szaybo, the resident art director at The Clash's record label, CBS, incorporates just about every element of punk design that you can think of – except the 'ransom-note' style lettering cut from newspapers and magazines, which Jamie Reid used to such sensational effect on the sleeve of the Sex Pistols' first album. The cover of *Never Mind the Bollocks* also employed the garish neon colours that were the signature of 1977, although the hues used have not been consistent in the many subsequent pressings and CD releases over the years. (Of course, the sleeve of *Bollocks* was nothing in shock-value compared to the sleeve of the single 'God Save the Queen', which featured the publicity portrait of Her Majesty taken especially for her Jubilee year, with her eyes and mouth covered over with the name of the band and the title of the song, again in the 'ransom-note' style lettering.)

To illustrate their love of slapstick, the front of The Damned's first LP, *Damned Damned Damned*, portrays the band in the aftermath of a food fight, with Rat Scabies caught in the act of licking squashed cream-cake off Captain Sensible's head (it was indeed cream-cake but less optimistic observers may have perceived it as vomit). In a spectacularly 'punk' promotional stunt, a limited number of the records were distributed with a photo of Eddie and the Hot Rods on the back, instead of the intended photo of The Damned playing at the Roxy, with a sticker saying 'erratum' on this edition to draw attention to the 'mistake' (these, if you're lucky enough to have one, are worth a pretty penny nowadays).

The sleeve art of The Stranglers' second album consists of a coffin adorned with a brass plaque engraved with the legend 'No More Heroes' and surrounded by a wreath of red carnations. Today this may not seem shocking but in 1978, in the 60th anniversary year of the 1918 Armistice and when many First World War veterans would have still been alive, it was considered to be deeply offensive. Likewise the affront caused by the sleeve of X Ray Spex's one and only album, *Germ Free*

Adolescents, is difficult to appreciate today. On it each of the band members appears to be trapped in and trying to escape from their own giant test tube. It's a very attractive image, with the band clothed in the fluorescent colours for which lead singer Poly Styrene was famed, but it caused outrage in the hysterical tabloid press at the time because it makes reference to assisted conception (the first 'test-tube baby', Louise Brown, had been born in Britain in the year of the album's release). The Slits' only album from the Seventies, *Cut* (which in the 21st century is a euphemism for female genital mutilation, though it's not clear whether it would have had this association in 1979), is adorned with a photo of the band naked except for loincloths and a generous slathering of mud. This image *does* retain a little of its ability to cause consternation today, when Page 3 photos of topless models have been banned from the tabloids and Benny Hill (in the sped-up 'chase' sequences that closed every episode of his eponymous Seventies show) is considered to be an unreconstructed sex pest rather than the nation's lovable comedy uncle. It is alleged that Palmolive, The Slits' drummer, found this sleeve design so distasteful that it may have been the reason why she left the band soon after the release of their debut – born in 1954, she would have grown up in the puritanical and (certainly towards women) repressive Francoist Spain.

Meanwhile, the sleeve of Buzzcocks' first album, *Another Music in a Different Kitchen*, was silver – that most un-punk of colours, harking back as it did to the Space Age of the Sixties, when it was envisaged that by the year 2000 we'd all be making our way to work with rocket-powered jet packs and taking our holidays on the moon. The typography, too, was cool and classic – neat sans-serif typefaces, arranged vertically at 90 degrees as well as horizontally, to form elongate lines that were accentuated by delicate black ruling. The photo of the band on the front of the album was pleasing and uncomplicated: the four members were dressed in matching black shirts, looking quizzically at the camera, with no evidence of the dishevelled states that The Damned or The Slits were posed in on their debut LPs. They looked like a brood of similarly aged cousins, snapped in a corner at a family gathering, rather than a gang of drunks caught in flagrante at the end of a particularly indulgent night out.

This, like all the band's other sleeves from the United Artists years, was designed by Malcolm Garrett. Malcolm was a graphic-design student at Manchester Polytechnic when he was introduced to Richard Boon, Buzzcocks' manager, by Linder Sterling, an illustration student a year above Malcolm at the poly (Richard Boon himself had studied fine art at Reading and contributed many ideas to the formation of the band's record sleeves). This was around the time that the band recorded *Spiral Scratch* at the end of 1976. To save money, Boon wanted to commission a poster advertising Buzzcocks' gigs that would be printed without the details of the date or venue, so these could be added later with marker pen. Malcolm produced these posters – the famous 'Love Battery' design – using the college's screen-printing equipment. He also devised the logo the band continues to use to this day. It was created using Letraset (dry transfer-lettering that is rubbed on to paper from its plastic sheet) in a typeface called Compacta. The type was cut up and redrawn, so it appeared stretched and quite different from the original, with the staggered Zs that are its distinguishing feature. (The BBC would attempt to pastiche this effect in the altogether less elegant logo used for the long-running music-quiz show *Never Mind the Buzzcocks* – although, if they'd just asked nicely, Malcolm or Pete would probably have granted them permission to use the real thing.)

Malcolm Garrett designed the band's other two album covers from the United Artists period, as well as all of the band's singles sleeves – in some cases once he had heard the songs and in some cases not. An enormous amount of thought and labour went into the concepts for the album sleeves – for example, all the 'brush script' lettering on the sleeve of *Love Bites* (which you could probably just download as a font these days) was all meticulously painted by hand, while there was some devilish trickery involved in posing the front-cover photo of the four guys. The band was photographed in front of a mirror so you can see the backs of their heads behind them. Also behind them is a backdrop painted with the name of the album – but, in order for the backdrop to be shown in the mirror, it had to be hanging in front of them, so a hole had to be cut in it through which the photograph could be taken. This sleight of hand also meant that the words *Love Bites* had to be painted in reverse on the backdrop. Malcolm says: 'I'm mildly surprised that no-one's ever commented on that photograph or asked how we did it – I mean, it's a little bit odd! But we were satisfied that what appears to be a straightforward portrait of the band has got this weird twist to it.'

Malcolm explains, in relation to the designs for the singles sleeves: 'I attempted, where I could, to illustrate the lyric of the song – for example, the graphical device on the reverse of "Promises" is a cross superimposed over a circle, to represent a kiss ["Lipstick" being the B-side to "Promises"].' A prevailing (and unusual) feature of Buzzcocks' singles sleeves is that the design extended over both sides. About this Malcolm says: 'All the sleeves have an interplay between the front and the back. Lots of people – including the record company – can be quite precious about what's on the front, so you can have more fun with the back. You can be more playful.'

Another example of a sleeve that illustrates the song is 'Harmony in My Head'. Malcolm says: 'It's a graphic head with esoteric "atoms" circling the eyes and the composition is quite "harmonious". It's a combination of straight lines and curved lines, so on the back it's just redrawn with the straight lines drawn as curved lines and the curved lines drawn as straight ones – to illustrate the B-side because, graphically, "something's gone wrong". It's ironic that the entire debacle of printing the sleeve in the wrong colours (see page 181) is a further example of "Something's Gone Wrong Again".'

The most 'punk' of Buzzcocks' record sleeves is, of course, the instantly recognizable 'Orgasm Addict'. The sleeve is printed in a strident combination of acid yellow and navy blue, complete with a montage of a naked woman with smiling, lipsticked mouths for nipples and an electric iron instead of a head, assembled by Linder Sterling, the band's illustration student friend. This iconic design makes a powerful commentary on the phenomenon of consumerism, as well as the commodification of sex and the exploitation of women, while referencing the style of early pop artist Richard Hamilton (particularly his 1956 work, 'Just What Is It That Makes Today's Homes So Different, So Appealing?').

Yet, in its own way, the sleeve of the single 'I Don't Mind' is equally subversive, belying the apparent demureness of the design. The band didn't like the idea of songs that had been released as singles appearing on their albums – they wanted to give their fans maximum value for money by releasing 'stand-alone' singles, which The Beatles had largely tried to do. The record label insisted that 'I Don't Mind' also be included on the album *Another Music in a Different Kitchen* – so, to register the band's displeasure at this decision, Malcolm designed the sleeve of 'I Don't Mind' with nothing on the front but the United Artists logo, while the catalogue number and the titles of the songs were on the back. To emphasize the statement, the sleeve was printed in the United Artists corporate colours of cream and brown. Unfortunately, when Malcolm sent the artwork to the printers, they thought he'd got the back and the front mixed up and so it was printed, incorrectly, with the titles of the songs on the front instead of the record label's logo. (The press ad for 'I Don't Mind' was even more seditious – it featured a huge United Artists logo that had been cut up and rearranged with the strapline: 'Marketing Ploy: the Single from the Album'. It even included the message: 'This single out now: new single out soon'.) Sly digs at the corporate world such as this would only ensure Buzzcocks' growing popularity within punk.

Punk, in the summer of 1977, had found its footing, facilitated by the furore caused by the Sex Pistols' 'God Save the Queen' and controversially titled *Never Mind the Bollocks*. An obscenity case taken out against a record-shop manager who displayed the offending disc in a prominent position was unsuccessful as 'bollocks' was deemed (by a university professor called as an expert witness at the trial) to be merely a good, traditional Middle English word that had for many years been used in the King James Bible.

The tabloid press went wild over the 'moral panic' they believed to be posed by punk, and the Pistols were the obvious whipping boys. The broadsheets, too, thought there may be a cause for righteous vexation but reported their fears in a suitably more restrained manner: in 1977 there were 14 articles about the Sex Pistols in the relatively sensible *Times* compared to 53 in the *Daily Mail*.

The *Times*, in January of 1977 (only a few weeks after the notorious Bill Grundy interview was aired), quoted the Conservative MP for Christchurch in Dorset – a small, attractive and affluent southern seaside town with one of the most elderly populations in the country – as branding the Pistols 'a bunch of ill-mannered louts'. The *Daily Mail* vilified punk as being 'the sickest, seediest step in a rock-world that thought it had seen it all', while the *Sun*, which was probably more obsessed with punk than even the *Daily Mail*, granted the Pistols a double-page spread in January 1978 that condemned the band as musical 'morons...[who] spit at [their] audiences' and vomit 'for the amusement of the customers'. The *Sun* seemed outraged at the band's behaviour and the corrupting effect it might have on the nation's youth, yet its writers seemed to have forgotten, ironically, what every student of journalism learns in the first week of their degree course: that 'there is no such thing as bad publicity'.

There was even an episode of the BBC's documentary programme *Brass Tacks* in August 1977 dedicated to the discussion of punk. It took the form of a live debate with a panel of authority figures who had had some experience with punk rock – including a Christian pastor and a committee of local councillors whose councils had banned punk groups from performing in their areas – opposing a panel of punks and champions of punk, including Pete Shelley, DJ John Peel and a handful of the regulars of Manchester's famous alternative-music venue and second home to Buzzcocks, the Electric Circus. The presenter, Brian Trueman, opened the show by postulating that punk is seen by some as 'a bigger threat to our way of life than Russian communism' – quite a claim in the years of the Cold War. There was even a bank of telephone staff in the studio, ready to take calls from indignant members of the public – although member of the punk defence team Ian's mum rang in to say, 'He doesn't smoke, he doesn't drink...they're not harming people.' In response to accusations that punks are vile and obscene, Pete Shelley – looking his most fresh-faced, affable and appealing – retorted, 'Do I *look* vile and obscene?'

So, while the Pistols and their followers were being denigrated by the British media, Buzzcocks were on the crest of a PR wave. They were featured frequently – and favourably – in the music press. They were guests of Tony Wilson on Granada TV's *So It Goes* and appeared several times on BBC's *Top of the Pops*. There was even a documentary made about Buzzcocks by Granada in 1978, *B'dum B'dum*[16], at a time when a programme dedicated to a single band would be a considerable rarity (although they did have to share the limelight in this 45-minute chronicle with Howard Devoto). Unlike other punk bands, Buzzcocks also popped up in some quite unexpected places – even on Saturday-morning children's TV. Maybe even more unexpectedly, Buzzcocks – or individual members thereof – were pictured many times as pin-ups in teenage girls' magazines: appetizing eye-candy for the newly hormonal. You wouldn't have seen Johnny Rotten, with his dodgy dentition, or The Damned's Dave Vanian, who looked like he'd just got out of the wrong side of the coffin one imagines he might have slept in, as a centrefold in *Jackie* or on the back page of *Patches* – but Buzzcocks were there, occupying the same spot that maybe David Cassidy or Donny Osmond had inhabited four or five years earlier.

So how did Mr and Mrs McNeish feel about their son being a key player in a movement that was considered to be more dangerous than 'hyper-inflation' (another Seventies bugbear) and which threatened to debauch and debase the nation's youth?

Pete's cousin Howard says: 'Pete's mum and dad didn't object to him being involved in punk but they never thought it'd take off like it did – and they were also a bit worried for him as there was a stabbing at one of the gigs. Me and Pete's younger brother, Gary, went to see Buzzcocks play at the Students' Union in Manchester. It was in the early days of punk and there were a lot of people spitting – Pete was covered in it and our Gary actually punched someone for gobbing at the stage. But Pete said, "At the moment it's a hard and aggressive movement but it'll settle down eventually." He was very tolerant, very understanding of people. And he was right – the spitting thing soon died out. You see, Buzzcocks were different from a lot of the other punk bands, as they were real musicians, they had proper songs and people went to their gigs to listen and to watch, not to kick off.'

Other questions were raised in the family, though, after a certain article was published in the music press. Howard remembers: 'A funny thing happened in the early days of the band. A picture appeared – I think it was in the *NME* – of Pete and Steve [Diggle] where it looked like they were kissing. I think it was taken at the Electric Circus. When Pete got home my mum demanded to know if he was "really a puff"[17]. His reply was: "It doesn't do you any harm in the music industry if people think you're gay." She was satisfied with that and I don't think his sexuality was ever discussed in the family apart from that time – it just wasn't seen as being an issue. Pete fought passionately for gay rights, as it was something he felt very strongly about – although he never found the need to pigeonhole himself as far as his sexuality was concerned.'

Howard says about punk: 'Of course I got into punk because of Pete. When I was 15 he invited me to a gig that he was putting on – but he said that he couldn't tell me who was playing; it was a secret. I didn't go in the end because I was afraid of going into Manchester on my own and having to make my way back home late at night. I wish now that I'd gone, though, because that was one of the nights when the Sex Pistols played at the Free Trade Hall!

'We'd go early to watch the support band and Pete'd be there in the audience, because he always liked to give the support act some feedback. Pete gave a lot of younger bands a leg up whenever he could.'

Of course, one of those younger bands was Joy Division, who would – certainly in their later incarnation as New Order – eclipse Buzzcocks in terms of popularity and outstrip them in volume of sales. Howard adds: 'Hooky says that Joy Division didn't even have a full lineup when Buzzcocks first invited them to support them on tour but they had to get their act together as it was an opportunity too good to miss.'

John Maher takes up the story: 'We already had connections with the lads who became Joy Division – Peter Hook was at those Sex Pistols gigs at the Lesser Free Trade Hall in 1976, as was Ian Curtis. Those shows served as an inspiration for a lot of people to start a band.

'As we were fellow Mancunians, and as we'd already had some experience by that time, they came to us for advice. For example, there was a lad called Terry who was going to be their drummer. He didn't end up drumming with them but he did become their roadie. When they were buying a drum kit that was advertised in the *Manchester Evening News*, Terry took me with him to advise them. My abiding memory of that trip is a certain member of Joy Division continually winding down the car window and catcalling at women! I can't tell you what he was saying but it was pretty saucy.

'Before they were called Joy Division they went under the name Warsaw, and before that Stiff Kittens – that was a name that Pete had suggested for them, not entirely seriously! They probably did the right thing by changing their name.'

Maher says of touring with Joy Division: 'They had this air of being quite serious and dour – the long overcoats and the moody black-and-white photos taken on the bridge in Hulme – but when we were on the road with them it was like going on tour with a bunch of football fans. They were big drinkers; they got turfed out of one of our hotels because they'd broken into the bar after it had closed for the night. It was lad culture – a total contrast to what they were on record.

'They were keen practical jokers and there were some high jinks on some nights of the tour. Legend has it that they tipped live maggots on us from above on the last night at the London gig. We don't remember that happening, though! And the same "legend" has it that they bought mice from a pet shop and let them loose in our tour bus...'

It was around this time, in 1979, that Buzzcocks were at their zenith. They toured Europe, they toured the States, and they made TV and radio appearances on both continents. They were at the top of their game and they couldn't put a foot wrong. Punk survived the initial explosion that could so easily have consumed it, although many of its adherents were branded after 1978 as 'post-punk' (one of the reasons being that 'real' punk was considered to have died in 1977, when the Pistols hit the big time in the summer of that year and the movement could no longer be considered underground). Buzzcocks can claim a generous amount of the credit for coaxing punk out of the seedy clubs of London – and for gifting the world the gothic-rock band fronted by the fragile Ian Curtis.

Of Pete's attitude to the fame he'd craved so much as a child that he'd deliberately got himself lost at the annual Miners' Gala, Howard says: 'We'd go backstage after the show and, although there was always a bottle of champagne as part of the "rider" (you've heard of "No Moët, no show-ay"), Pete would be there, just drinking a cup of tea and maybe eating a sandwich. It was hardly rock 'n' roll! After the show loads of fans would be badgering him for his autograph. We'd ask, "Don't you get sick of it?" and he'd say, "How could I get sick of it? These people pay my wages."'

Howard adds: 'Pete was known very affectionately by the kids in our family as "Peter Popstar" – but he was never "the pop star", despite his nickname. His thing was, he wanted to entertain people, but he never wanted to be an "entertainer". A few years ago we wanted him to sing at a family gathering. We'd been trying to persuade him all evening to get up there but he was really reluctant to do it – although he did in the end. We said, "Why are you so nervous? You were playing to 12,000 people last night in Sweden." His reply was: "Yes, but I didn't know any of those people."

'I think the reason why people loved him and his music was because he wrote about stuff that was real to them: he wrote about the way that people feel. And he'd sing about stuff that had really happened to him, stuff that everyone can relate to.

'Pete would've been flabbergasted at the outpouring of grief that there was when he died. He was appreciative of his fans and yet at the same time he was very modest. At the end of the day he was a simple Leigh lad who just wanted to make people happy.' And, with the succession of divine pop delicacies that Buzzcocks dished up over their long career, you can safely say that he succeeded there.

So let's blow the digital dust off these 'lost tapes' and let Pete tell you the story of Buzzcocks' songbook from those fruitful years when they were signed to United Artists – in his own words and with his characteristic warmth, wit and wisdom. (You'll just have to imagine the gentle Lancastrian accent, the self-deprecating and sometimes salacious chuckles, and the occasional taking of comedy umbrage.)

Take it away, Pete...

Notes

1 The Parsonage Colliery was one of the deepest coalmines in the country and in the 1930s employed 1,500 workers. It closed in 1992.

2 The Women's Land Army consisted of young women who were sent to farms to do agricultural work that had traditionally been done by men, as the young men were being called up to fight in the Second World War.

3 In Northern English, 'to mither' means 'to make a fuss' or 'to irritate'.

4 A bus or coach taken for a recreational excursion.

5 *Cosmos: A Personal Voyage.*

6 Sex was the boutique run by Sex Pistols' manager Malcolm McLaren and designer Vivienne Westwood. It sold rubber, fetish and bondage wear and helped define the punk look. Female punk icon Jordan and Sex Pistols' bassist Glen Matlock were employed as sales assistants in the shop, while the other Pistols, Adam Ant and Siouxsie Sioux's Bromley Contingent were regular customers.

7 Like Sex, Granny Takes A Trip (meaning an LSD trip) was another boutique at the less fashionable end of the King's Road. It sold genuine vintage and antique clothing as well as cutting-edge 'designer' wear (it was still possible to get 1930s' wedding dresses and Victorian nightdresses at jumble sales at this time). Although most associated with the hippies of the late Sixties and the rhinestoned and dandified rockers of the mid-Seventies, GTAT didn't cease trading until 1979.

8 John Lydon has since claimed that the band's title was not alluding to pornography or violence but was in fact named for the reproductive parts of a plant – the 'sex pistils'.

9 In later years, Buzzcocks' protégés Joy Division and New Order performed their own, mercifully shorter covers of 'Sister Ray', maybe as much in recognition of the song's formative influence on the early Buzzcocks as in tribute to Reed, Cale et al.

10 With Richard Skinner on BBC Radio 1, 3 August 1991.

11 The hall was built in 1846 on the site of the bloody Peterloo Massacre of 1819. It was the subject for Romantic and revolutionary poet Percy Bysshe Shelley's 'The Masque of Anarchy', an epic of 91 stanzas.

12 Which in themselves would have drawn attention on a warm June evening in Manchester – and the summer of 1976 was, at that point, the hottest on record.

13 Wythenshawe was at one time the largest social-housing project in Western Europe and extends over two postcode areas.

14 They, like Buzzcocks, were produced by Martin Rushent.

15 One of the residential areas in south Manchester favoured by students.

16 The programme was named after Howard Devoto's creative pronunciation in 'Boredom' on Buzzcocks' *Spiral Scratch* EP.

17 In the 1970s in northern Britain a 'puff' was a homosexual man. Southerners favour the spelling 'poof', but in the north a 'poof' is what you sit on at your gran's when there's not enough seats.

the tapes

Pre-Punk

You were from Leigh, about 15 miles from Manchester city centre – what was it like when you were growing up?

Leigh when I was growing up was a coal mining town. There were 30 or 40 pits in the immediate area. My dad used to work at a mine in Astley Green, my mum was brought up in Pit Yard in Astley – how northern is that? – and my first proper job was at the National Coal Board[1].

When I was in the first year at grammar school there was still a railway in Leigh. I used to get 3 shillings a week pocket money (the equivalent of 15p today) and it was 2 and 11 pence for a return ticket to Manchester. We'd have 1 penny left over and so couldn't buy much when we were there. We used to go round the food hall in Lewis's department store and take samples of cheese and pies and things. We also used to go round the libraries – the Central Library and the John Rylands[2] – and museums, or we'd go and look at the Pre-Raphaelites in the gallery on Mosley Street because they were free as well. There was a lot to see and do without spending any money.

When I was a teenager they closed the railway station in Leigh and I used to go into town on the bus. There used to be a lot of record shops in the streets where the Arndale Centre is now. We used to satisfy ourselves by looking at the sleeves – we didn't really have the money to buy anything.

I used to go with my friends and we'd spend the day wandering round Manchester. We used to go to Kendals, the department store on Deansgate – they had a trendy boutique which used to sell clothes and which also had a record stall. It was called Way-In. So we'd hang out there because they played music in the shop. One of my favourite records at the time was 'Badge' by Cream and they used to play that. We'd spend hours browsing round but no-one ever asked us what we were doing or if we were going to buy anything. Then they had the David Bowie album *The Man Who Sold the World* – the one where he's wearing the dress on the cover. If you went shopping in Leigh all there was really was Woolworths – pick 'n' mix was about the greatest variety that there was – and so Manchester was the place where things happened.

In my early youth, Manchester was the musical rival to Liverpool. Lots of bands came out of Manchester in the sixties – The Hollies, Herman's Hermits – you name them. Then *Top of the Pops* was recorded in Didsbury[3] – they chose Manchester over London for this flagship music show, which says something.

What did Manchester have to offer in the way of nightlife in the early days of punk?

In Manchester, if you were dressed up – as a punk, or just not following the norms of fashion – there were very few places where you could get a drink. At that time I was living with a guy who knew lots of drag artistes, so we used to go to this club called Dickens on the top floor in a building at the wrong end of Oldham Street [now in Manchester's trendy Northern Quarter]. It was a gay bar, a drag club. It was a club that they'd let us in!

Manchester's changed a bit since then, though, hasn't it?

When I lived in Manchester, what's now called the Northern Quarter was a run-down area of town where all the rag-trade businesses were [even by that time Manchester was still a centre for textile and clothing businesses]. A lot of the buildings in Manchester were blackened with soot – you can only see the brickwork on Victoria Station and the tower at Strangeways now because they've been sandblasted. On a Sunday, at one time, the city centre used to be a desert, a ghost town – there were whole sections of the city centre that were offices so it'd be dead at the weekend. But now the offices are apartments, so it's got a whole new lease of life and some of the emptiness and rough edges have gone.

Buzzcocks played at Planet K in the Northern Quarter at the end of 1999 – it was our Christmas-party show. I think Planet K had previously been a furniture shop. They've tarted up the Oldham Street area and it's now a magnet for music fans from all over the world – a place of pilgrimage. I suppose you can say it's been gentrified. You've got it in London, in places like Hoxton and Dalston and Shoreditch, where people take a run-down area and breathe new life into it and then all the creatives colonize it. And Salford Quays, that used to be the docks – like Albert Dock in Liverpool, and Canary Wharf. That can only be an improvement, can't it? The centre of Manchester's now all very sophisticated – it's all street cafés and conference centres and that. And the canal that runs under Deansgate and past the back of what used to be the Haçienda – that used to be an absolute eyesore, but it's been urban-regenerated now.

Tony Wilson's idea was for the Northern Powerhouse – where the Northwest would be devolved from the rest of the UK and Manchester would be the region's capital[4]. His dream was that the area would be independent economically and politically and that its cultural scene in particular would be heavily funded. I don't think this is anywhere nearer to happening – it was a typically ambitious idea of Tony's – but there are plans for a major arts venue, the Factory, to be built in Tony's honour so perhaps this is the beginning of the cultural aspect of his dream being realized.

Manchester is famous worldwide for its record shops. Piccadilly Records was handy, being next to the bus station. You could pop in and browse while you were waiting for the bus. They'd usually have whatever it was you wanted. I used to buy CDs in there, in about 1984 when CDs were still new – when you're fed up of your crackly old vinyl and you want a nice, clean sound. I remember getting some Roxy Music CDs there. And Virgin Records used to be on...was it Newton Street? Before they moved to the Megastore at the bottom of Market Street. The old one was less corporate than the shiny new one. I think it might have been Virgin where Howard Devoto advertised for musicians to join him in Magazine. There were lots of good bookshops in Manchester as well – like Grass Roots, the radical bookshop just off Piccadilly. They weren't cathedrals of consumption; they were places where you could meet people and hang out with friends.

When did you move from Manchester and what made you leave? You resisted it all the time you were in Buzzcocks Mark I.

I only moved from Manchester in 1985 because I'd signed a contract for my solo album, *Heaven and the Sea*, and the commuting to London didn't agree with me. A flat became available in my friend's building in London – it was because the tenant had died. I moved into it on what was supposed to be a temporary basis – and 19 years later I was still there! I didn't have anything against Manchester; I wasn't trying to escape or anything. It was just the chance to do something different: a new chapter in my career.

Why do you think Manchester became such a hothouse of musical talent?

The reason why Manchester is a good place for stuff to happen is because the centre is so small – you can walk across the city centre in under an hour. It's compact; it isn't sprawling like London is. I remember hearing in the Seventies that within a 30-minute journey of the centre of Manchester there were 9 million people – and there are probably even more now. There's lots of nightlife and lots of shopping places – that's what makes cities vibrant. So when people from the surrounding areas go out, or want to do anything creative, they choose Manchester. A lot of people get condensed into a small area – so the chances of meeting up with people with similar interests and a similar viewpoint are far greater than they would be in a bigger city. A lot of people who were instrumental in the punk and post-punk scenes in Manchester weren't even from Manchester – including myself, Howard Devoto (from Leeds) and Ian Curtis (from Macclesfield). In Manchester you're bumping into people all the time – it's a lot less diluted than London.

What makes Manchester and its music special?

Manchester stands shoulder-to-shoulder with London but it also has its very own unique character. What defines the Mancunian spirit? A good sense of humour – that and stoicism. I mean, you have to be stoical with the rain, don't you? All my memories of Manchester are of people making the best of what there was. So Manchester bands capture the spirit of the city – the creativity, the maverick spirit, the unique northern-ness and the determination and the stoicism. And Manchester bands have the Mancunian mindset – making the best of what there is, and if you can't find something good in it, at least finding the humour in it.

How did you first get into music?

I was born in 1955, and by '63 and '64 you had The Beatles – they were the first pop group that you could relate to. You knew who everyone was: they had their own cartoon personalities – they did their own variety performance. My favourite was probably Paul, then I'd gravitated towards John by the time the band had split up.

My auntie used to live in Scotland; my uncle had a tied cottage near Loch Lomond and we used to go up there in the summer. They had a big radiogram in the sitting room with a load of 78s and singles. They had stuff like Patsy Cline, Elvis and of course The Beatles, and I used to pretend to be a DJ. I'd amuse myself like that because it was out in the country and there wasn't much else to do – and quite often it was raining. We listened to the radio at home as well: this was in the days before Radio 1 and at the time the only way you could hear popular music was on the BBC's Light Programme[5].

My other auntie, my mum's sister, went to live in Australia and didn't like it. They went on a £10 assisted passage, but they had to pay the full fare on the way back – it took them about three years to save up for it! On the way back the ship stopped at Hong Kong and she picked up a couple of transistor radios for me and my brother. Transistors were groundbreaking technology at the time, compared to the wireless or radiogram that was like a piece of furniture: they were made from wood and they were as big as your sideboard. It was about 1964 and we could get the pirate stations on our transistors, Radio Luxembourg[6] and Radio Caroline[7] – still in the days before

Radio 1; that didn't start until 1967. Then of course we'd watch *Ready Steady Go!* and *Top of the Pops* on TV.

Who were your own musical heroes?

The Beatles were an important part of my interest in music. For Christmas 1968 my brother and I got a Bush record player – one of the old ones, with the auto-changer. I got *Sergeant Pepper* as another Christmas present – we always used to hear it when we went to other people's houses, when they had parties because their mums and dads had gone out. My brother got 'Urban Spaceman', the single by the Bonzo Dog Doo-Dah Band. Around September or October that year I'd bought 'Hey Jude', knowing that I was going to get a record player for Christmas. By the time The Beatles split up I'd got a stereo.

Around 1969 I started buying music magazines and newspapers and I kept a ring binder of cuttings and interviews. Then in 1970 I got a guitar and I had these books of easy-to-play Beatles songs. The Beatles came as an all-round package: they were cultural icons. If you read about The Beatles it would introduce you to other stuff, like meditation – of course there was no internet at the time and listening to music was the way you found out about things. The Beatles were a fountain of new ideas and experiences.

I was a big fan of Yoko Ono as well – I used to sing along to Yoko. One time my parents gave me a pound to get my hair cut and I bought a poster of John and Yoko in bed instead. When I was listening to Yoko my parents thought I'd gone properly mad – they couldn't understand it at all! I had so many posters and press cuttings that there wasn't an inch of wall space showing underneath. There was a secondhand record shop in Leigh, on Church Street near the parish church, and they had records that were 10p and 15p (this was, of course, post-decimalization[8]).

I used to go in there every week and browse; you know, as you do when you're 14 and 15, just seeing if they had a copy of the album in because I didn't have enough money to buy it. I managed to amass the entire collection of Beatles singles from there. The ones I paid full price for were 'Penny Lane' and...just one other one, I can't remember what it was now.

What was the first live show you attended?

In 1971 T.Rex were touring: it was around the time that 'Hot Love' was released. I bought the single when it came out and I went to the concert – it was on the 16th of May at the Free Trade Hall in Manchester. It was my first proper gig. It was seated and I was right at the front. I saw them and that was it – The Beatles were no longer going and this was something that I could be part of. I became a Bolan fan. I took all my Beatles singles in to the record-exchange shop and traded them in for *Weasels Ripped My Flesh* by Frank Zappa – they didn't have anything by Bolan. I didn't like *Weasels* that much – it was weird, kind of jazzy-type rock, and there was no satisfaction in it for me. I bought T.Rex's *Electric Warrior* when it came out and I got tickets to see them again but it wasn't quite the same: it was all screaming teenage girls and I wasn't at the front. I took my girlfriend, who was also a fan. I was mostly into Bolan from around 1972. In 1973 they released all the four Tyrannosaurus Rex albums – I got them all. I'd got my electric guitar and amp by then and I could play all the songs. A lot of my rhythm-guitar playing is influenced by Marc Bolan.

Then in 1972 I went to the Bickershaw Festival. Bickershaw is a small mining town between Leigh and Wigan, and I believe [late TV personality] Jeremy Beadle was one of the organizers. The Kinks played, and Hawkwind, the Grateful Dead, Donovan, Captain Beefheart...it was a real music festival: the Woodstock of Wigan! There was even a documentary on it. It was on the 5th to the 7th of May 1972: three days of mud, rain and music. On the first night my friend and I just walked round the perimeter fence because we didn't have the money to get in. You know how it was at festivals back then: the security wasn't that good, and people were prising open the fence and getting in, but we were too scared to do it. Then on the Saturday a gap had been left open in the fence and we got in for free! I didn't have a hippy outfit, though; I had a duffel coat. And yes, of course it was in black and white – everything was in those days.

I'd been listening to a song on the radio before I left the house that day and I heard it again at the festival: it was 'Star Man' by David Bowie. I'd bought 'Space Oddity' when it came out in 1969 after seeing it on the *Tonight* programme, then a friend at school had *Ziggy Stardust*. I'd tape albums I'd borrowed with headphones on and write down the lyrics from the lyric sheet in a foolscap ledger while sitting on a little stool in the front room. I had an arrangement with the record exchange where I could buy a record on Saturday morning, tape it and take it back later that afternoon and get back the price, minus 50p. This was in the days before shrink wrap, of course.

It was 1972 and Bowie and Mick Ronson had a lot of coverage in the music press. I had the front page of *Melody Maker* on my bedroom wall, the one where Bowie was saying he was bisexual, and my father disapproved, so that was great. It was perfect, packaged rebellion! The week after 'John, I'm Only Dancing' came out, Bowie was playing in Manchester at a club called Stoneground – I think it was somewhere in Stretford. The opening music at the show was Beethoven's Symphony No. 9, which was used in the film *Clockwork Orange* – that was all the rage at the time as well. Bowie played stuff from *The Man Who Sold the World* as well as *Ziggy Stardust*. I became a big Bowie fan. Bolan had gone off the boil a bit; his stuff had become really simple. Bowie was a far better songwriter.

I went to see David Bowie again in Stretford – it was at the Hardrock on Greatstone Road, one of Manchester's great forgotten venues. I don't think it was open very long. That was 1973 as well. I got the tickets from Paperchase in St Ann's Square. We used to go there a lot because they had a lot of bootleg records. And when I bought the tickets for Bowie the tickets were numbered 1 and 2!

My girlfriend in 1972 had moved to Atherton from Malvern in Worcestershire and she knew this guy who was a bit like Morrissey: he was really way-out. Bowie in his interviews was always coming up with these references to bands like Velvet Underground that you just couldn't get hold of at that time – and this guy had two of their albums! I went to see Lou Reed when he played at the Palace Theatre in Manchester. It was quite exotic for a teenager growing up in Leigh – I was always interested in stuff other people wouldn't like. I liked Sparks as well. I saw them in '71 or '72 on *Old Grey Whistle Test*, at about the same time that Alice Cooper was on the show, and he became huge...He was another oddball that not many people where I lived liked.

Some music fans liken being a fan to being in love, or like a religion. Was it either of these things for you?

Being a fan for me wasn't like a religion, and it wasn't like being in love either. If you'd've asked my parents they'd have said I was obsessed, but for me it was the music: about listening to other people's and learning how it was done so that I could write my own. I had an admiration for The Beatles: they were something that occupied me, inasmuch as I was occupied by the music – I liked music, and these were the bands that I liked. But I mean, I like Beethoven and Wagner and Mahler as well!

If I had fans, I think I'd be frightened of their ardour, yet you seem to take it in your stride.

I like having fans. They're our customers, and of course it's great to know that your customers are satisfied. It's interesting to meet fans, to get to know people. When I'm on stage I don't just see a sea of faces – I try to spot people that I know and sing to them. I don't find [being the object of adulation] a burden, no – I don't think we're that famous that it's a problem. When people recognize me in the street they say hello, but that's all – we don't have stalkers or anything. And I mean, everyone likes to be liked, don't they?!

Notes

1   Another proud northerner and erstwhile employee of the National Coal Board was the gay-rights activist Allan Horsfall. In the mid-Sixties (when he lived in Atherton, next to Pete's hometown of Leigh) he joined the Homosexual Law Reform Society to campaign for the decriminalization of homosexuality and allowed his home address and phone number to be listed as their branch contact details. This represented a tremendous personal risk at the time but Horsfall's activism eventually contributed to the passing of the Sexual Offences Act of 1967.

2   Always progressive and keen to educate and improve its citizens, Manchester was the first local authority in the UK to open a public library after the Public Libraries Act was passed in 1850, which benefitted Pete as an autodidact.

3   *Top of the Pops* was actually recorded in Rusholme, another suburb of south Manchester, in a repurposed Methodist chapel that had previously served as the studios for Mancunian Films. This company specialized in making entertainment for northern audiences and in 1934 produced a film starring the young George Formby, *Boots! Boots!*

4   The dream of a devolved Manchester has been partially realized by the appointment of Andy Burnham (coincidentally a former MP for Leigh) as Mayor of Greater Manchester, a position with considerably more power than the traditional, mostly ceremonial role of town mayor.

5   The BBC's Light Programme was a radio station that broadcast 'light entertainment' and music from 1945 until 1967, when it was superseded by Radio 1 (young people's music) and Radio 2 (middle-aged people's music). *Pick of the Pops*, the UK's first 'chart' show, was broadcast on the Light Programme.

6   Radio Luxembourg was broadcast from the small European country because commercial broadcasting was not permitted on the UK mainland due to the monopoly awarded to the BBC. It first started broadcasting in the Twenties and by the Sixties was famed for its emphasis on pop music and its appeal to the teen market (on which the BBC was slow to pick up).

7   Radio Caroline was a pirate radio station that first broadcast in 1964 and circumvented the regulations surrounding commercial broadcasting by operating from a number of different ships based in international waters. It specialized in groovy music that appealed to the Sixties pop-pickers.

8   Decimalization Day in the UK was 15 February 1971.

Orgasm Addict

Stand-alone single
B-side: 'Whatever Happened To?'
Recorded: September 1977, TW Studios, Fulham, London
Mixed: Advision Studios, Fitzrovia, London
Released: 8 October 1977
Songwriters: Howard Devoto and Pete Shelley
Producer: Martin Rushent
Sleeve designer: Malcolm Garrett; collage by Linder

You recorded this at TW Studios in Fulham?

Well, we started doing it there. It was the first recording session that we'd done with Martin Rushent. We came down to London and Martin had used TW with The Stranglers who were also signed to United Artists[1]. It was underneath a music shop in the basement and he'd used that and thought, 'Here's another punk band, we can put them in there.' So we went down to it and it was like a dingy basement really and we did the two tracks – 'Orgasm Addict' and 'Whatever Happened To?'. We did the basic recording and a rough vocal on it but we weren't really happy with the studio – it was dank! We thought, 'We've just signed a record contract – we want a proper studio.'

We'd signed on the 16th of August – the day Elvis died – and a couple of days later we did a session for Piccadilly Radio[2] where we played 'Whatever Happened To?' and 'Orgasm Addict', although I don't know if they ever played 'Orgasm Addict'! So I went down to London on the 16th of September – the day Marc Bolan died – and for some reason the record company sent along a chauffeur-driven Rolls-Royce to pick me up at the station to drive me down to Barnes, where Olympic Studios was. As we were driving to Barnes the driver said, 'Have you heard? Marc Bolan's died.' And in fact, coincidentally, he'd smashed his car into a tree near the studio[3]. It was a big shock to me because

I was always a big Bolan fan. T.Rex was the first proper concert I went to see in Manchester's Free Trade Hall. I was on the front row: 16th May 1973. That was when I decided that I wanted to do something in music. So it was a big shock to me to find out he'd died – especially as Kevin Cummins had recently shown us a photo of him holding up a copy of *Spiral Scratch* and smiling.

So I went to the studio and did the vocal and the backing vocal. I think we were in Studio 2 – a smallish studio, rather than the big room, which is Studio 1, the one that's on the cover of *Singles Going Steady*. We were getting much better results in there and it felt more like a proper studio, rather than a makeshift thing. I mean, The Stranglers were happy at TW but we weren't, and the rest is history.

There was an incident when we were in Studio 2 – Andrew Lauder, the A&R guy, came along with a crate of Tennent's super-strength lager, which ended the evening with an argument with Garth throwing his new Thunderbird[4] bass down a flight of stairs – luckily it was in a case!

PHOTO BY DAVID CORIO

Pete and the avuncular Martin Rushent. They were very close and enjoyed working together. Pete was devastated when Martin died in 2011.

Alan Winstanley was the engineer...

He'd worked with Martin Rushent on The Stranglers' *Rattus Norvegicus* – he was the house engineer. They went on to work on all The Stranglers' stuff together, and a lot of other stuff. And of course Alan went on to work with Clive Langer with Madness.

Putting out 'Orgasm Addict' must have been a tremendous risk for United Artists, knowing that it wouldn't get any airplay.

It was a brave move on United Artists' part to release as the first single for a new band a single they knew would never get played on the radio. But I suppose part of the selling point was the notoriety. The reason why we chose this as the first single on United Artists was we had a poll when we went into the studio to record *Spiral Scratch*. We thought the fairest way to do it is for everyone to choose four or five songs and the top four that get voted will appear on *Spiral Scratch*. The fifth one to be chosen was 'Orgasm Addict' – so we'd always decided that that was going to be the next single, regardless of who we were signed to. We were going to put it out ourselves but the money we were making from *Spiral Scratch* only helped to pay for our expenses for touring with The Clash on the 'White Riot' tour. The tour soaked up all the money we'd made on *Spiral Scratch* but the tour and the EP led to us being approached subsequently by record companies. The tour wasn't so much about promoting a record – it was a way of introducing people to punk.

It couldn't be played on the radio and it probably wasn't displayed in shops at the time because of the sleeve design?

Well, you see we went even further. Not only did we have a
record which was controversial but it had the sleeve that was

designed by Linder. It sold because of good marketing –
and because it was a good song. United Artists had a brilliant
marketing and press department. John Peel still played it –
it didn't get played on daytime radio but Peel's programme
was on late at night.

**Is it true that it got past the BBC's board of censors because
it came to them as a white label so they didn't know what the
title was, didn't see the sleeve and couldn't decipher the lyric?**

I don't know about that – that might be part of the good publicity
and marketing! After all, it's record companies that sell records,
not bands. The BBC did ban my solo single 'Homosapien'
though. They objected to the line that says, 'Homo superior/
In my interior'. I don't know what they read into that!

**Andrew Lauder was noted for his 'adventurous' signings,
wasn't he?**

Andrew Lauder signed Can and Neu! and Hawkwind.

You had offers from other labels at the time?

We had other offers but the reason why we liked Andrew Lauder
was because we were quite adamant about having full artistic
control – including the sleeve designs. Especially the sleeve
designs! And Andrew just said, 'Yes – no problem.'

On the day that we signed the contract, 16th of August,
I received a phone call at Richard's and Howard's house – they
had rooms in a house owned by a philosophy lecturer at Bolton
Institute of Technology and we used to rehearse in the basement.
It had a phone wired in because all I had in the place I was living
in down the road was a coin-operated phone box. That flat was

like Buzzcocks Central! Anyway, it was Maurice Oberstein on the phone, the managing director from CBS, saying that we shouldn't sign with United Artists but sign with them. I told him we'd had negotiations with other record companies but we were quite happy with United Artists because they were prepared to give us what we wanted – which was full artistic control.

Where were you living at the time?

I moved from Leigh probably a couple of days before the first gig in July 1976. I lived in Higher Broughton, Salford, on Lower Broughton Road, and I was in a windowless basement flat at the start of Buzzcocks. I got kicked out in about the April and had to move back to my mum and dad's because I hadn't paid the rent. I'd gone for a night out at the Ranch and I came back to my flat with a few people to find the door had been taken off its hinges and all my stuff had gone – the landlord had taken it round to my mum and dad's. So I moved back in with them.

It was quite a busy time because we went on the 'White Riot' tour through May 1977 and just before the tour I'd been signing on [for unemployment benefit]. The Labour Exchange tried to make me take a job as a bran packer, but thankfully I didn't get the job.

After I got kicked out of the flat and went back to my mum and dad's I started signing on in Leigh. I think it was in early April [1977] that we appeared on *Granada Reports* at the invite of Tony Wilson – at that time he was still a TV presenter and he used to have a music slot, *So It Goes*, on the early-evening local news programme. And after the 'White Riot' tour I went back to try and sign on again and they said, 'You've been working.' I told them I hadn't been paid for it! It seemed that a 'concerned citizen' had actually shopped me to the Social to say I must be a multimillionaire because I'd been on TV and played at the Rainbow in London. So they stopped my dole! They were trying to get me another job but this was at the end of July, early August, just before we were due to sign to United Artists, so I said, 'I'm signing a record contract next week.' I mean, they weren't paying me – and they were expecting me to go out and find a job!

Had you been working up until that time?

I gave up my job at the National Coal Board officially the day before I started with Buzzcocks. And I've never had a proper job since!

That was fortuitous then!

Yes, things like that happened a lot – a nice dovetailing.

Did you get a big advance?

I haven't really checked how much it would be today if you worked it out with inflation – but it's still far bigger than any advance we got on the more recent albums. But we still only paid ourselves £30 per week. We were trying to be sensible. It's not all for spending on fast cars as soon as you get it! You've got expenses – which a lot of pop stars these days forget about. But it did work out quite well.

How did you meet John Maher?

A girl had put an ad in *Melody Maker* saying she wanted musicians to play with, but she didn't say she was a drummer. I told Howard to get in touch with her in case she's a drummer because The Velvet Underground had a female drummer and

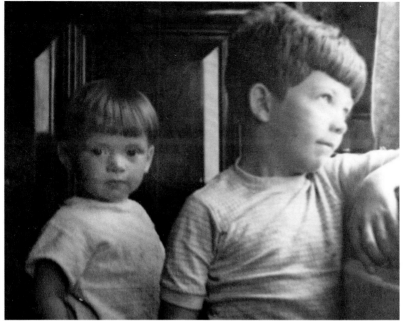

Pete and his cousin Howard Lycett, *c.*1964 – when looking out of the window was one of the only things there was to do.

The Electric Circus, Collyhurst Street, Manchester – formerly a bingo hall, then a heavy metal club. The venue closed down in October 1977.

Pete shares 'a moment' with Steve Diggle in the dressing room at London's Roxy club while Garth Davies looks on aghast (or jealous).

Signing the contract on the bar at the Electric Circus. Andrew Lauder is the guy on the left with the moustache and glasses who looks like he doesn't belong in a punk club.

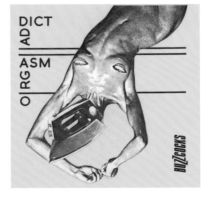

Malcolm Garrett's sleeve design, incorporating a collage by Linder, with a selection of 'official' and 'unofficial' badges.

Isn't it for this kind of moment that everyone wants to be in a band? Taken in what is now Manchester's Northern Quarter, 1979.

Malcolm Garrett's sleeve design, with official badges. The 7-badge set was available to buy from the *Secret Public* for the princely sum of £1.50 – plus 25p for p&p.

Malcolm Garrett at his final year show at Manchester Poly, June 1978.

In the studio at the recording of the video for 'Lipstick', produced by a team from Granada Studios, 1978.

Malcolm Garrett's sleeve design. Embossing – an expensive process – made the album sleeve that extra bit special.

Malcolm Garrett's sleeve design. Compare with Duchamp's 'Coeurs Volants', produced for the cover of a 1961 arts revue.

On Lever Street, Manchester, just round the corner from the New Hormones office, 1979.

we thought it'd be cool to have one. Anyway, this guy who'd only been playing drums for six weeks had got in touch with her and she thought he might be more suitable, as she just wanted people to play with and we were looking for a serious drummer, because we had these gigs with the Pistols lined up. We went round to meet him and we saw him and that was it. He'd only got the kit six weeks earlier for his 16th birthday – he was just a natural.

Had Martin Rushent worked in A&R at United Artists?

Yes. He started off as an engineer and along the way he met up with Andrew Lauder. The MD at the time was Martin Davies, who used to produce Shirley Bassey, and I think that's how he met Martin Rushent. When United Artists signed The Stranglers Martin said, 'I wouldn't mind producing them!' And likewise when Buzzcocks came into the United Artists stable. So he was a bit like a stable lad turned jockey.

Can you remember where and when 'Orgasm Addict' was written?

I wrote the music and opening lines and Howard wrote the rest. You know 'Orgasm Addict' is a line from William Burroughs – orgasm addicts are referred to in many of his works. Howard heard about William Burroughs through David Bowie – Bowie used the 'cut-up' technique to write his lyrics, the technique that Burroughs popularized, where you write words on scraps of paper and throw them in the air and see how they land. The Dadaists had devised the method by pulling words out of hats as a means of writing poetry, and it was later used by Kurt Cobain, Genesis P Orridge and Thom Yorke of Radiohead. It's copying and pasting, basically, before there were computers[5].

I'd read about William Burroughs because I was a big fan of Bowie, and when I used to go round to Howard's he had loads of Burroughs' books. I'd borrow his and then I ended up buying my own. Burroughs was like a big dressing-up box for phrases. Out of his works comes 'heavy metal', 'Steely Dan' – there's a whole list of them.

I remember times when you'd be at a disco and you'd realize that just before closing time there'd be a mad rush of people trying to get off with whoever they could – and it was out of that was born the idea of the Orgasm Addict. It was long before the idea of sex addiction as being a medical condition. The brief was about someone who's obsessed with – addicted to – having orgasms. So all Howard did was to write out a list almost from the thesaurus. Years later he confessed to me that he'd made a mistake, because on the recording it says, 'You're a kid Casanova/You're a no-Joseph' and he realized that because he'd gone through a thesaurus to find 'no Joseph', meaning he isn't as pure as Jesus' stepdad, he's thought the term would be a 'no-Joseph' – but then years later, perhaps 20 years afterwards, he realized it should be 'You're no Joseph'. I do sing that now, since he's pointed it out to me, but on the original one I sing 'You're a no-Joseph'.

And what's the 'sex mechanic' – in the line 'The sex mechanic's rough'?

The first time I heard it I thought it was a sex mechanic – i.e., someone to just tinker with your bits – but subsequently, thinking about it, I think it's 'the sex mechanics, rough' – so it's not a sex mechanic who's being rough; it's the mechanics of sex that are rough.

'Sex Mechanic' was later the name of a tune by Manchester electronic dance act 808 State, whose Graham Massey used to be in Biting Tongues – another of the bands on New Hormones, the label that you set up to release *Spiral Scratch* on.

I was at an event in Brazil with him around 2009, 2010, a seminar about music grassroots. There were different panels and we spoke about how we started out and that. Viv Albertine from The Slits was there as well. We were there for about a week. But I wasn't part of Manchester's electronic dance music scene in the early Nineties because I was already living in London.

Who were the Children of God?

Well, as a student there were always people trying to convert you at college. Howard may have been alluding to the Children of God's alleged practice of Flirty Fishing[6], where young women in the cult would try to lure young men into the fold by promising them sexual favours.

And what about The Joy Strings?

They were a Salvation Army beat group; they used to appear on TV on Sunday evenings at about the time of The Beatles and Dave Clarke Five. They used to perform in their uniforms and the woman had the bonnets on and they'd sing pop songs about how the Lord loves you. They had a contract with EMI and got into the charts with 'It's an Open Secret' and 'A Starry Night'. So the idea was that this person had actually worked his way through them all.

And where it says 'International women with no body hair' – I used to think it said 'nobody hair'. I thought, what a strange concept...then I realized it was 'no body hair'. That's just routine now but it would have been quite exotic at the time!

Did United Artists commission Malcolm to design the sleeves?

No, we told them that that's what we wanted. You see this was what we'd agreed with Andrew Lauder – that United Artists would let us do what we wanted to do. We came up with the ideas and they were happy to let them happen, so they were great facilitators in that way. We spent a lot of time thinking about what we did – it was more studied than thrown together. We had a vision of the whole package and how we wanted it to be – even down to insisting on having picture sleeves. Picture sleeves were not the norm at the time – they cost more to produce. We'd already had the luxury of making our own record (with *Spiral Scratch*) and making it how we wanted it. We specified in the contract that we wanted full artistic control and this is what they gave us. It was a deal-breaker!

Where was the photo on the back of the sleeve taken?

The photo was taken by Kevin Cummins, who had become our court photographer. He was the person we knew who had a camera. His day job was taking pictures of industrial machinery for catalogues. He was Paul Morley's sidekick. It was taken in a bus stop in Manchester somewhere – not central Manchester; somewhere weird, like Stretford Road[7]. We were just walking round and we saw the bus shelter had four separate windows, so the four of us each stood in a separate window for the photograph. It transpired that Malcolm had actually given instructions to take a photo like that so it would fit the rectilinear sleeve design.

Kevin Cummins took the photos of us signing the contract with United Artists – on the bar at the Electric Circus. The Jam played there that night as well. It was the day that Elvis Presley died – doing a final dump. It was somehow fitting.

Next day we did an interview at the Piccadilly Hotel with Caroline Coon for *Melody Maker*. So it was all happening.

Where did you know Garth from[8]?

Garth was an old school friend of mine who I'd been playing with since 1973. Last time I saw him was when Iggy Pop played at the Factory in, I think, 1978. He was a good bass player – very melodic. He's in a pub band now in Tyldesley, his hometown. I believe they do all the northern pub staples, including 'Matchstalk Men and Matchstalk Cats and Dogs'[9].

Steve Diggle described Garth as a 'punk monster' – and on a track on the *Razor Cuts* bootleg recorded at Leeds Poly Garth can be heard threatening people in the audience and calling them 'Yorkshire Bastards'.

That all started because I didn't know what to wear for the evening. I was staying at my mum's, sharing a room with my brother, and I looked in his drawer and there was this nice red top with a white collar. It was only later that it was pointed out to me that it was a Manchester United top – so certain sections of the audience, presumably Leeds United fans, started chucking stuff and making a fuss and that was when Garth chipped in with, 'If any of you White Rose[10] cunts want to come up here I'll knock you all round fucking Leeds!' – but they'd started it first. And it's Steve who's singing 'Red Sails in the Sunset' [recorded by Bing Crosby, Louis Armstrong and Nat King Cole, among others] and 'Angelo' [by the Brotherhood of Man] on that bootleg to make things proceed smoothly.

As we were leaving Leeds Poly that night Garth was sitting near one of the windows in the back of the car and as we were trying to get out of Leeds someone knocked on the window. We of course said, 'Don't wind down the window!' And as he wound it down a fist came through and punched him in the face. He wasn't the world's luckiest man.

So when did he leave the band?

On the 6th of October, just before 'Orgasm Addict' came out, we played in Coventry – Mr George's or something, the venue was called. We went to pick up Garth at his house on Astley Street [in Tyldesley] and we were told he was in the pub. So we went to the Miners Arms in Astley and picked him up. He was very drunk and as we were driving along the motorway he started a fight with me in the back (it was a Peugeot estate car, with a fold-down seat in the back – something like a people carrier is now). It started after we'd stopped at the services to buy some batteries for the cassette recorder. The driver, Pete Monks, pulled over on to the hard shoulder and Garth was trying to kick in the windows. He was in an awful state.

Anyway, Garth calmed down a bit and got back in the car and we made it to Coventry. He went in the pub again after the sound check and then he was very drunk during the gig – he was finding it hard to play or even stand up. He just took off his bass – the Thunderbird – threw it on the floor and walked off the stage, leaving me, Steve and John to do the rest of the gig. So I said to Steve, 'Turn up the bass on your amp,' so at least it sounded a bit fuller. That was on the Saturday and by the Monday, when everything had cooled down, John said, 'If Garth's going to be in the band then I'm not going to be in the band.' So it was a simple decision[11].

So we needed to find a replacement bass player. In the meantime we had some dates in Scotland to start off the 'Orgasm Addict' tour so we brought in Barry Adamson. He played all the Scottish gigs and one in Stoke. By that time we'd met Steve Garvey. He came to observe the gig in Stoke and then after that we had Garvey all the way[12].

How did you meet Steve Garvey?

After Garth had left, we needed a bass player because 'Orgasm Addict' was due to come out and we had a tour lined up. We had these auditions at a church hall in Didsbury – we'd advertised in Virgin Records in Manchester, *Melody Maker*, and probably the *New Manchester Review*. We had loads of people turn up[13] and some of them would say, 'Why can't you play songs that I know?' – so they were non-starters. Then there was one guy who came in and he had his bass up here like Mark King and we thought, 'No, he won't do.' And some people were so bad that Steve, John and I would sneak off to the toilets and lock ourselves in the cubicles and not come out until they'd gone. There were two people who were contenders: one was Steve Garvey and the other was – what's his name? Mog? Ian Morris who used to be in The Smirks – they were a comedy new-wave band from Manchester who had a bit of a cult following. Mog played on what was the demo for 'Jilted John'.

According to Steve Garvey he got the job because when they were walking back from rehearsals he bought John Maher a Mars Bar (nice to have a chocolate bar named after you!). At the time he was working in a brass-instrument repair factory, although he didn't play brass. Steve Garvey knew Karl Burns from The Fall; he later played with Karl Burns in The Teardrops. He came and he could play and he looked OK and we got on with him...so he joined.

How had you met Barry Adamson?

I'd met him at the Ranch and had always got on with him. Then when Howard was putting together Magazine he asked me if I knew Barry Adamson and what he was like – so I gave him a character reference. He hadn't been playing very long but he was certainly competent; he could play what we wanted him to play.

Factory Records was established in about January 1978. Do you think Tony Wilson would have wanted you for Factory if you hadn't already been signed?

He never said anything! He used to try and wind me up subsequently by saying that we'd sold out by signing with one of those record companies in London. But he never asked us.

Factory was famous for using 'house' designers and producers and assigning each item a catalogue number – but this was what you'd already done with United Artists and Malcolm.

Well, yes. But this is what happens when you innovate – there are always people who come along later claiming that it was their idea.

Notes

1   United Artists was founded in 1919 as a film production company by actors Charlie Chaplin, Mary Pickford, Douglas Fairbanks and film director D W Griffith. The aim of the organization was to allow actors to retain their independence, rather than having their interests controlled by the studio. The UA record label, established in 1957 – initially for releasing film soundtracks – continued this tradition by affording Buzzcocks the creative freedom they demanded.

2   Manchester's premier commercial radio station began broadcasting from studios in Piccadilly Plaza in 1974. It was founded by Radio London's Philip Birch after the newly passed Marine Offences Act of 1967 closed the pirate stations down.

3   Bolan was being driven in a Mini by Gloria Jones, his partner and the mother of his son, Rolan. Jones is best remembered for singing the original gutsy, ballsy soul version of 'Tainted Love', a song that so epitomized the Detroit sound that she became known as the 'Queen of Northern Soul'. Wigan Casino – which until its closure in 1981 was the beating heart of Northern Soul – was just six miles from Pete's hometown of Leigh.

4   Steve Garvey says: 'One of my heroes growing up was Martin Turner, the bassist and singer out of Wishbone Ash. He played a Gibson Thunderbird, like the one Garth played, and when I joined the band that bass was still around. It wasn't Garth's own instrument – it had been bought with the advance, so it belonged to the band. But when I got to play it I didn't like it.'

5   Burroughs was a believer in magical thinking, claiming that 'there are no coincidences...and no accidents'. He used the cut-ups for divination and 'conjuration', among other purposes, as he believed they 'break down the barriers'. He warned sternly that they were not to be used for 'artistic purposes'.

6   Flirty Fishing was initially used to attract men into the movement, and then there was a further degeneration when women members were expected to engage in paid sex work to raise funds for the group. The cult disallowed birth control and many 'Jesus babies' were born as a result of these encounters. Children of God (which currently exists as the Family International) has been dogged by accusations of abuse and exploitation by past members, including those who were children at the time.

7   Stretford Road starts at the area near the university buildings and runs through Hulme and Old Trafford, to the southeast of the city.

8   Pete's cousin Howard says of Garth: 'He's still local – funnily enough, I coached his son at rugby! (Union, not League.) Garth plays in a pub band round here now – they dress up in zoot suits and he plays the double bass. They look like something from that film *The Mask*.'

9   A dreary novelty folk song that reached No. 1 in the UK Singles Chart in 1978 and celebrated the work of Salford artist L S Lowry.

10 In reference to the Wars of the Roses: the white rose has traditionally represented the House of York and the red rose the House of Lancaster.

11 A source close to the band says: 'Garth just walked away. They used to tease him terribly. It was all intended to be in good humour but Garth had had enough. In gangs of guys, if you show any weakness they lay into you.'

12 Steve Garvey says: 'I'd seen Buzzcocks I think three times when Garth was in the band. My friends, the guys in The Fall, opened for them once and I went with them and I said, "I'm so much better than he is!" So when Garth got kicked out I made sure I got an audition. I knew they were good; I knew that Pete had tremendous charisma. So when I joined I was over the moon: that was my dream. I would get up and do encores on those few gigs when Barry Adamson played with them because they didn't think I could learn all the songs...'

13 Steve Garvey: 'They did audition quite a few bassists but perhaps not as many as it says in Steve's book!' At the audition Garvey played a fretless bass, a Longhorn, which is trickier to play than the more popular fretted bass; maybe it was this quirky choice – as well as his proficiency on it – that impressed the band.

Whatever Happened To?

B-side to: 'Orgasm Addict'
Songwriters: Alan Dial and Pete Shelley
Producer: Martin Rushent

How did you come up with the idea for the song?

Well, I said to Richard Boon that I was thinking of writing a song
about 'Whatever Happened To?' – like, whatever happened to
Oxydol (a soap powder that they don't make any more). It was
really a list of things that are no longer in existence – like Spangles
(remember those sweets, Spangles? I used to like the Old English
flavour ones[1]). I mentioned it to him but then I didn't do anything with
it. Then one day he said to me, 'Have you got any further with that
song? Because I've written some lyrics for it.' So I put them to music.

This was the way I used to write with Howard – for a lot of the
songs he'd already have the lyrics, and I'd write the music. Like
when we wrote 'Boredom', he'd been on the nightshift at the tile
factory – not a tie factory, as recorded in Jon Savage's *England's
Dreaming*! It may be that he didn't get my accent right. It was in
Salford – Howard was living in Salford at the time. His job was, if
a pallet of tiles collapsed in the kiln he had to don the spacesuit
and go in and clear it out. So he came back from work one
morning and no pallets must have fallen over that night because
he'd written these lyrics. And while he went up to have a wash
and a shave before going to bed I had a look at them and came
up with 'Boredom'.

Instead of going under his own name Richard went under the
name Alan Dial. It's something to do with the Situationists, the art

movement that was later a source of inspiration for a lot of Tony Wilson's ideas for Factory Records.

How did you meet Richard[2]?

Richard was a friend of Howard's from Leeds. I first met him at a party in Bolton. His abiding memory of that night is that I was wearing too much make-up!

Howard and I stayed at his house in Reading (where he'd been a student) when we went to try and find the Sex Pistols. He'd finished university – he'd done a degree in fine art – and was looking for a project, so he moved up to Manchester to be our manager. Because of his artistic background he was up with all the weird and wonderful ideas, so he was a good person to bounce ideas off. He made the Jackson Pollock shirts and the Mondrian shirts. We wore the Mondrian shirts for the first time at one of The Clash shows at Hounslow Coliseum on the 11th of March 1977 – it was a dry run for the 'White Riot' tour. I wore a black shirt and the rest of the band wore these shirts that had been white but had been painted with the Mondrian design with poster paint or something – it was in the days before fabric paint. So when they took off their shirts after the gig the paint had soaked through the fabric and the design was stuck to their skin.

Why did he write 'Whatever happened to the cow'?

Yes, I often wonder when I'm singing it what it actually means. It does seem to fit when we do these little festivals up and down the country – they probably have to move the cows out while we play the festival. They're probably sedated in a shed down the road!

At this point, when Steve Garvey had joined the band, you're

playing as a four-piece, rather than as a three-piece with

a vocalist, so the arrangements are different. How do you separate the guitar parts – one rhythm, one lead, like a traditional setup? Or do you and Steve lead on the songs that you've written?

It means that if I play a lead line, then the rhythm guitar part doesn't just disappear! I mean, when we recorded *Spiral Scratch* we did overdubs. I suppose that's why there are not a lot of solos in those earlier songs.

Does one of you play lead and one of you play rhythm?

Well, Steve'd like to think that he's the lead guitarist but actually I tend to play more lead than he does during the set.

Do you play lead on your songs and Steve play lead on his?

No...it's more random than that. It depends on the song and what parts there are. There's no hard and fast rule – it depends on the song. And sometimes we both play lead. For example, I'm playing the lead on 'Alive Tonight', which Steve wrote, and on 'Autonomy'. I'm playing all the riffs. We tend not to have the rock-cliché type of leads anyway – I tend to play melodies. Part of the distinctive nature of Buzzcocks' sound is that you've got two guitars playing a similar rhythm – the 'buzz-saw guitars'. It's double the power.

And it's hard to play lead and sing – it's like patting your head and rubbing your stomach at the same time!

What gigs were you doing at this time?

We played Leeds Poly, the Electric Circus, the Marquee, Doncaster, Westcliff-on-Sea...When we did the tour with

The Clash that got us national exposure. That September we played at Eric's in Liverpool, then the Greyhound in Croydon, then Barbarella's in Birmingham. The first gig we played without Howard was one of The Clash's.

Had punk gone national by that time? I mean, at these provincial shows you were doing, were there punks in the audience?

Yes, because as soon as the Bill Grundy thing happened with the Sex Pistols, kids saw it and thought, 'Wow, this is great. This is a way to annoy your parents.' So it had become a really big part of the musical landscape. I mean, it had been building, but the petrol on the fire was the Bill Grundy incident. Even though no-one outside London had seen the actual TV programme, everyone had heard about it because it was in the national press – it was reported as 'The Filth and the Fury'. So the time was right for taking punk to the provinces.

Notes

1   Pete was still a fan of boiled sweets and sucked many herbal Ricola drops during the recording of these interviews. He felt they improved his voice.

2   A source close to the band says: 'Richard was the sweetest guy, the nicest guy.' It's not certain whether these are the most important qualities required by the manager of a band.

What Do I Get?[1, 2, 3]

Stand-alone single
B-side: 'Oh Shit'
Recorded: January 1978, Olympic Studios, Barnes, London
Mixed: Olympic Studios, Barnes, London
Released: 3 February 1978
Songwriter: Pete Shelley
Producer: Martin Rushent
Sleeve designer: Malcolm Garrett
Run-out-groove message: 'A love story'[4]

When was this written?

I seem to remember writing it somewhere around December 1976.

And was it written about someone specific?

It was slightly written about Linder, because she was going out with Howard at the time and that's why it says, 'For you things seem to turn out right/I wish that only happened to me instead'. It wasn't really a love song in that way; it only becomes that with the addition of the 'I don't get you' at the end[5], which makes it into a traditional type of love song. It's an afterthought really. It's like you've been just talking to somebody, pouring your heart out to them, and then the bombshell's dropped. I see it as a subversive love song. But that wasn't based on real life – I didn't really fancy Linder.

We used to hang out a lot, though. Howard was at college in Bolton and she was an art student at Manchester Poly and I was unemployed in Salford – so we used to hang out at Howard's in Salford. Linder and I used to see a lot of each other but it wasn't anything romantic.

It was written originally as a punk love song – 'I only want a friend who'll fuck to the end' – so I cleaned it up a bit to make it so it could achieve its full potential. There was no way you could change anything about 'Orgasm Addict' to make it more palatable. And it said, 'I get nothing: fuck all, fuck all, fuck all, fuck all...' But I don't think we ever played it with those lyrics. And it was going to have three verses: the first one saying, 'I only want a friend who'll stay till the end'; the second one saying, '...love till the end'; and the third one saying, '...fuck till the end'. It was Howard who said it needed jazzing up, fleshing out a bit. In fact it was Howard who came up with the second verse: 'I'm in distress, I need a caress/I'm not on the make, I just need a break.' I wrote it at about the time that Howard was leaving the band, so originally it was meant to be Howard who sang it. I think we did one rehearsal with Howard singing it. I wrote it in the December and round about the January or February was when Howard left – just a few days after *Spiral Scratch* had been released.

So really it's talking to someone who's in a relationship and lamenting one's lack of a relationship. Not so much that you wish you could be with them, just that you envy them – 'For you things seem to turn out right.'

This was recorded at Olympic?

Yes, I think we may have done the demos at TW, though. We did quite a lot in there – we did the first two albums in Olympic and all the singles from then on.

Olympic was one of the biggest studios – The Rolling Stones recorded there, as well as The Yardbirds, Jimi Hendrix and Dusty Springfield. The Rolling Stones recorded 'Sympathy for the Devil' in the big room where we recorded 'What Do I Get?' and everything after that. It was a big room, in an old red-brick schoolhouse, where you could get a big sound. We could set up in the middle of the room, as a band – not like in Indigo, where we recorded *Spiral Scratch*, all in separate rooms.

Olympic has closed in recent years – I think it's been

converted into flats now[6].

It must have cost quite a bit more at Olympic than it cost at TW.

Yes – but the gamble paid off for the record company, didn't it?!

This was when a lot of things started happening for you...

Yes, a lot was happening for us at that time. We were on the front cover of *NME* around then. It was just after Steve Garvey had joined the band. Then the 28th of December was when we started recording our first album, *Another Music in a Different Kitchen*.

On the 16th of January we filmed the video for 'What Do I Get?'. It was filmed at the ITN [Independent Television News] studios. Because the ITN news used to be on at lunchtime and in the evenings, in the afternoons when they weren't using it they used to hire it out to anyone who wanted to use the facilities. The video was more of a publicity device than for showing on TV.

And at the end of the year was when Andrew Lauder left United Artists to start his own record label, Radar Records. We got the last four months of his time at United Artists!

And Doug Bennett[7] was the engineer. Is it true he used to sleep in the studio?

Doug had worked with Martin Rushent before. Yes, sometimes he slept in the studio so he could continue working – he was working on other sessions as well. It was all go at the time.

So you beat Howard in the charts, because 'What Do I Get?' got to No. 37 and Magazine's 'Shot by Both Sides' only got to No. 41!

Yes, well...Not a lot to crow about, really! Especially as they were both my songs.

You were on Tony Wilson's *So It Goes* with 'What Do I Get?'.

That was the footage that was taken at the Electric Circus on the 16th of August, the day we signed to United Artists, with Garth playing.

So Steve Garvey was with you by the time you recorded 'What Do I Get?'?

Yes, he fitted right in. Steve played the basslines more or less as Garth had played them[8]. Garth was very melodic as a bass player, and so was Steve[9].

Where did he learn his craft?

I don't know. He used to be mates with The Fall – but he didn't learn it off them[10]!

PHOTO BY KEVIN CUMMINS

Tony Wilson on bass at the Electric Circus, Collyhurst Street, Manchester. No-one knows whether he could really play or if he was miming.

Who made the 'What Do I Get?' shirts?

Janey Collings made them. She was a friend of Richard's. They didn't have the lettering on, just the green diagonal. They pre-dated the release of the single[11].

I wore one of the shirts at a gig at Manchester Poly.

Did you record a demo for 'What Do I Get?' with Garth?

After we signed to United Artists we did a demo session with him in Manchester and we did it again with him when we were at TW, but by the time we went to Olympic and Steve Garvey was with us it was a completely different recording.

'What Do I Get?' was used in the film 'Ghost World' eventually? I expected a lot from it because it's got that song in it but I was a bit disappointed with it when I saw it.

It was based on a comic book. It's not Dostoevsky or anything!

The sleeve for 'What Do I Get?' is a design classic – it's timeless.

Malcolm would try and capture what we were trying to convey in the music – and transforming the auditory into the visual is quite a skill[12].

Was there an alternative sleeve design for 'What Do I Get?' – a black-and-white geometric one?

No, that was a press ad – for in the music press. We – well, us and Malcolm Garrett – were responsible for making up the ads as well so he would theme everything together.

It's a beautiful lyric – heartrending.

A funny thing happened with the lyric in Japan. On Japanese releases they print the lyrics in English and then supply a Japanese translation so that the fans can understand what the song is vaguely about. Whenever we used to have a release in Japan they'd ask me to supply the lyric and I used to say to them, 'No, I want to see what you come up with.' So they'd get someone to listen to the record and write what they'd think they were hearing, then they'd translate it. On this occasion they got it a bit wrong. The line 'For you things seem to turn out right' is translated as 'The entrance to the tender bride'. It's like *Fifty Shades of Grey*, isn't it? It's highly charged.

In another [Japanese] transcription of the lyrics it says, 'Alone here in my hoppity bed'. That's a surrealist interpretation. I always enjoy the misheard lyrics.

Notes

1 'What Do I Get?' was used in a UK TV advert for McDonald's Big Flavour Wraps in 2016. Morrissey was a keen fan of Buzzcocks in the United Artists years (he was allegedly often to be found using the phone in the New Hormones office) but as a committed vegan was less than pleased about this advert. He is quoted as having written, on his fan site true-to-you.net, that he hoped he'd seen it only in 'a bad dream'.

2 In a 2019 poll by the Pete Shelley Memorial Campaign, 'What Do I Get?' – not 'Ever Fallen in Love' – was found to be the favourite track of the most loyal Buzzcocks fans.

3 On the version of 'What Do I Get?' that is included in the 'Live at the Lyceum' section of the 1995 box set *Product* (recorded 10 March 1978), Pete announces the song with: 'Now, the moment you've all been waiting for – no, it's not the spot prize...'

4 Some of Buzzcocks' singles feature a relevant message on the run-out groove and some just the initials or name of the technician responsible for cutting the disc at the pressing plant. Some are marked 'A Porky Prime-Cut' – the signature of lacquer-cutting and mastering engineer George Peckham, who was very prolific over the years.

5 John Maher's voice can be heard in the call-and-answer section towards the end of the song. Steve Garvey says: 'They had me go in the booth but after the one take they said, "No, you're out, you can't sing!"'

6 The red-brick building started life as a theatre for Barnes's own repertory company in 1906 and later served as a cinema then as television studios. Fortunately, the planned development was abandoned and the building now houses a two-screen cinema and café as well as a small recording studio.

7 Bennett's surname is variously spelled this way and also Bennet.

8 Steve Garvey says: 'When I joined the band, Garth had played on "Orgasm Addict" and the B-side, "Whatever Happened To?". I tried to follow what he'd played but not note-for-note.'

9 Garvey also says: 'Nobody ever told me what to play, except Pete gave me the riff for the bridge in "What Do I Get?" because I had to follow the guitar in that. That's the only time they ever told me what to play.'

10 Steve Garvey: 'He [Mark E Smith] was a nasty piece of work but he was funny. If he didn't like you, you'd know about it! I probably would've ended up being in The Fall if I hadn't've ended up in the Buzzcocks, if truth be told. I might've stuck around longer than some of the other members stayed for, as I'm very affable – it takes a lot to push my buttons.'

11 In some of the studio shots taken of Pete and the guys wearing the 'What Do I Get?' shirts, the diagonal appears left-to-right, instead of right-to-left, because the photos were taken in a mirror as part of the shoot for the cover of *Love Bites* (as discussed in the Introduction, see page 41).

12 Richard Boon's intention had been to use a photo on the front of the sleeve to illustrate the concept of 'What Do I Get?' and one on the back to illustrate 'Oh Shit'. Malcolm Garrett didn't have the photos to hand when he made the visual for the sleeve (maybe they hadn't been taken) so he made the mock-up using two shades of green paper and Letraset lettering. When the band saw it they said, 'That looks great – we'll go with that.'

Oh Shit

B-side to: 'What Do I Get?'
Songwriter: Pete Shelley
Producer: Martin Rushent
Run-out-groove message: 'Another music'

When and where was it written?

I seem to remember writing it quite early in 1976, before we'd done our first gigs. I remember when I was writing it I was in my bedroom singing away and I went out to the kitchen to make a cup of tea. My mum was doing the ironing and she said, 'Ooh, do you have to swear so much?' So I thought, 'Well, I must be doing the right thing.'

How many gigs had you played by that time?

We played 12 gigs if you include the one at the youth club. At the house where Howard lived we used to rehearse in the basement, but it was still noisy – it wasn't soundproofed. Howard's next-door neighbour was a bit fed up of his Sunday afternoons being disturbed by this racket. He was the caretaker of this church hall, St Boniface, nearby so he let us rehearse there. As a thankyou for letting us use it we agreed to play at the church youth club. I say 'youth club'. I use the term loosely – most of its patrons seemed to be between the age of about 8 and 14. Howard was in a bit of a quandary about swearing in front of the kids. He said, 'Well, we can't do "Oh Shit"' – so I said, 'We could change it to "Oh Spit"' – which seemed equally punk. But we didn't play it in the end.

It's about a theme that everyone can relate to.

Yes, it's about the aftermath of a relationship break-up. It's simple in its form but it tracks the different stages that you go through. The denial – 'the bolt out of the blue' – then remorse – 'Oh, nothing's ever going to be good from now on, my love life's over' – and finally acceptance – 'Well, it was your fucking fault; I wish I'd known before that you were such a cow.'

I've always thought of it as being the flipside of the 'What Do I Get?' scenario – a few months down the line when it's all gone wrong.

Yes, well you can put a narrative to it. It was good to have the pairing of the yearning of 'What Do I Get?' with the B-side that you couldn't play in polite company – the juxtaposition of extremes.

Was it about someone in particular?

No, it was just an exercise in…profanity. My mother didn't approve. But there was no other way you could write a song like that. And of course everyone's been there.

It's one of those songs that's like a conversation. Most of my songs are conversations – some of them internal. But the song resolves itself as it travels through time. 'What Do I Get?' too is a conversation, apart from the artifice of it rhyming. But it's written in everyday language; it just happens to rhyme.

Even the rhymes are very natural, though – it sounds like speech.

That's what I try and do in songs, because if it becomes too involved it puts a distance between you and the listener. Part of the thing with punk was that you were supposed to be expressing everyday mundane things that were important to the individual but you weren't preaching or waving a flag. It was my opinion that a lot of the world's problems would go away if people would just shag each other more – or learn to love each other more. It was the Seventies, you see.

Steve said that in the early Seventies people were singing songs about mushrooms and castles – like all the Yes albums. What we were singing about was more pared down – like music was in the Sixties with, say, 'She Loves You'. Good pop songs are not rocket science but it's good how it works.

Did it cause some controversy at the time, then?

I do remember that 'What Do I Get?' fell foul of the women who stuck the labels on the singles at the pressing plant because they objected to working on a record with a song entitled 'Oh Shit'. There were white-label copies, where labels were stuck on single-sided discs by Martin Rushent and his assistants in the A&R department. They're probably worth a fortune today. Unfortunately I don't have a cupboard full of them!

It was supposed to come out on the 20th of January but because of the dispute and having to stick on the labels it was the 3rd of February when it was released. It got to No. 37 in the charts.

Those women would have objected to it even more if they'd heard it, wouldn't they? They were only objecting to the title – they'd've been horrified by the lyric!

Oh no, they hadn't heard it. It was another bold move on the part of United Artists. They sent out radio copies that only had one side so it would still get lots of radio play.

In *Sounds*, Savage Pencil did a little cartoon strip about it,
I think I've got a copy of it when it appeared in the *LA Times*.
I suppose it was a way to get in the music papers at the time.

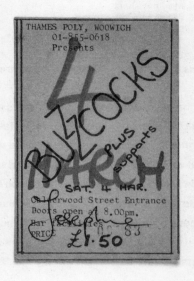

I Don't Mind

Single
B-side: 'Autonomy'
Recorded: 1978, Olympic Studios, Barnes, London
Mixed: Olympic Studios, Barnes, London
Released: 14 April 1978
Songwriter: Pete Shelley
Producer: Martin Rushent
Sleeve designer: Malcolm Garrett

This was the first single that also appeared on an album...

Part of the philosophy was that the singles that we released
wouldn't be on the albums; however, the idea of releasing the
single after the album had been released was more palatable
to us – it was a marketing tool and if you'd bought the album then
you didn't need to buy the single. But if you heard the single on
the radio you might then go out and buy the album. It wasn't like
now when they try and rip people off as much as they can!

When and where was it written?

I can't really remember when I wrote it – it might have been the
summer of '77.

'Nostalgia' was a 1974 song, so when the gambling metaphor
appeared in 'I Don't Mind' it had been recycled. But at the time
of 'I Don't Mind' I didn't know that 'Nostalgia' would be coming
out as well.

It's a theme that constantly recurs in my songs – that being
in two minds, not knowing whether a relationship is working out.
There's always that thing when you fall in love; you worry that
you're not worthy. There's that suspicion in the back of your mind
that you might be reading it all wrong and you think, 'Why me?'
It's about the uncertainty, doubting oneself as much as doubting

the relationship. As a love interest gets stronger there's always that tendency to worry that you're going to be found out: 'I don't know if I'm an actor or ham/A shaman or sham.'

So who were you going out with at this time?

I was probably going out with lots of people – the songs were written over a number of years – but it wasn't written about someone specific. The songs are very rarely written about a person; they're inspired by my reaction to the situation, rather than the person, so really they're autobiographical – about me rather than about the other person. Other people are like archetypes which I'm subjected to. And often they're a kaleidoscopic mixture of people and relationships and things I've read in a book. It's like in an American biopic where they write a special character who's a composite of lots of different people just so it makes sense to the narrative of the fiction.

If I see somebody I fancy I'll fall in love with them straight away! It depends how much I dwell on it and how many nights I spend lying awake thinking about it and how much it's unrequited.

It's about being paranoid and finding situations hard to read. It says, 'I used to think you hate me when you call me on the phone' – but of course, if they're ringing me up why would I think they don't like me? So it expresses the vulnerability of whether the other person's leading you on.

As an aside, the fair used to come to town every year when we were teenagers and me and my friend used to go. One time there were these girls there – we ended up talking to them and my friend ended up dating one of them. There were two other girls in the group and I fancied one of them and so in order to try and get her to go out with me I spent a lot of time with her friend. It was only years later that the penny dropped and I realized that it was the *friend* who fancied me – but I didn't see that at the time because I was interested in someone else: someone who wasn't interested in me. I'm sure Shakespeare has written a play about this – is it Rosalind in *As You Like It*, or *The Comedy of Errors*? Or perhaps *Cyrano de Bergerac*. I just didn't read the signs.

Your relationships at this time must have been tested because you were on the road quite a bit.

Yes – being subject to adoration as well! I'm not saying there wasn't temptation – you'd see lots of nice people every day. But we'd usually drive back home after gigs whenever we could, so there wasn't much opportunity for acting on it. It was like it is now when we're on the road: you finish the show, hang out in the dressing-room, have a drink in the hotel bar and then go to bed – on your own! It wasn't wild debauchery every night. I think if people had been more direct to me rather than waiting for me to make the first move there might have been more of it! You see, I wouldn't want to take advantage of being *me* – as an object of admiration in a band – unless I was directly propositioned: made an offer I couldn't refuse. The theme appears again in my solo song 'If You Ask Me I Won't Say No'.

That insecurity strikes a chord with everyone.

Everyone's insecure – unless they're a psychopath. We've all been let down – all thought one thing and it's turned out to be completely different from what we thought. And we try to avoid that hurt and embarrassment in the future. I was writing songs for people who were like me, who'd had similar experiences. When they heard the songs they all started coming out of the woodwork! People come up to me and say that the words that I write in songs are the things that they feel but they can't write – so you give words to the feelings that they have. That's what you do as an artist; even instrumental music can encapsulate what you feel.

That's why I tend to write in the first person and keep it general by not giving too much detail – so the listener can imagine themselves into the situation. It's not about me; it's about the listener. And it'd all be very boring if it *was* all about me and what's happened to me!

Autonomy

B-side to: 'I Don't Mind'
Songwriter: Steve Diggle

So this was the first song of Steve's that you played – at one time his only song?

Well, he and I had co-written 'Fast Cars' as well. This song came about before Howard had left. I came up with the solo to put on the end bit.

You sing it as a sort of duet.

It's call-and-answer and I do the 'answer' part.

It was a favourite of both Tony Wilson and Joe Strummer.

Did you get that from Joe Strummer or did you read it in Steve's book? [laughs]

It's stayed a constant in the set for years.

I like it because of its angularity. It always reminds me of the *William Tell Overture* – there's something about the rhythm that's similar.

The Factory nights at the Russell Club were going on at about
this time. Howard got a cameo in *24 Hour Party People*

in a scene that's supposed to be in the club[1]. Were you approached to appear in the film?

I had received a letter from the director, Michael Winterbottom, asking me to take part in it but I didn't follow it up. I can't remember what part they wanted me to play.

And you were also playing with The Tiller Boys at about this time. The Tiller Boys' first gig was featured on the iconic Peter Saville poster for the first Factory night, which wasn't produced until after the event.

So much for deadlines! The Tiller Boys was me, Eric Random and Francis Cookson – we had weird tastes in music. Eric Random had been a Buzzcocks' roadie and I met Francis when he put on a Buzzcocks gig at Parr Hall in Warrington, on May 13th 1977. He was a student. Then I used to see him in Rafters in Manchester.

The Tiller Boys was formed one evening at a night called the Beach Club, which was run by New Hormones. I'd recently found out that the dance troupe the Tiller Girls were from Manchester – so we had the idea of calling ourselves The Tiller Boys.

I knew a girl called Carol at the time who had a council house in Stretford and we used to stay there when we'd all been out in Manchester at the Ranch (I was living in Leigh at this time – that's too far out of town to get back after a night out). There was another bloke called Fran Taylor who I used to see at the Electric Circus who later became a roadie for us.

Carol ended up getting thrown out of her council house so the four of us decided to rent a house in Gorton[2] – me, Carol, Francis and Fran. The rent was about £14 per week. We lived there for about two and a half years. So Eric used to come round and we used to play music and there was talk of us getting a band together. Buzzcocks were by this time playing the big gigs – the top ranks and theatres. We knew Tony Wilson – he used to come round a lot to the house in Gorton – and he said he was opening this Factory club so we said *we* could play! There was a Mini Pops drum machine and we had loads of tape recorders; it eventually became Groovy Records. I used to play guitar, Eric played guitar and Francis was mostly drums and tape loops. So on the night, just to antagonize the audience, we'd got all the stools from around the club, piled them into a wall at the edge of the stage so you couldn't see us, and we got Richard Boon to tape a sign, written on a piece of A4 paper, to one of the chairs saying, 'Name That Tune'. And we just made loads of noise.

I was operating a tape recorder that was playing all these tape loops and at one stage I just rewound the tape and put it on 'play'. I was standing at the bar ordering a drink and Howard said, 'I thought you were on the stage!' So it was that kind of thing: stretching the boundaries. It was an 'experimental' outfit and it was instrumental: it didn't have any vocals in it.

We went into the studio later and did an EP – *Big Noise in the Jungle*.

How did you fit it all in with your Buzzcocks commitments?

Well, we weren't touring or in the studio constantly – and back then, the telly shut off at about midnight, so there wasn't much to do in the small hours. And it wasn't anything we rehearsed! It was more about performance than rehearsal.

I understand you sing an alternative lyric when you perform 'Autonomy' live.

What?

At a certain point in it you make eye-contact with someone in the audience and sing, 'I...I want you...on top of me'.

Yes, it's a joke that me and Steve have. It works every time!

Notes

1   In *24 Hour Party People*, the comedy-drama film centred around Manchester's music fraternity in the Factory Records era, Tony Wilson (played by comedy actor Steve Coogan) has been caught by his wife, Lindsay, 'getting a blowjob off a hooker in the back of a van' (his words). Lindsay takes revenge by shagging 'Howard' in a toilet cubicle. The real Howard Devoto is dressed as a plumber, unblocking a washbasin, and he says, 'I definitely don't remember this happening!' Of course, much of the action in the film is fictionalized. Apparently, the scene was filmed in the toilets of Jilly's Rockworld (where the plumbing was, indeed, often faulty).

2   Gorton is a district to the east of the city and was distinctly down-at-heel in the Seventies – and far less desirable than the areas to the south of the city favoured by students and creative types.

Another Music in a Different Kitchen

Studio album
Recorded: December 1977–January 1978, Olympic Studios,
Barnes, London
Mixed: Olympic Studios, Barnes, London
Released: 10 March 1978
Producer: Martin Rushent
Sleeve designer: Malcolm Garrett

So when was this recorded?

We recorded the demo on the 14th of December. We recorded for
the album on the 5th of January, three weeks later. We used to have
Martin Rushent there when we recorded demos – mainly because
the things we were trying to do weren't the kind of things that were
usually done in the studio. The energy levels were totally different
to what other bands at the time were like. He'd come along to
make sure that the engineer wasn't making us sound like the last
band who'd been in – we needed someone like Martin there.
We'd have an idea of what we wanted to do and we'd stick with it.

I have quite an economical method of writing. I'm not one for
trying out 20 different versions of something – I have one version
in my head and that's the one I'll do. Very little rewriting or even
tweaking went on. It's a very cost-efficient way of working for
whoever's paying for it.

It only took about two weeks to record – the last week of
December and the first week in January: coincidentally, exactly
a year after we'd done *Spiral Scratch*.

What was Martin's background musically?

He'd been on *Top of the Pops* in the Seventies with a song called
'Give It All You Got'[1]. He was singing on it. He could play bass

Tag from a *Daily Mirror* balloon race. Steve Diggle was famously pickpocketed at the Liverpool one.

and keyboards – he had a good working knowledge of music. He started off as a tea boy then blagged his way into being a tape op. He used to work on lots of sessions – he had loads of anecdotes to tell. In the early Seventies he worked at Advision and he was the engineer when Marc Bolan was making *Electric Warrior*. So he picked up a lot of experience of how bands work in the studio. He was also very good at reading people, so he could always make it a fun experience rather than a headache. He could always get the best out of us – we looked forward to going into the studio with him. And it was more organized than when we were working with Martin Hannett – that was a bit more freeform.

If you look on the sleeves it usually says 'Produced by Martin Rushent, arranged by Buzzcocks'.

You got quite a generous advance? I read that it was £75,000. That was a lot of money at the time.

Well, yes, but it was for the three albums that we'd been contracted to do, it wasn't just for *Another Music in a Different Kitchen*.

The cover shot was taken at Olympic?

Yes, in the kitchen – it turned out to be fitting for the title of the album but at the time the photo was taken we didn't have a title in mind. And we did the photo shoot to promote the album with Kevin Cummins in Kitchen Queen in Manchester. They had all these kitchen setups in there – it was one step up from a builders' merchants.

You were a fantastic-looking bunch of lads, weren't you? You looked like you all belonged together – like brothers or something.

Well, we were a band!

We always thought Steve was half-Chinese. I think we were a bit disappointed when we found out he wasn't.

So did lots of people. In fact there was someone in Japan who appeared on TV doing a cover of 'Telephone Operator' and my Japanese ex-wife said everyone thought he looked like Steve.

What guitars were you playing at the time?

I think it was a handmade one, a Gordon Smith – named for two guys called Gordon and Smith. They're made in Partington, Manchester.

Before that I'd had the red Starway guitar, the one that's credited on *Spiral Scratch*. I got it in Leigh, secondhand, for £18. It was light and it played well: it had a 'dirty' sound. I suppose it was a cheap alternative to a Fender Jaguar or Jazzmaster.

It got broken when we were rehearsing in the church hall in Salford in the summer of '76. I threw it down and the top section of it snapped off. It still played well but it was better because it was lighter[2]. Howard kept the broken-off bit. The two parts were united at an exhibition of music memorabilia as part of the opening of a Doc Martens shop in Manchester, years later.

Wasn't a copy of your Starway made in later years?

A copy of the original broken instrument was made by Eastwood in 2007, complete with a custom-made case. The case is imprinted with the original Buzzcocks logo on it, as used on *Spiral Scratch*.

Fans clubbed together to buy me an unbroken vintage Starway – red, like the original – in 2007. Some of these vintage instruments are very much in demand now, even the ones that were cheap at the time – you see, they don't make them like they used to.

How did the album get its name?

Just before we started recording *Another Music in a Different Kitchen* in December 1977 we did a group of shows where we had badges made. We'd had some stickers made some time before, which said 'Another music in a different kitchen'; that was a phrase from one of Jon Savage's and Linder's collages, which was called *A Housewife Choosing Her Juices in a Different Kitchen* (we liked the slightly salacious sound of that). When we were asked by United Artists what we'd like on a sticker that's what we came up with.

You had badges made to promote the album as well?

We played three gigs in December '77: one at the Roundhouse, one at Brighton at this little grotty pub-type place and one at the King's Hall, Belle Vue, Manchester, which was going to be the big end-of-the-year party show for the band. A guy called Alan Edwards used to do our press (he's a PR big shot now – he works with The Rolling Stones, among others) and he'd arranged for a coach full of journalists to come down from London for the Brighton gig.

The venue in Brighton was only small and it was crammed – it was the week before Christmas, so the world and his wife were out. In those days we didn't have electronic guitar tuners; they didn't exist. So I used to tune all the guitars and bass by ear in the dressing room before we went on. I haven't got perfect pitch but it's close. The dressing room was a shed built on to the back of the pub – a lean-to with a corrugated tin roof. It was freezing. Then when we got into the pub it was packed, and obviously very hot. The guitars went out of tune instantly and the condensation was pouring off them. We had to tune again on stage. Our performances in those days were full of those little incidents. There was none of the slickness that you see today!

So for these three dates we had these badges made that said 'Another music in a different kitchen' and the date, and we gave them out at the gigs. This was the start of us doing the badges that accompanied each new release. We used to have big boxes of them on stage and grab big handfuls of them and throw them out into the crowd – something that health and safety would never allow these days! People didn't care – it was a punk gig. I suppose it's better than buckets of blood!

Side 1

It opens with the guitar solo from 'Boredom'. Whose idea was that?

Mine. The idea was that a lot of people might have only heard *Spiral Scratch* so it was a reintroduction to the world of Buzzcocks. Howard had once told me that when he used to listen to albums of The Beatles or The Shadows he thought they must just be being very quiet in the studio before they started to play the next song – so the spaces between tracks was something that we tried to avoid. There's a repeat echo at the end of the excerpt from 'Boredom' so that there's no empty space before 'Fast Cars'. Then after 'Fast Cars' it's got the sound of the car accelerating, then it goes straight into the ringtone at the beginning of 'No Reply' – so it's more like a soundscape than just a collection of discrete tracks.

Fast Cars

Songwriters: Howard Devoto, Steve Diggle, Pete Shelley

Was it originally Steve's song? He says he'd written the lyric but left it at home on the day of the recording.

He said that about 'Promises' as well! As far as I know he didn't have a lyric for it. Howard wrote two verses of it and I came up with the verse about Ralph Nader. Steve should just take his lyrics with him.

It was inspired by Ralph Nader's 1965 book, *Unsafe at Any Speed*, which claimed that many US cars were unsafe to drive. As a result of it Congress established the National Highway Traffic Safety Administration, introducing safety measures such as safety belts and stronger windscreens.

And cars that didn't disintegrate, leaving loads of jagged metal. It was a bit of an issue at the time – Andy Warhol was doing screen prints of fatal car crashes and J G Ballard's *Crash* had come out in 1973. David Cronenberg made a film of *Crash* in the Nineties that was considered to be really shocking at the time. It was about people who'd been in near-fatal car crashes and found themselves turned on sexually and they'd then stage car crashes to satisfy their lusts. I don't know whether it's a real fetish that people have but the book was good.

Seatbelts weren't mandatory in the UK until about 1979 or 1980 – despite all those advertising campaigns in the Seventies with Jimmy Savile urging us to 'Clunk Click Every Trip'. You didn't have to wear a helmet on a motorcycle either until the early Seventies.

Ralph Nader is still a consumer advocate and activist for a number of other causes. He's also more recently stood for president.

It isn't meant to be a deep song, though.

Did you have a car yourself at this time?

No, I didn't learn to drive until I was quite mature – and I tried it for a while and didn't like it! I prefer to get the bus or to let someone else drive.

No Reply

Songwriter: Pete Shelley

When was this written?

I've got the feeling I wrote it when Howard was still in the band but it was one he never got round to singing.

It was basically a song telling a story of the frustration of trying to get in touch with a loved one and them 'not returning your calls', as they say nowadays. It was harder in those days – there were no mobiles, no emails and no answering machines, and in fact a lot of people didn't have a landline. You could either go and knock on the door or send a letter. At that time you could send a letter in the morning and get a reply in the afternoon as there were two postal deliveries a day. You could write to someone in the morning and ask them to meet you that night – it was almost as quick as email. It was a whole different means of communication.

But in those days it wasn't as easy to tell if someone was deliberately avoiding you because you wouldn't know if they'd been in the house when you rang or even if you'd dialled the wrong number – not like nowadays when you can see all your 'sent' emails and all the calls you've made in your call log.

So it's an angst-ridden song about the failure to communicate – it's about that paranoia.

Where did you record the ringtone?

We recorded it on the phone in the studio at Olympic; we just put a microphone on it. And then at the end of the song the phone's slammed down.

It's a good song, still good to play – although it's also very much of its time.

Another Music **is like a concept album, isn't it? Or the soundtrack to a film about a week in a teenager's life. I've always had a kind of kitchen-sink drama running in my head when I hear it.**

Well, that was the whole idea of punk, wasn't it? The idea was that you sang about things that excited or exasperated you. And in some ways we did link it all together.

You Tear Me Up

Songwriters: Howard Devoto and Pete Shelley

Where and when was this one written?

Well, that was another early one with Howard – I did the music and he wrote the words. It was written at the end of '75.
　　Howard conjures up the sick teenager well, doesn't he?

The drumbeat in this is very distinctive. It has an urgency about it: it's very punk[3].

I've since found out that that drumbeat is now referred to as 'D-beat' – a lot of second-generation punk bands have that as the main beat that they've used. It's particularly associated with Discharge.

So you know where it says, 'All this slurping and sucking/ It's really putting me off my food' – it says in Paul Morley's autobiographical *Nothing* that you kissed him. Is that true?

Oh, yes. We used to do that sort of stuff all the time. It was the kind of thing that happened in those days.

He says he's never kissed another man since.

Perhaps I put him off – or perhaps he thought no other man would ever match up!

Get on Our Own

Songwriter: Pete Shelley

Can you remember where and when this was written?

I seem to remember it being written some time in '76. It was one of those that for some reason or other Howard never wrote lyrics for.

It's a cheeky, flirty song. It wasn't written about someone in particular – it could have been written about anyone. It's got a very wholesome Sixties sound about it, like an old-fashioned love song.

What can you tell us about the Pete Shelley 'yodel'?

I was always a fan of Frank Ifield. He was an Australian country singer. He had a big hit in the early Sixties with 'I Remember You' – I used to listen to it on the Light Programme. He followed it up with a novelty song called 'She Taught Me How to Yodel'. I don't know if it was a euphemism for something.

And I'd seen a BBC anthropological programme about a tribe in New Guinea or somewhere who did a kind of yodelling – perhaps as one of their war cries – so I purloined that.

The vocalization is quite jazzy: it isn't just sticking to the black-and-white notes; there are bits in between. There are stretches... It's quite sophisticated musically in a way that astounds even me.

Love Battery

Songwriters: Howard Devoto and Pete Shelley

You and Howard wrote this together?

Yes, it's another one of Howard's creations that I provided the music for.

I think Howard must have been very frustrated sexually. All his songs are either about people pissing him off or about him being fit to explode.

I didn't get the impression it's about having a romantic encounter with a female lover...

You'll have to ask Howard about that!

Talking about 'fizzing at the terminals', my gran read in an interview that you said that a 'Buzz Cock' was something you get when you sit on the back seat of a bus, with the engine throbbing beneath you. I thought it had the ring of authenticity about it because some people from your neck of the woods say 'buzz' instead of 'bus'.

I've read this. It's gained ground because people think it could be true. But it's not. We got the name from that line in *Time Out* about that TV show *Rock Follies*.

This song reminds me of a George Formby number. He was from Wigan, next to your hometown, Leigh. Was he an inspiration?

I am aware of his work but I've not modelled myself on him. I know 'Little Stick of Blackpool Rock' was banned by the BBC, though – 40 years before 'Orgasm Addict'! If you listen to it now it's surprisingly saucy[4].

Sixteen

Songwriter: Pete Shelley

What's the background to this?

I wrote it when I was round at Howard's one day – he used to keep a guitar in the spare room in case I came up with a song while I was there. It must have been before April '77 because I remember I was 21 when I wrote it (as it says in the lyric).

It's a bit of an odd song. It's in 3/4 time, for a start, and there are all sorts of angular, disjointed bits, including the bit in the middle where it goes wild.

We'd got to know Jon Savage by then – he'd been working with Linder on some collages. He had a car and he used to drive us around everywhere. One night during the recording we had a night off and we went to see *Star Wars* at the cinema. We'd bought these H&H amps – the special, V-S Musician ones – and they came with a flanger pedal. The way that flanger pedals work nowadays, it's a separate thing that you plug your guitar into. But this H&H one, it connected to the amp, so there was circuitry inside it so it was more like an effects unit. The next day we were recording the chaotic bit in 'Sixteen' and because there's all the electronic noises in the film, the firing of the ray guns and things like that, we found that if we turned up the amps really loud these effects boxes would start feeding back and making these god-awful noises. So that was our homage to *Star Wars*.

When we first started playing it John Maher didn't have many cymbals. When we were rehearsing in the basement at Howard's there was a brass coal scuttle and the lid made a similar sort of noise to a cymbal when you hit it. So John 'borrowed' a clamp from the chemistry lab at school and made this contraption. He even used it when we played live. This was another case of us being experimental. There were hints of Captain Beefheart in what we did, that type of strangeness.

I don't think 3/4 time is common in rock, is it? Although The Stranglers have used it.

No – that's why 4/4 is called 'common time'! But then the waltz, which is in 3/4 time, was the mainstay of European music for hundreds of years.

You've said it's got similarities to Ravel's *Bolero*?

Well, it's on two chords, isn't it, and it's got that similar, lilting feel.

Did you really hate modern music: disco, boogie and pop?

Well, I'm not really a dancer. I've always seen it as being one of those odd things to do – a bit like sport. I did have a girlfriend once who used to win medals ballroom dancing. We used to go to the church hotpot supper dances – so I learned a few ballroom dance steps. And when you used to go to the youth-club disco when you're a teenager – girls dancing round their handbags and that. I never pulled there; I was never that trendy kind of guy. That's why I put myself permanently behind the guitar – then they come flocking.

It was railing against all sorts of things. 'And I don't like French kissing/'Cause you swallow my tongue' – that was written from a personal experience with someone who was like a vacuum cleaner.

The irony is that you can't dance easily to this song because it's in 3/4 time – unless, of course, you were waltzing.

'Sixteen' is a song by Iggy Pop, isn't it?

Is it? I don't know it, so it wasn't an homage to that.

I read that Paul Morley covered it with his band The Negatives – yet I've read elsewhere that he was never in a punk band and it's just a myth that he invented.

No, they were real. I seem to have vague memories of seeing them play – perhaps at the Electric Circus. People were starting bands all over the place at that time. Things didn't have to be done in the standard way – that was the whole idea of punk.

Side 2

I Don't Mind

See page 98.

Fiction Romance

Songwriter: Pete Shelley

How did you come to write this?

On the day when we signed with United Artists we did a photo session with Kevin Cummins in a library. We'd been at the Electric Circus so it was going out towards Oldham: Collyhurst or somewhere. And there was a bookshelf with a sign above it saying 'Fiction/Romance'. But that came after the song. You can see the photo in the book that accompanies the *Product* box set.

It's got that jerky riff and at first it had no lyric. The lyric evolved as we were playing the song live – I'd improvise the words almost every night and it finally coalesced into what it is on the album. It's about how fiction romances don't happen quite the way they do in books, although it's got the ray of hope at the end. Even though life doesn't turn out the way it does in books it still has elements in it that can make it better than it would be in a novel.

Had you read many of those kinds of books yourself – or did your mum read them?

No, I didn't read them and I don't think she did either. She used to knit a lot.

Autonomy

See page 102.

I Need

Songwriters: Pete Shelley and Steve Diggle

How did you come to write this?

At the sound check before that gig at the Roundhouse we started playing this riff – it was just something we put together on the spot. But then we opened the show with it. We played it as an instrumental; there was no lyric for it. Because it was something that came out of a jam it was difficult to say who had the complete ownership of it. At the same gig we also played 'I Don't Mind', 'Get on Our Own' and 'Autonomy' – we were trying out the new songs that were going to be on the album.

I started writing the lyric when we were in the studio, about three weeks later. The lyric is an exploration of the fact that there's a difference between what you want and what you need and what you crave for – and perhaps what's good for you. Each line was answered with the words 'I need', which seemed to be in the music. And then there's a bass-guitar solo in the middle, which worked really well.

We were doing loads of travelling at the time – we had to drive straight from gigs drenched in sweat, even at this time, in the winter – and so about every six weeks I'd have a cold. And in fact I had a cold when I was recording the vocal for 'I Need'. I can hear it when I listen to it now, although I think most people just thought I was nasal and northern.

So I list all the things I need – sex, love, drink, drugs, food, cash, 'you to love me back' – and in the last section it says 'I need flu...I need drugs'. I needed flu drugs, you see. I was really suffering.

It's just a little fun song that was born out of a jam.

Moving Away from the Pulsebeat[5]

Songwriter: Pete Shelley

That's an imaginative title for a song.

That was a line of Paul Morley's – it came from a review. He was making the point that some of the songs that we did were not to the regular rock 'n' roll 'formula'.

Where and when was it written?

I think I wrote it in about December '76 – that's when the initial riff and structure came about. It was at about the time when we were rehearsing in a disused office space at Lifeline on Mosley Street, a drop-in centre for drug addicts. Richard Boon fixed us up with it. It wasn't a dedicated rehearsal space; it was just somewhere where we could make plenty of noise.

It seemed like a showcase for John's drumming.

Even though it's set to a Bo Diddley beat it stands out as being different from other songs. The drums make it. And we played a lot of the chords with the harmonics – so it's mainly an instrumental. You could say it's an instrumental with a lyric. It isn't really a melodic song – it's mainly about the rhythm and it has a jerkiness about it. Like a Cubist composition. It sounded modern, which is partly the theme of the album.

In the studio we decided to double-track the drums – so it wasn't a studio effect; it was really him playing it twice.

Would it have worked out differently if you'd had a different drummer?

I suppose so, yes. We were lucky with John. Even though he had no experience he had a lot of innate talent.[6]

The way we used to work, it's not like nowadays when you go into your home studio and make a demo then play it to the band. We'd just go into rehearsal and go, 'I've got a song, it goes like this' – and we'd work it out there and then. In conversations that I've had with John subsequently he says he plays the drums to the melody of the song – he's listening to what's being sung and emphasizes bits in that so it's hard to think of the song without the drums.

Yes, the drums in 'Pulsebeat' are absolutely intrinsic to the song, aren't they?

Drumming was becoming more high-profile at that time. The Burundi drummers[7] were getting people into the more ethnic, more primitive side of drumming. We were trying lots of different things with the album. It was good recording with Martin Rushent, in the same way that The Beatles were well paired with George Martin. George Martin had worked on novelty records with people like The Goons[8] and Charlie Drake[9] so he was used to coming up with things that weren't the regular kind of thing – and working with Martin Rushent was a bit like that. And I was coming in with all these ideas from left, right and centre, stuff that wasn't regular rock 'n' roll – odd time signatures, avant-garde stuff, free-form jazz – and he helped us realize our ideas. Some producers wouldn't even know what to do with that stuff but he could always make it sound good.

It was recorded for a Peel Session...[10]

On the Peel Sessions they didn't want us to play songs that we'd had out as singles, so we always used to use them for trying things out – it was almost like doing a demo. We used to use the Peel Sessions as a testing ground; that's why things like 'Late for the Train' were recorded for it.

The End[11]

What's this about?

'The End' is the bit on the play-out groove, where it's the reprise of 'Boredom' followed by the repeating scale. There's a story about that in itself. The recording of the repeating scale was given to us by a friend of Richard's – he was an art student with an interest in pataphysics, where you use scientific principles in creating art. It's two different scales: as the notes get higher the notes from the bass come in as well, an octave below, so it's two scales overlapping. It sounds like it's getting higher and higher but it never actually gets any higher because, by the time it's doing the high thing, that's fading out and the low one has come in, so your ear follows that. It's an auditory illusion – like an M C Escher print where you follow the stairs that never take you anywhere.

Pataphysical science, incidentally, is mentioned in the opening lines of 'Maxwell's Silver Hammer' by The Beatles.

Another Music got to No. 15 in the UK Album Chart. That was quite respectable for a debut punk album, wasn't it?

Yes, I suppose so, but we had no idea what to expect. We'd only really had one single that could be played on the radio, because the first one was 'Orgasm Addict' and the second was 'What Do I Get?', which we didn't go on *Top of the Pops* with. It was exciting to find we'd got into the Top 20.

We'd been doing lots of gigs, including on the 'White Riot' tour, and we'd built up quite a following, so I suppose that's how the album sold. We'd done a few singles with Martin Rushent as well, so we knew what we were doing by then and everything was fine – we were in a good space.

You must have had to sell a lot and, more crucially, sell them quickly to get to No. 15?

That was the joy of having a decent record company, because that's what they're good at doing – selling records and making sure that the shops have got enough of them. Nowadays it's a struggle just to make sure when you walk into a record shop you can actually find what you're looking for.

We didn't get a silver disc or anything for it, though – that came later with *Love Bites*, because that sold a lot more. It was only a few months later but by then we'd become regulars on *Top of the Pops*.

Notes

1 'Give It All You Got' is quite anonymous-sounding, easily forgettable Seventies fodder but the B-side, 'Why Bother to Fight', is an altogether much more punchy, pacy number, teetering on the edge where punk meets heavy metal.

2 Many myths have sprung up about how this modestly priced Japanese guitar – probably originally bought in bargain chain store Woolworths – sustained the transformative damage. Pete's cousin Howard says of the Starway: 'He bought it from a place on Leigh Road – it used to be a music shop but I think it's a hairdresser's now. A lot of people think he smashed it up on stage, but he actually snapped the top off so he could balance the setlist on there – you can see it in some of the photos from that time.' The Sex Pistols' manager, Malcolm McLaren, meanwhile, referred to the Starway as the 'sawn-off guitar' (the wood had broken so cleanly at the point where it was glued that you could be forgiven for thinking that it had, indeed, been sawn off).

   Pete himself said in an interview with Mark Page on Radio 1's *City to City* programme on 25 October 1986: 'It's a very mythical guitar: a lot's been written about it...I'm thinking of having a special presentation case made for it and donating it, along with all the press cuttings [about it], to the V&A [London's Victoria & Albert Museum] for posterity.' He was obviously joshing – the idea of this must have seemed fanciful at the time when he said it – but now the Starway is in fact in a glass case in a museum. It's on display at the British Music Experience, a permanent exhibition in Liverpool's historical Cunard Building, which traces the history of rock and pop throughout the years, particularly charting times of change within British popular music. The Starway is there to represent punk and the metamorphoses engendered by the new genre.

3 Steve Garvey says: 'We played very in front of the beat – it was push, push, push. Nothing was behind or on the beat, everything was in front – typical of punk-rock bands but we mastered it. The Ramones were the key to it – they were a bigger influence on what we were doing than the Pistols. But we didn't sit down and discuss it – it just happened.'

4 A stick of rock is a candy cane, for Stateside readers, or lolly for Australian ones, with the word 'Blackpool' or some other message embedded throughout its length. The euphemism in 'With My Little Stick of Blackpool Rock', released as a B-side in 1937, is so transparent as to be patently see-through. Formby sings: 'It may be sticky, but I never complain/It's nice to have a nibble at it now and again...' And when the conductor's baton somehow 'flew out of his hand' at a seaside concert, the song's protagonist cheerfully assists by conducting the band with his 'little stick of Blackpool rock'.

   Incidentally, much fun can be had if one sings along to some of Pete's songs using George Formby's vocal style. The more Music Hall numbers work particularly well using this trick.

5 'Moving Away from the Pulsebeat' was released as a one-sided 12-inch promotional disc. It can fetch up to £100 today.

6 Pete has said elsewhere, and Steve Garvey agrees, that John had an almost telepathic understanding of what was required of him and an ESP-like rapport with the other members of the band.

7 The Royal Drummers of Burundi had started touring the world in the Sixties but the 'tribal' sound may have first come to popular prominence in the west after the release of 'Burundi Black', the 1971 single by French pianist and producer Michel Bernholc (dubbed 'Burundi Steiphenson Black' for the release of the record), which featured a sample of aboriginal Burundi drumming recorded by French anthropologists in 1967.

8 *The Goon Show* was a radio programme broadcast on the BBC's Home Service throughout the Fifties. Its surreal and absurdist humour – much of it created with bizarre sound effects and silly voices – heavily influenced Monty Python and also, perhaps more unexpectedly, was cited as an influence by The Beatles.

9 Charlie Drake was a singer, actor and slapstick comedian. Songs he recorded with George Martin include 'Splish Splash' and 'My Boomerang Won't Come Back', which was considered to be politically incorrect even in 1961.

10 John Peel was one of the first DJs to join Radio 1 in 1967. The new station was aimed at the younger audience and its daytime programming consisted mostly of chart fodder, but Peel's evening show was respected for playing a more-than-eclectic mix of genres and helping to 'break' many new artists. The 'sessions' (so-called because they were recorded by 'session men': artists other than the BBC's own 'house' bands or orchestras) consisted of four tracks that had been laid down over just one day, resulting in a sound that was pleasingly halfway between that of a studio recording and a live performance. During Peel's tenure (until his untimely death in 2004) 4,000 sessions were recorded by over 2,000 artists.

11 'The End' is not actually listed as a separate track on either the sleeve or the label. It is an undocumented addition after the final track. It matches the opening snippet of 'Boredom' before the first track, 'Fast Cars'.

Love You More

Stand-alone single
B-side: 'Noise Annoys'
Recorded: EMI Abbey Road Studios, St John's Wood, London
Mixed: Advision Studios, Fitzrovia, London
Released: 30 June 1978
Songwriter: Pete Shelley
Producer: Martin Rushent
Sleeve designer: Malcolm Garrett
Run-out-groove message: 'The Secret Public'

This was recorded at Abbey Road?

Yes. We went into the studio that The Beatles had recorded in and then we mixed at Advision, which is where they used to record advertising jingles in the Sixties – another studio that's sadly no longer there.

Recording at Abbey Road must have been a buzz for you.

Well it was – but it was just a studio really! I don't remember it as feeling like hallowed turf. Steve was probably thrilled, though.

Was it written about a girl who worked in Woolworths?

Yes. At the beginning of '74 I started going out with this girl who lived between Leigh and Bolton. I was living in a student flat in Bolton but still spending time at my mum and dad's in Leigh. We'd arrange to meet and I'd get the bus from Leigh – was it the 82 or the 582? – and she'd know what bus I'd be on so she'd get on it and we'd travel to Manchester together. We'd only started going out on New Year's Eve and it was a Saturday – whatever the first Saturday in 1974 was. I'd been at my mum's over New Year and we travelled together in the morning for her to start work at Woolworths and then I met her at lunchtime to tell her that I'd just written a song, which was 'Love You More'.

I'd known her probably just over a week. The line 'Don't want to end up like no nine-day wonder' isn't metaphorical –

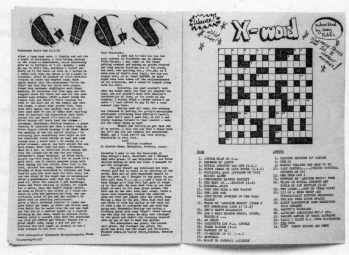

'The Secret Public', as inscribed on the run-out groove of 'Love You More', was the name of Buzzcocks' fan club, its newsletter (above) and a one-off, glossy art publication featuring collages by Jon Savage and Linder (above, top).

I was worried it might not make it to the nine-day point! That was because in a previous relationship I went out with someone I already knew and it had only lasted nine days.

It's very intense – it sounds like it's about someone who you've been with for years.

That's what passion's like, isn't it? It intensifies everything. And a couple of weeks can feel like a lifetime when you're in love.

What counter did she work on?

Oh, I can't remember now. She just worked there on Saturdays – she was a student.

So she didn't get you free pick 'n' mix?

No, no...unless that's a euphemism for something.

Was it played on the radio much? I thought it might be a bit short for radio and ends on rather an abrupt note.

I'd imagine it got lots of airplay as it went up the charts.
   I always like those sudden endings to frighten DJs. Like in 'Are Everything', where it fades then comes back in really loud. There's a similar thing that The Beach Boys do in 'Help Me, Rhonda' (that's not a song about the Welsh Valleys!).

It got to No. 34 in the charts.

That might not sound that high but 1978 and 1979 were the biggest years for sales of singles and you might have had to have sold perhaps 100,000 records to get to that number.

You were asked to appear on *Top of the Pops* before it was actually released...

It was supposed to come out earlier but it was delayed. We'd begun recording it on the 13th of March – about a month before 'I Don't Mind' was released.

Did someone at *Top of the Pops* have a bit of a soft spot for you?

No, we had a good plugger – a guy called Mike. He always used to take us out for Chinese meals – that's where I learned to use chopsticks; very sophisticated. And he introduced us to snow peas [mangetout].

Is it sped up for the record? If you play along to it seems to be in the key of F rather than E, which is what you'd expect.

Martin Rushent would record a track then, when he was in the cutting room, he used to tweak it so that it was at the level of energy that he wanted it to be at. I had a cold at the time – you can hear it more on 'Noise Annoys'.

So why on record do you always do your own backing vocal rather than have Steve do it?

Because usually I have an idea of the harmonies I want to do, and it's easier and quicker for me to do it and to teach it to him between the time of us recording it and him performing it.

Whose idea are the 'Oh-ohs'?

Mine. It was in the original song.

I mean, where did you get the idea from? They're one of your trademarks.

Well, for a start they're 'Oh-ohs', not 'Whoa-whoas'. In America they seem to think it's 'Whoa-whoa'. A few times when we've been playing live I've stopped the song and said, 'It's not "Whoa-whoa"; I'm not rounding up cattle or trying to stop my horse! This is "Oh-oh" – as in, "it hurts".' I didn't get the idea from anywhere – it's something I dreamed up. It is one of our trademarks – you can stick it almost anywhere.

What gigs were you playing at this time?

We did a tour for every one of the singles – so that was the 'Entertaining Friends' tour.

And you performed it on *Revolver*? That was a strange show, wasn't it?

Yes. It's supposed to be in a fictitious ballroom but it was actually in the ATV studios in Birmingham. You'd be backstage with your gear set up and then suddenly the stage would revolve round into the studio – that's why it was called *Revolver*.

The comedian Peter Cook is supposed to be the ballroom's manager. He looked over at me and winked! I'm not sure what he meant by it – I never got the chance to ask him.

They had no idea how to do a pop show. We got there at a god-awful time like 9am on a Sunday and with rehearsals and camera rehearsals you'd be doing it for most of the day. Generation X were on the show with us and they pissed off all the production people because they wouldn't play the song the same twice – but we were good: we were professional. While we were singing it a couple of guys in the audience were holding up pictures from a gay porn magazine. I don't know what that was about either! People could be very saucy with me.

Howard came along for this recording. We played 'Noise Annoys' on *Revolver* as well.

And what about that film called *Love You More*?

It was originally a short story by Patrick Marber called 'Peter Shelley' and was made into a short film by Sam Taylor-Wood. [Patrick Marber used to play the student in Steve Coogan's Paul Calf videos.] It was included in a book of short stories that novelist Nick Hornby compiled to raise money for an autism charity. It's about a guy called Peter who loses his virginity with a girl from school on the day that 'Love You More' comes out. They end up having passionate sex in her bedroom and it's the start of a beautiful relationship. The ages had to be changed for the film – they were about 14 in the book. I have a cameo role in it as a man browsing in a record store. It won awards in Japan and was nominated for the Oscars for the short films but it didn't get the gong.

What happens in the film in the end?

In the end they decide to meet up again and listen to the B-side. They've just had 'Love You More' on repeat while they've been making love. Although I'm not sure you need longer than 1 minute 58 when you're 15!

The lyric in the last verse is quite unexpected.

It ends with 'Until the razor cuts', but originally when I wrote it I didn't have it ending there. It's quite dark compared to the previous two verses but matters of the heart are very strong and can be very violent in people. It's something that society tends to gloss over. The general view is that the love song is frivolous and people – at the time of punk in particular – wanted to do something more political. But to me there's nothing more political than the way people treat each other. That's of greater importance than the class struggle or the socio-economic climate because it's something that affects people in the here and now, day to day.

Noise Annoys

B-side to: 'Love You More'
Songwriter: Pete Shelley
Producer: Martin Rushent
Run-out-groove message: 'The crossover market'

When and where was it written?

I used to go out with a girl from Hazel Grove, a posh bit south
of Manchester and, like a lot of girls that you go out with,
they've got a mate. This mate was called Cathy West and we
used to joke that she was very drunk all the time – which she
usually was whenever I saw her. Once on the 192 [the bus that
runs between Hazel Grove and Manchester] when we were
on our way to the Ranch I just started making a jokey song
[to the tune of 'Noise Annoys']: 'Cathy West, Cathy West, Cathy
West, Cathy West, Cathy West, you are a lush' – so that was
where the music came from. Then when we played at the
beginning of May '77 at the Band on the Wall we went to a
pub around Oldham Street and someone had left a copy of the
Daily Mirror. I was flicking through it while I was waiting for my
drink to be brought over and the headline read, 'Noise Annoys
Neighbours'. And I just loved the sonorance of the phrase
'Noise Annoys'. That fitted in with the Cathy West song and all
I needed then was a rhyme for 'noise annoys' – and I thought
of 'pretty girls, pretty boys'. So it's a song about your mother
screaming at you to keep the noise down. It wasn't meant to
be any great philosophical treatise.

So it starts off with a very rock opening. There's a saying
about heavy metal – they say: 'It's a big opening, a big finish

and something to keep them apart.' So it opened with these huge power chords and it almost degenerated into this freeform jazz section and the song emerges phoenix-like out of the rubble of the heavy-metal chaos. The guitar solos are supposed to be badly played – kind of monotonous with missed notes and discordant things because it's supposed to be a noise.

It's only a little, short piece – even though it's longer than 'Love You More' – but it's a nice, fun song with instrumental chunks in it.

When we get to the bit where it says, 'Do you ever hear your mummy scream...?' we made that noise when we were mixing it at Advision. We got a tea tray with bottles and cups and things on it and went into the vocal booth and threw it on the floor at the cue – so that was fun to do.

We were always trying to get little quirky things into the songs whenever we could.

I suppose when I was a kid and I used to listen to it on vinyl I thought it was a bit of a novelty song, but now that I've heard it played live I can see the sense in it.

All the songs at this time were played live before they were actually recorded, so that's how they evolved.

Was it at about this time that the *B'dum B'dum* documentary was aired?

I suppose so because it was made during the summer, although it may have been shown later in the year. At Granada all the main anchor people like Bob Greaves would be allowed to each make their own little programme during the summer – and Tony Wilson decided to make one about Buzzcocks and Magazine. We recorded the live portion at the Lesser Free Trade Hall gig on July 20th 1978 – so that was two years exactly after the first

Buzzcocks gig there. I was interviewed in the café in Woolworths (which used to be on the corner of Oldham Street), which I used to go in a lot, and Howard was interviewed in the royal box at the Palace Theatre – quite a contrast.

Ever Fallen in Love
(With Someone You Shouldn't've)

Single
B-side: 'Just Lust'
Recorded: 1978, Olympic Studios, Barnes, London
Mixed: Advision Studios, Fitzrovia, London
Released: 8 September 1978
Songwriter: Pete Shelley
Producer: Martin Rushent
Sleeve designer: Malcolm Garrett

I read that this was inspired by watching the film *Guys and Dolls* when you were staying in a guesthouse in Edinburgh.

That's correct – on the tour where Barry Adamson was playing bass. We went out to get haggis suppers. We were staying in a hotel and it was before they had colour TVs in every room so they had one in the lounge downstairs. There was a little bar built into the corner of the room and I was drinking beer from one of the old-fashioned, dimpled pint pots and *Guys and Dolls* with Marlon Brando and Frank Sinatra was on. Frank Sinatra plays Nathan Detroit and his girlfriend is Adelaide, a showgirl, and she's bemoaning the fact that they've been going out for so long and he hasn't proposed yet. At the end of the scene she says, 'Have you ever fallen in love with someone you shouldn't've? Wait till it happens to you.' And I thought, 'That's a good idea for a song...' The chorus is basically just what was said in the movie.

The next day our driver, Pete Monks, had to go to the post office, so we were sitting outside the post office in the van and I was thinking about how to start the song. Originally I'd thought of, 'You piss on my natural emotions', but after a while I thought 'spurn' is better – it'd be more likely to get played on Radio 1. I was very influenced at the time by the notion that relationships would be much better if people would just realize that it's better to be in one with me. And if you make a fuss about it you jeopardize the relationship you have got.

Like the other songs, I tried to make it sound like speech – it's just that it has to rhyme.

Was it written about someone in particular?

Well, like I said – they all are, and they're all not. It doesn't need to be explicitly about one person. And to sing about any one person would be to give them too much credit!

A lot of songs, especially love songs, are about getting people to change their mind – because without a lot of coaxing a lot of relationships would never get off the ground.

Is it true that it's the longest song title that's ever appeared in the UK charts?

No, I think there have been others. That might have just been part of the publicity!

The full title is actually 'Ever Fallen in Love (With Someone You Shouldn't've Fallen in Love With)'. But a longer song title is a song from the Seventies by the Faces – 'You Can Make Me Dance, Sing or Do Anything' (that's the abbreviated version, anyway)[1].

It's that constant shifting between major and minor that gives it the universal appeal to people.

In 2004 I met a band from LA in New York – The Adored. I sang backing vocals on two of their songs (both on record and when they accompanied us as support on the 'Flatpack' tour in 2006). In a rehearsal one time, the first song starts off with a chord and then the music comes in, and as the guitarist played the chord the band all looked at me expectantly and one of them said, 'Don't you recognize the chord?' I said no and he said, 'It's C-sharp minor – from "Ever Fallen in Love"!'

In some ways it's like it begins on a false start. We play a B and then when it goes down to the E it releases all that tension: it's resolved. It's taken you to the place where it was hinting you might be going to. I've seen someone on YouTube showing people how to play it and he's doing it all wrong. He makes it all difficult for himself because it isn't a fancy thing; it's just moving a few fingers here and there – just picking. And it works well with me and Steve doing the chords – when it goes down to the E he starts playing the riff and then I come in and play the riff. But it's quite a simple song – there's no solo in it and no middle eight. There's just the verses and the chorus and the bit with the E – and the riff[2].

And where it ends on the major chord it kind of changes the sense of everything that's gone before – although the song's been heartrending it's as though you're saying, 'Shit happens, and you live to fight another day.'

I always like having happy music, even with wrist-slitting lyrics.

What about that cover of 'Ever Fallen in Love' by Fine Young Cannibals?

Roland Gift went to art college in Hull with Phil Diggle, Steve's brother, and Phil used to sublet him a room. I heard that Fine Young Cannibals had been playing it live. So I was in Bumblebee's, an organic grocery store on Brecknock Road in Camden, and he was in front of me in the queue and I said hello to him. And he said, 'We've just done a song of yours – we've just done "Ever Fallen in Love".' They'd recorded it for a Jonathan Demme film called *Something Wild* and their record company,

London Records, had suggested releasing it as a single. So it wasn't *their* intention to release it as a single; it was their record company's idea.

It ended up getting to No. 9 in the charts, so it must have been better than our version of it, because that only got to No. 12!

It's a version of the song that a lot of your fans object to.

They did it sounding like themselves, which is what you're supposed to do with a cover version. It became a huge hit and the album sold by the van-load, which provided us with some money from royalties with which we were able to finance the re-formation of Buzzcocks in 1989.

So what happens when someone wants to cover one of your songs? They don't need your permission or approval?

No, unless they want to put different lyrics to it. Someone did a Hawaiian-surf version of it that said 'Ever Fallen in Love with a Hula Girl?'

I've heard cover versions of this song where they mangle the lyric.

The Noisettes sang it on one of Jonathan Ross's shows and Will Young sang it and in the second verse they sing, 'Unless we find out who's to blame'. But I wrote 'what's to blame'. I mean, we know who's to blame – and it's not me!

What did you think of the Nouvelle Vague version?

Well, that's been good as well. They do songs that you wouldn't expect to be done in that style, in that style. It's appeared in adverts everywhere and has reached a wider audience. People like that version of the song where they might not like a punk-rock version of it. That's the thing with songs – they can be done in any style.

So what about the version of it that was used in *Shrek 2*?

For the film it was sung by Pete Yorn, an American singer-songwriter. But people got to hear it, and it helps keep you out and about without having to do anything.

Do you know why they didn't want to use your version of it?

They may not have thought of Buzzcocks as saleable. It could also be that it would be cheaper to record a new version of it than to use the original. We heard once that a company wanted to use 'Ever Fallen in Love' in an advert and to use it they'd have to pay synchronization fees. And I heard that the price the owner of the copyright quoted was £250,000 – and this was quite a few years ago.

Who would choose what would be put out as a single?

Well, it was basically us but there'd be input from Andrew Lauder as well.

When we were in the studio recording all the songs that went on to *Love Bites*, everybody's girlfriends and significant others came down to London for the weekend and they all went shopping in the West End. In the meantime Martin decided that he and I should have a 'vocals day' – working on the vocals for all the songs. Up to that point 'Ever Fallen in Love' had never had any backing vocals – there are no backing vocals on the demo. You can hear on the version of it that's on the *B'dum*

B'dum programme that there were no backing vocals on it. So I recorded some backing vocals and Martin did some as well – it's like a three-part harmony, but not in a Crosby, Stills & Nash kind of way. We'd been working on it all day and we were quite pleased with ourselves. Then when the others came back from shopping Martin said, 'Listen to this...' – and he always used to monitor incredibly loud – and blasting out was the track more or less as it is on the record. And the rest of the band were dumbstruck. It was only really then that we thought it could be a single.

It was re-recorded for a benefit single after the death of John Peel, wasn't it?

Amnesty International had the idea of doing a charity single as a tribute to John Peel, to celebrate the many years that he'd been on the radio. His family agreed as long as it wasn't 'Teenage Kicks', which they thought had been over-played. 'Ever Fallen in Love' was John Peel's other favourite track and we all agreed it was an excellent choice. So I went in a studio in London one Sunday morning with members of The Datsuns and El Presidente from Glasgow. We established a tempo and I laid down a basic guitar track to act as a guide for the other musicians to add to later. I left and that was the last I heard about it until it was actually completed and it was ready to come out. They got Sir Elton John and Robert Plant and Roger Daltrey and Dave Gilmour to contribute to it. Elton John did his bit by a transatlantic link. It was an all-star cast but there was never a point where everyone was in the studio at the same time.

Another guitar luminary was chosen to be involved but he doesn't actually appear on the record. It was all going well until Andy Gill (from Gang of Four, who was producing it) said, 'That's great but remember there's no guitar solo in the middle.'

So the guitarist said, 'If you take off my guitar solo you take off everything' – so, as the song doesn't have a guitar solo, Andy Gill took off 'everything'.

At the UK Music Hall of Fame in 2005 they decided to give John Peel a posthumous lifetime-achievement award. To commemorate it, a 14-piece Buzzcocks – with Jamie Cullum, Peter Hook, Andy Gill and some of The Datsuns, as well as me, Steve, Tony and Phil – played a version of 'Ever Fallen in Love' and it

PHOTO BY CHRIS GABRIN

Malcolm Garrett and ladyfriend Jakki at a Buzzcocks gig at the Roundhouse in London, probably 28 May 1978.

was televised. We were on last and, as with all things broadcast live, it was very rushed and I think we were playing as the final credits went up.

Can you tell me a bit about the sleeve design?

It was a really striking image – I've always liked the red and blue. The second Amon Düül II album, *Phallus Dei*, uses the same red and blue colourway and Malcolm had done something similar on the sleeve of The Tiller Boys' *Big Noise from the Jungle*, with a radiating design in red and blue[3].

You got a silver disc for 'Ever Fallen in Love'?

On Martin Rushent's study wall there was a silver disc for 'Ever Fallen in Love' – that was for 25,000 copies. I didn't get one, though, for some reason!

Notes

1 The full title is 'You Can Make Me Dance, Sing or Anything (Even Take the Dog for a Walk, Mend a Fuse, Fold Away the Ironing Board, or Any Other Domestic Shortcomings)'. Released towards the end of 1974, it was the Faces' last single. The words of the full title do not appear in the song.

2 Steve Garvey says of his bass part: 'Generally I did try not to "pedal", which is just playing the root note, although there are some exceptions to that – the most obvious one being "Ever Fallen in Love". I swing with the song, and I don't add anything – I felt like I didn't need to: it didn't need anything else.'

3 Malcolm Garret says: 'I was a huge Marcel Duchamp fan. Richard Boon had the idea of using something based on *Fluttering Hearts* for the sleeve of "Ever Fallen in Love". He described it over the phone and I produced a drawing from his description that was remarkably similar to the actual one, although I'd never seen it.' When Pete's *Collected Lyrics* was published in 2018, the same heart design was used for the cover of the book but with the colours reversed so it was even more intense.

Just Lust

B-side to: 'Ever Fallen in Love (With Someone You Shouldn't've)'
Songwriters: Alan Dial and Pete Shelley
Producer: Martin Rushent

**This was another collaboration between you and
Richard Boon...**

Yes, I'd mentioned the idea to Richard of writing a song called
'Just Lust'. He put pen to paper and came up with the words and
I supplied the music. It was a lyric with which I could identify.

**'There's bed in your eyes but there's nothing there to trust' –
that's just like something you'd write.**

Richard was our manager and so I used to talk to him a lot
when we were on the road. He'd obviously been paying
attention to some of the things I'd been saying! And at this time
he was living in Howard's house, so he was often there when
we were rehearsing.

**It's a great take on a punk love song – it's up there with
Alternative TV's 'Love Lies Limp'.**

Well, it's not all hearts and flowers, is it? There's compulsion
and obsession, betrayal and exploitation, disappointment and
regret – things The Beatles didn't really sing about. Punk gave
us the freedom to discuss human relationships in a way that
no other genre had done previously and to consider themes
that hadn't previously appeared in popular songs – not just

the comedic aspect, like in 'Orgasm Addict', but the darker, more complex aspects of love. Punk was about openness and honesty and confronting the truth of things, even if the truth wasn't that attractive.

Was it just this and 'Whatever Happened To?' that Richard wrote with you? Has he written songs with anyone else?

Yes, it was just those two with Buzzcocks, although he may have written songs with other bands on New Hormones.

Steve says he was writing a song with Richard as well: 'She's Got a Brother'. You can picture the scene – meeting a girl but fancying the guy. He says Richard loved the title but it never manifested.

Which other acts were on the New Hormones label?

When money started coming in Richard found he had more money to spend on the project so there was quite a lot of activity on the label in the early Eighties – The Tiller Boys, which was my side project with Francis Cookson, were on New Hormones; Eric Random, who was also in The Tiller Boys with us; Alberto y Lost Trios Paranoias, who were a comedy music act who did parodies of punk songs; Ludus, which was the band that Linder fronted; and numerous other post-punk acts, like Dislocation Dance and The Diagram Brothers. It was all good stuff. Some of the people in these bands went on to bigger things: some formed other bands that had chart success later on, like Simply Red and 808 State; and some became known for other stuff, like C P Lee from Alberto y Lost Trios Paranoias, who became an academic at Salford University – he wrote a book about that time when someone shouted 'Judas!' when Bob Dylan played the Manchester Free Trade Hall.

Richard famously turned down The Smiths because he felt they needed a more high-profile label than New Hormones. Things could have turned out quite differently if he'd signed them! As it was everything went a bit pear-shaped towards the end of 1982 and the label was wound down.

So would you say New Hormones was a rival to Factory Records?

We didn't draw those parallels at the time but in retrospect that seems fair to say, yes.

I believe that, like with Factory, not all the releases were records?

Some of the releases were on cassette only. Also, the second release wasn't music at all but a collage produced by Linder and Jon Savage – *The Secret Public*.

What's Richard done since Buzzcocks?

He worked with Rough Trade in the Eighties but more recently he's worked as a senior librarian at Stoke Newington Library. He runs a reading group there and is involved in the running of a literature festival. I don't think he's been involved in music for some time, although we see him at gigs every now and then.

What was that talk show that you and Richard spoke at that was held at the British Library in 2016?

It was me, Steve and Richard being interviewed about the early days of the band. We were sitting on comfy chairs on a stage in front of an audience – it was just like being on *Parkinson*! It was

fun but I'd rather be playing songs.

We've done a few of those talks over the years. Once in Brighton I did a lecture before the gig. They're good in the fact that they can help you to crystallize your ideas, but I don't feel all that comfortable doing them. I'd rather be on stage with my guitar and a band behind me.

Love Bites

Studio album
Recorded: 26 July–6 August 1978, Olympic Studios, Barnes, London
Mixed: 11–16 August 1978, Advision Studios, Fitzrovia, London
Released: 22 September 1978
Producer: Martin Rushent
Sleeve designer: Malcolm Garrett
Run-out-groove message: 'A spiky spectacular' (Side 1) and 'What?'
(Side 2)

Where was this recorded?

It was recorded at Olympic, where by that time we were quite
used to working. And we'd done the demos at Arrow Studios in
Manchester, just off Deansgate, going out towards Hulme.

It only took a couple of weeks to record – we were on a roll
by then.

The tape op kept a diary of what was going on in the
studio, which every now and then we'd read out – it was done
very wittily. One of the things that happened was that the tape
machine blew up when we were recording the first song on the
first day! But it was a good, playful atmosphere in there.

**Where did you stay for the couple of weeks you were
recording?**

For the recording of the album we moved to this house in
Chiswick, West London. It was a big house with lots of bedrooms
– I think these arty types lived there. They'd left all their stuff there
so we took this big bag of hats into the studio and everyone was
wearing them for the first few days of the recording.

We had a slight break between recording and mixing, which
I used to make my first trip to the Continent – I went to Paris

with Richard and some friends (I'd never been abroad before).

I've been many times since: I like it. It reminds me of something that happened when we recorded *French* – a live album recorded in Paris in the early Nineties. It was the early days of the internet and we'd used it to promote the album. A year or so afterwards we were in Washington and we decided to do a press conference because we used to have all these fanzines that wanted to interview us. The first question one of them asked us was, 'When did you move to France?' You see they'd read on the internet: 'Buzzcocks live in Paris'.

Had you not been tempted to move to London at this time?

Not really, no. Up north it was seen as being 'that London'.

It got to No. 13 in the UK Album Chart...

We got a silver disc for it, for sales of 60,000 in the UK. You could get copies made, so I got one for my granny, which went on eBay after she died, and one for my mum and dad, and one for myself, and all the band got one. In the late Eighties there was a lad that was writing to me that had bone cancer and he was going to do an auction to raise funds for a charity. So I just sold it to a collector and made a donation to the charity.[1]

Of course, we've sold many more than that since. The albums have been reissued in many different guises since then – although now when CDs are sold it barely covers the wages of the person in the shop who's selling it.

So although *Another Music in a Different Kitchen* got to a similar position in the charts, it didn't earn you a silver disc?

Well, possibly not – or the cheapskates at United Artists didn't
150   bother to get us one made.

**The sleeve design is somewhat reminiscent of The Beatles'
White Album.**

Well, it was, kind of coincidentally. It was later that we started
making the specific Beatles references – see the reverse of the
sleeve of *Singles Going Steady*[2]!

Where were the photos taken?

In a photographic studio. They were taken by Chris Gabrin –
he'd photographed us a few times before for the music press.
He was a rock photographer but also acted as a tour manager for
Blondie when we played with them in Europe in either '78 or '79.

It was supposed to be a bit like the cover of *With The
Beatles*, where their faces are half in shadow. Our faces were
made up differently on each side – a heavy make-up on one
side and a lighter one on the other (we had a professional
make-up artist).

Then on the insert there were some photorealistic,
airbrushed paintings done by Robin Utracik who played in
The Worst, a legendary punk band from Manchester who were
proud of the fact that they couldn't play and yet – or perhaps
that's why – they were revered (they supported us at a few
gigs, including one at Foxes in Croydon and one at the Electric
Circus in October '77). In fact the photo of me that the painting
was done from was taken at the Rock Against Racism gig at
Alexandra Park in Moss Side. We were on early in the day and
I got completely off my face on drink. (This was the gig where
Steve played with Steel Pulse and ended up falling off the
stage.) So I'm throwing up behind one of these caravans and
I hear someone say, 'Hey, Pete!' And I turn round and he took
my photo there and then – when I was looking up, having just
151   spewed my guts up.

What guitar were you playing on this album?

I was playing the Gordon Smith. They're handmade in a workshop that's like a garage – very artisanal. I mean, the way that most guitars are made nowadays, they send off the specifications to a firm in China and they send back a container-load of them. So it's more bespoke than that, there's a lot of detail – they used to hand-wind their pick-ups and that. The instrument I had was the body off one guitar and the neck of another – they had examples there and you could pick the ones you wanted. I liked the shape of one but I liked the feel of the neck of the other, so they married the two together. The last one they made me was just a couple of years ago – you see, I don't use tone controls, I never have. I've never seen the point of them: they just make everything sound more 'muffley'. And I don't really adjust the volume; I only use it as an on-off switch. So instead of having two controls, volume and tone, it's just got volume. Custom-made guitars can be very expensive but Gordon Smiths are quite reasonable.

Onstage at Rock Against Racism, Alexandra Park, Moss Side, July 1978: an event that has gone down in history. This was before Pete threw up behind the Portakabins.

And you yourself played with John Cooper Clarke at this time, in his backing band, The Invisible Girls?

I did but I'm not sure which tracks I played on – they were late-night sessions! It was just in the studio; I didn't play live with him. Martin Hannett would just play the track over and over again and I'd just play along to it and he'd use which bits he wanted. There were people coming in and out of the studio all the time; it was a bit of a party atmosphere[3].

***Another Music in a Different Kitchen* was a hard act to follow. If you sign a contract for a certain number of albums, how do you know you can necessarily keep on producing songs? It seems like a hell of a gamble and also a lot of pressure on you.**

Yes, it's a gamble, because you're bound to it – the record company will always want its pound of flesh. But you have to follow the muse!

Side 1

'Real World'

Songwriter: Pete Shelley

I've read that you wrote this when you were on tour with Penetration.

Yes, I might have done. It would have been the 'Entertaining Friends' tour that we did to accompany 'Love You More'. They were good to tour with.

What's the lyric about?

Lyrically it's this idea that people would get along better if they just cooperated – 'We both win when we play the same game'. We're not here for long and we have to make the best of it we can – it's hard enough as it is! Lyrically it's not that strong but it didn't need to be. We didn't have a lot of time when we were making that album so in some ways the album is a bit of a mixed bag.

It was good as an intro for the album because it builds – that's why we chose it as the first track. It's got the guitars playing those harmonics and there's a nice bassline[4] – it's like an overture.

Who used to decide the track listing?

We used to decide between us. Because this one was a slow builder it was an easy choice as the intro. And we knew 'Late for the Train' was going to be last because it'd be hard to put it in the middle of a side. Because in those days, don't forget, an album had two sides so you needed something good to open up a side, then something that'd close that side – then the same for the second side. So it was like doing a play in two acts, rather than the one act that it is on a CD. There was something good about working within the constraints of that 17 and a half to 22 and a half minutes that you'd get to put on each side – getting that flow.

We used to open the live show with 'Real World' as well and when we did the 'Another Bites' tour in 2009 it was still as powerful – it still had the same excitement and dramatic tension.

'Ever Fallen in Love (With Someone You Shouldn't've)'

See page 137.

'Operator's Manual'

Songwriter: Pete Shelley

This, like 'Sixteen', also seems to be in 3/4 time.

It's another one that's jerky – it's in a peculiar time signature, then it goes into a waltz. It's in 3/4 time but in part of it the accent falls in an odd place – on 3, rather than on 1.

Everyone's familiar nowadays with the idea of an operator's manual but it seemed quite cutting edge at the time. You had quite an interest in tech?

I'd always been interested in computing and at Bolton Institute of Technology I was studying for an HND in electronics[5]. I used to build my own kit, which you could in those days (before the days of integrated circuits), as evidenced on *Sky Yen*. And my first proper job was as a computer operator.

You were a pioneer of early computer programming for music purposes.

When my solo album *XL1* was released in 1983, it came with a program for the ZX Spectrum, an early home computer. It was coded by Joey Headen, a friend who had a degree in computer science. The code was included on the run-out groove and you had to record the music on to a cassette to load it into the computer, which would then display the lyrics and graphics on the screen. The graphics were quite simple but they were colourful and moved in time to the music (it was a bugger to program!). It was cutting edge at the time and still has a certain retro charm to this day. All the people who missed out at the time because they didn't have a ZX Spectrum can now watch it on YouTube!

So how did 'Operator's Manual' come to be written?

I'd bought a new amp for my hi-fi and the instruction booklet said 'Operator's Manual' – so I thought, wouldn't it be good if you had one that helped you sort out all your emotional stuff? It also has a slight suggestive ring – it calls to mind a marriage manual. 'If only I had a mechanic'! It harks back to the 'sex mechanics' in 'Orgasm Addict'.

There's something quite erotic about the idea of man-as-machine, people's sex lives being something you could code for – and it'd be handy if you could just refer back to the user notes every time you had a problem.

'Nostalgia'

Songwriter: Pete Shelley

When was this written?

I wrote this in 1974 so it pre-dates Buzzcocks. It was already fully formed – so it was just a case of playing it to the band and working up a version of it. It was written for my first band, Jets of Air. We never played it live – it was when they were still in the bedroom phase! It sounded pretty much the same then, except in Jets of Air I was playing it on a 12-string guitar.

What were you thinking of when you wrote it?

It's about how ice cream tasted better in the past – or how it might taste better in the future. How everything was great in 'the past' – but 'the past' has become 'now'. And that feeling of nostalgia for something that you can't put your finger on. It was in my poetic student days. I was very much into the Romantic poets – hence my name, Shelley.

You were young to be having those kinds of thoughts, though, weren't you? You must have only been 19 when you wrote it.

Yes, 'Sixteen' and 'Sixteen Again' are about the same theme – about being dissatisfied with your current life. But, as I say, not every song is autobiographical!

'Nostalgia' was covered by Penetration[6]. You were quite friendly with Pauline Murray?

Well, I don't know if they 'covered' it, as it appeared on their album that came out at about the same time as *Love Bites*! It was a song that I felt suited her voice and I was happy for them to play it.

Yes, they still come to the gigs, her and Rob. They have a rehearsal-studio complex up in Newcastle. I've seen her play recently. She couldn't quite get the high notes in 'Nostalgia', though.

'Just Lust'

See page 145.

'Sixteen Again'

Songwriter: Pete Shelley

Again you're talking about being 16. Was it a good time in your life?

There's a sort of convention in songs – like 'the moon in June', there's a lot of songs about being 16. It's just an artistic device rather than something that was necessarily true. Sixteen is the age when you begin your adult life, isn't it – as per the age of consent and being able to run away to Gretna Green. And this one too is quite poetic. You don't get many songs that include the words 'A la carte'!

This one was also written in 1975. There wasn't really enough time between finishing *Another Music* and then doing all the touring and promoting 'Love You More', so when we came to record *Love Bites* I had a cache of songs that I'd already written. We used to do it live so by the time we recorded it I was used to playing and singing it – in true *Blue Peter* fashion it was one I'd made earlier[7]. It had had time to develop, to mature.

You played it on *Whistle Test* in 1978...

Yes, we did that and 'Nothing Left'. It's a good song. We might have chosen it as a single if we hadn't gone with 'Ever Fallen in Love'.

Side 2

'Walking Distance'

Songwriter: Steve Garvey

This was the only Buzzcocks song that Steve Garvey wrote that found its way on to record at the time (although there are a couple of demos for songs which he wrote, which are on *Chronology*[8]). Do you know when and where it was written?

He just turned up at the studio with it one day. He did his thing and I played along with it and embellished it and it just worked out. It was nice doing an instrumental. We were still finding our feet as musicians and exploring what was possible[9].

Did he play guitar, then, as well as bass?

Well, like most bassists he could play guitar as well. Chris [Remington] is probably the only bassist I know who doesn't have pretensions of playing the guitar.

I believe the guitar parts are somewhat reminiscent of Can?

Yes, maybe – perhaps more Neu! than Can.

So was Steve Garvey a Krautrock fan as well?

I don't know. Steve and I worked out the guitar parts anyway, so if there's any Krautrock influence it's come from us.

It's a song that's driven very much by the bass part...

That was Steve Garvey's style: very tuneful. There are no chords in it; it's just guitar lines and bass, no rhythm guitars on it. It's one of the few songs that we've done in that way and it's a radical departure from our usual style.

This was played in a Peel Session as well.

We used to use the Peel Sessions to try out new things. They used to be recorded at the BBC studios at Maida Vale. They had a big room where they'd record symphony orchestras but we were in a small studio that was especially for bands. The Musicians' Union had an agreement with the BBC that there would only be so much 'needle time' – Radio 1 only play so many hours of records a day, so they had to get musicians in to make up the rest and that's how they came up with the Peel Sessions. We'd get paid a fee and go and do a three-hour session. The people in the studio were very good at what they did but I think they were a bit under-utilized. They were just used to doing the same thing all the time, so when we came in and wanted to do something a bit different they seemed quite excited about it.

'Love is Lies'

Songwriter: Steve Diggle

This seemed like a bit of a diversion for Steve – very different from 'Autonomy'.

I suppose it's meant to be a pastiche of traditional, Sixties love songs. It's got a bit of a cod-Elvis thing going on, hasn't it? His voice, I mean. Elvis meets Bryan Ferry!

It was made before the vogue of doing acoustic – 'unplugged'. I'm not sure how well it suits Buzzcocks. But when we played it on the 'Another Bites' tour it showed a tender side of Steve that he often neglects.

'Nothing Left'

Songwriter: Pete Shelley

I've heard that this is another one for which you had music but no lyric.

I'd tried the lyric at around Christmas '77. It was about unmarried mothers and stuff and it just wasn't working out. Thankfully I left those lyrics at home!

Did you have to wait to be dumped before you could complete the lyric?

Not really – it's more a theoretical dumping. It's another transitional song, like 'Oh Shit' or 'You Say You Don't Love Me', where you go through those stages. In each verse it's like you've moved on that little bit further – from self-pity, to rationalization, to realization. It shows a progression – the healing of time.

When I saw you play this live recently I noticed that you made a musical reference in it to 'Strangers in the Night'.

We've always done this, even in the Seventies. Have you noticed it's not a very good version of 'Strangers in the Night'? It's a bit disjointed – like an homage to Les Dawson[10]. Remember when he used to play the piano in that god-awful tuneless way?! Even though I could learn to play it properly I never do. I've learned to play it improperly!

'ESP'

Songwriter: Pete Shelley

Where and when was this one written?

I had the tune from 1974 and I think I might have put the lyric to it at the Peel Session that we did at about this time.

It's always struck me as a very clever song, musically.

The riff goes round and the chords change underneath it, and this changes the nature of the riff. It's like a musical trick.
    The lyric's about ESP and trying to connect with people, about how we're all isolated from each other – the usual themes.

So do you believe in ESP?

Not really – otherwise I'd've got punched more! I mean, if people
could read your mind...

You had a badge that said 'Think...!' on it; that's in the lyric.

Yes, Malcolm Garrett designed it. It was another freebie
that we gave out at the end of gigs. It was realized that if
someone was walking round advertising us that was worth its
weight in gold. If you give something to somebody there's that
connection, isn't there? So it was quite cynical really, but in a
generous way. And if someone was wearing it someone might
come up and ask them what it was – or they might *know* what
it was – and it's like you're all members of a club, you've got
a secret connection.

'Late for the Train'

Songwriters: Steve Diggle, Steve Garvey, John Maher and Pete Shelley

This is another instrumental...

I had the idea for the chords and the starting and stopping,
although Steve might tell you different. It's got these great blocks
in it so it's very structural in its formulation. It's a bit Krautrock
and it's quite uncompromising. It was another that was recorded
for the Peel Sessions – you see they wanted us to play stuff that
hadn't already been heard, not the singles.

When we recorded 'Late for the Train' for John Peel we
were trying to figure out how we could do it. The staff at the BBC
suggested that we use tape loops, among other things – so this
is what we did when we were recording it for the album. We used
to use the BBC sessions to try out things that we hadn't done
before. They were very good technical boffins. Effectively they
gave us free consultancy!

**Instrumentals weren't common in punk at that time (with the
exception maybe of The Stranglers).**

It was the second instrumental on the album, which was a bit cutting edge for punk. But, you see, we were defining what the genre could be – there was no-one telling us what to do. And at that time we didn't really know what 'punk' was. Punk wasn't seen as being a straitjacket; no rules had been laid down as yet. It was more open; it wasn't as prescriptive as it was for the second-generation punk bands. In our day we could do what we wanted.

We did see ourselves as a punk band – after all, we'd played on the 'White Riot' tour – but at the same time we were kind of different, more what you'd call 'new wave'. There were other artists that were popular with people who were punks but at the same time you couldn't really pigeonhole them in that way. I mean, would you say Patti Smith was punk? Or Blondie? But they all came from the same melting pot. And not everyone was trying to be the Sex Pistols.

This is why journalists started writing about the 'new wave' – because there was a new wave of musicians coming up who weren't coming from the old Chapman and Chinn[11] route of readymade pop stars and the manipulation of the teen market. There were many diverse musical styles and the possibility of trying new things. Punk gave freedom to people. It made you listen to things and think, 'I could do that!'

I think of punk now as being more of an attitude, an attitudinal style than a form of music: it's a mindset.

Is this in an unusual time signature?

It's very distinctive – it's in 6/8, which is usually reserved for country dances! It wasn't always called 'Late for the Train'. While we were in the studio we went out to get something to eat and we had doner kebabs – so it was called 'Doner Kebab' for a while. But then it sounds like a train, so that's why we changed it.

I've turned up in my research that a 'synthed-up' version of 'Late for the Train' appeared on a LEGO advert in the Eighties.

Yes, that was me! It was for a battery-operated train that you could put together with LEGO. It was in 1984. It was at that time when people who'd been Buzzcocks fans when they were teenagers were being given jobs in the media and they could call the shots. So the guy who worked at the advertising agency was a fan. I did an electronic version – at that time I was doing my solo electronic stuff.

I'd done all the programming and I went down to London and recorded it. It took a while because the music has to be in sync with what's on the screen – it's not like nowadays when you can do all that kind of thing digitally. The visuals weren't cut to the music; the music had to be cut to the ad, and it all had to be done by ear. There was a lot of guesswork.

There was a part in the ad where someone was turning on a switch, so in the music I'd made a kind of fizzing noise, like static. But the compliance people said, 'No, you can't have that! Parents will be terrified of it, they'll think it's dangerous'. So I had to change it to a Flash Gordon-type noise.

It only lasted 23 and a half seconds but there was a lot of work in it.

I don't even have a copy of it – so if anyone from the advertising agency is reading this, get in touch!

Notes

1 This was only one of Pete's many generous charitable gestures over the years.

2 The reverse of the sleeve of *Singles Going Steady* has a photo of each member of the band each in their own pane, very similar to the sleeve of *Let It Be*. Some commentators have observed that *Singles Going Steady* was released at a point in Buzzcocks' career that had parallels with that of The Beatles in the *Let It Be* period – towards the end, when the edges were getting a bit frayed.

3 John Maher says of these sessions, which he also played on: 'The recording of The Invisible Girls' album at Strawberry Studios was another Martin Hannett "experience"! It was produced with a quite experimental approach – they'd record a basic backing track, then I'd add a drum track to that, not knowing what the vocal sounded like. It's quite tricky recording like that and as a consequence what you play live can be quite different from what's on the record.'

4 Steve Garvey says of 'Real World': 'The bassline on that was fantastic!'

5 Pete viewed computing as a leisure activity, something he did for fun. In a Radio 5 interview with Richard Skinner on 25 June 1983 he describes computing as being like 'a mental Meccano set' (alluding to the construction and engineering toy that had its heyday in the mid-20th century).

6 Penetration have also recorded a version of 'I Don't Mind', included on their 2015 album *Resolution*. John Maher played drums on this recording.

7 In the Sixties and Seventies, craft projects were a popular feature of the children's magazine show *Blue Peter* – and the much-parodied catchphrase 'Here's one I made earlier' was what the presenters would say as they set aside their own sad attempt at the intended project and reached beneath the worktop for another, better version that had patently taken a highly skilled art director hours to make. Steve Diggle used this expression as the title of a 1995 compilation album.

8 Steve Garvey says: 'Pete encouraged me to write songs. I'd bring music but it didn't work like Morrissey and Marr. And I was too shy to sing. Pete wanted us to be like The Beatles, with me like George Harrison!'

9 Steve Garvey: 'I just developed it during a jam. It was "out there" – but Pete and I used to listen to Can, to Krautrock – so there's nothing new under the universe. But it wasn't typical for punk.'

10 Mancunian comedian Les Dawson had his own BBC TV show in the Seventies and Eighties. One of his set pieces was to sit, immaculately dressed, at a grand piano and play a well-known classical piece or show tune but with many of the notes transposed, resulting in a hideously discordant – yet still recognizable – parody, all the while grinning smugly at his own 'prowess'. He was actually a very talented pianist.

11 The songwriting and production team of Mike Chapman and Nicky Chinn was responsible for some of the best-known hits of the earlier Seventies, including ones by Suzi Quatro, Mud, Racey, Smokie and Sweet (whose hits mysteriously dried up when they started releasing their own self-penned songs as singles). As a team they racked up over 50 Top 40 hits between them. They both still write songs and produce today, though separately now.

Promises

Stand-alone single
B-side: 'Lipstick'
Recorded: 1978, Olympic Studios, Barnes, London
Mixed: Advision Studios, Fitzrovia, London
Released: 17 November 1978
Songwriters: Pete Shelley and Steve Diggle
Producer: Martin Rushent
Sleeve designer: Malcolm Garrett

This was your second-biggest-selling single.

Yes – but that may have just been because it came on the
coattails of 'Ever Fallen in Love'!

**This is one of the only songs that you and Steve have
co-written. How did you come to write it?**

We'd been recording some demos for *Love Bites* in Arrow Studios
in Manchester in the summer of 1978. Steve had a tune but no
words – he said he'd 'left them at home'. He was improvising
them, as you can hear on *Chronology* (he's singing, 'All of the
children laying it down' and 'I'll make a cup of tea all on my
own'). He never did bring us the lyric for it so I wrote one for it.

STRAIGHT MUSIC PRESENTS

BUZZCOCKS

WITH GUESTS

SUBWAY SECT

CIVIC HALL
LONDON RD, GUILFORD
THURSDAY 9th NOVEMBER at 7.30 (BAR)

TICKETS £2.00 (INC. VAT) ADVANCE GUILDRAILS) BOX OFFICE: 9.00 a.m. - 5.00 p.m. MON-FRI (4.30 p.m. SAT)
TEL: GUILDFORD 67124 OR BONAPARTE RECORDS, TEL: GUILDFORD 33553, R & N TRAVEL, TEL: GUILDFORD 68171, OR
£2.00 (INC. VAT) ON NIGHT

I came up with the words in a flat that was being rented for us in Chiswick – at the time that we were recording *Love Bites*. We all stayed there instead of being put up in a hotel. It was quite a substantial house – I think the occupants had gone off somewhere exotic on holiday for a few weeks. Anyway, in the house was a copy of *The Art of Loving* by Erich Fromm. A lot of the themes of my subsequent songs may have come from ideas in this book. It's a philosophical treatise on the theory of love – it's not a marriage manual[1]!

The lyric seems quite bitter.

It's about how people make promises, then let you down – another 'before and after' scenario. The first bit is about the early days of a relationship: the smugness of thinking that everything is fantastic and that nothing can go wrong. Then as a middle eight it says, 'We had to change – but you stayed the same.' And the last verse is a mirror image – it's the words from the first verse slightly changed. It's lamenting the fact that the relationship is doomed and that the promises have been broken – and that people revert to type.

Now when we do the song live we only do three verses: two and a middle eight and then one at the end. This was partly to do with the nature of the way that you'd record in the days before digital recording. Unlike today, it used to be hard to put in an extra verse or chorus and it was also rare that you would edit down a song – the way it was laid down in the beginning is the way it would end up. Whereas nowadays you might write it with four verses but then take out a verse to make it snappier, in those days it was virtually impossible. I mean, you could do it but you were editing big reels of tape or the master – actually cutting and splicing it – so it was the angle of the cut that was the blend. Today you can edit it and blend the edge electronically. So if you made any changes on the master there'd be a danger you'd hear it – for example, if a cymbal was playing and it wasn't playing on the other bit then you'd notice it and so it wasn't something that was normally done. But since we've been playing it with only the three verses no-one's come up to me and said, 'You didn't play the last verse!' And so it must still work.

It's interesting to hear some of the songs in their nascent form as they appear on *Chronology* and also some songs that never made it on to record at the time. Whose idea was it?

Tim Chacksfield was responsible for *Chronology* – him and Tony [Barber]. He also helped us do the *Product* box set and the final versions of the albums that include the extra tracks. Even though he'd left EMI by that time he was brought in – he was good for that kind of thing because you knew you could trust him.

'Promises' had a very smart sleeve design.

Yes – but it's a bugger to autograph because it's predominantly black. Although nowadays people come armed with metallic pens, which makes it a lot easier.

Notes

1 Erich Fromm was a psychoanalyst who explored socio-philosophical topics, such as man's relationship with freedom, as well as human relationships. His *The Art of Loving* proposes the idea that love is a skill that we must learn or we will be prey to feelings of alienation and loneliness. He rejects the idea of sentimental or romantic love as a mere diversion. There *is* in fact a Polish 'marriage manual' titled *The Art of Loving*; it's subtitled *A Practical Guide to Married Bliss* and it's still in print today.

Lipstick

B-side to: 'Promises'
Songwriter: Pete Shelley
Producer: Martin Rushent

Where and when was it written?

Probably some time in 1977 – I wrote it on the way back from
the Ranch one night. I'd written a little ascending riff but I hadn't
written any words to it.

I was round at Howard's with my guitar one day and I started
playing it. He asked me if I was going to do anything with it and
when I said no, he brought out his book of song ideas and words.
He said, 'Is it OK if I use it for *my* band? I have some lyrics that'd fit.'
So that point was the parting of the evolutionary tree of 'Lipstick'
and Magazine's 'Shot by Both Sides', which I'm also credited on.

Then, while we were in rehearsals for *Love Bites*, I started
playing the riff and Steve Garvey asked what it was. We started
playing it initially as an instrumental and it seemed to work really
well, so I went off and wrote the lyric. To me it's a bit like a sung
instrumental.

The first part of it is quite frothy and lightweight. 'Does the
lipstick on your lip stick on my face?' – it's just a play on words
really. And then another play on words: 'It's the morning and
the mourning it is dawning on me too...' Although it starts quite
light-heartedly it does touch on quite a harrowing image. If you
were in a relationship with someone and then they die – and you
didn't hear about it until you got a condolence card from a friend
who thought you already knew...it'd be a bummer to say the

least. In those days – before mobile phones and the internet –
it could happen! But it didn't happen to me.

And that could be a good way to get back at someone who's
dumped you, couldn't it? To send them a condolence card saying
'You're dead to me', or 'The relationship is dead to me'.

What was the Ranch?

The Ranch Bar. It was next door to Foo Foo's Palace[1] on Dale
Street, in what's now the Northern Quarter. It was an underage

Still taken during recording at Arrow Studios, Manchester. The video for 'Lipstick'
was recorded that day.

drinking den. They used to play lots of Bowie and Roxy Music – it was quite alternative. It was only small but it became the hub of the punk scene in Manchester. The first gig we did on our own after the Sex Pistols gig was at the Ranch. Punk bands would be on at the Electric Circus and the Ranch was where everyone would go afterwards. It was one of the few places you could go and not have to worry about what you were wearing – unlike, say, Pips[2], which was more of a conventional kind of club. I went to Pips once after the Iggy Pop concert in '77 (it was the only place that was open at that time because it was a weekday) and they wouldn't let me in because I was wearing tennis shoes! The Ranch was the hangout of...well, if it had been a few years later it would have been the New Romantics. And it was where I first met Barry Adamson – it was just a fun place to hang out.

Notes

1   Foo Foo Lammar – Frank Pearson – was a famous drag artiste whose club was frequented by footballers and other Manchester celebrities as well as teenagers and punks. Frank was a tireless fundraiser for local charities and had a financial interest in many of Manchester's bars, clubs and restaurants, including ones in the city's Gay Village in later years. He was so notable that he received an obituary in the *Times* when he died in 2003.

2   Pips was in a nasty basement on Fennel Street, near Manchester Cathedral. It boasted four dance floors and, retrospectively, it's claimed to have been the northern equivalent of Covent Garden's Blitz club, home ground of the New Romantics. In 1989 it was rebranded as Konspiracy, purportedly the first club in Manchester to open specifically as an acid-house venue. The warren of tight corridors and dark corners in the Victorian undercroft made ideal spots for shady lizards to lurk in. The owner had managed to avoid paying the 'tax' that the thugs who thought they ran Manchester's night-time economy demanded of him by inviting them into his office and showing them the club's incomings and outgoings. When he could stall them no longer he cut his losses and closed the club down, without paying any of the 'back-tax'. Eventually the Hacienda, too, would close as a result of years of exploitation by Manchester's greedy gangsters, as detailed in Peter Hook's book, *The Hacienda: How Not to Run a Club.*

Everybody's Happy Nowadays

Stand-alone single
B-side: 'Why Can't I Touch It?'
Recorded: 1979, Strawberry Studios[1], Stockport
Mixed: Strawberry Studios, Stockport
Released: 2 March 1979
Songwriter: Pete Shelley
Producer: Martin Rushent
Sleeve designer: Malcolm Garrett
Run-out-groove message: 'Don't let the dark hair fool you'

Do you remember when you recorded this?

Martin Rushent came up to Manchester and we recorded it in
January 1979 in Strawberry Studios – where 10cc[2] used to record,
and later The Smiths. We had a couple of days of rehearsing the
tracks beforehand.

And where and when was it written?

Some time after us going on tour with *Love Bites*, which was the
previous September or October. It was an assembly piece.

It was the only song we appeared twice with on *Top of the
Pops*. (We were on more than once with 'Ever Fallen in Love' but
we only did the one recording and it was repeated.)

What's the lyric about?

'Everybody's happy nowadays' is a line from Aldous Huxley's
Brave New World. It's about a dystopian future where people
take a drug – a state-sanctioned drug called Soma – to be
happy, and that's the slogan for it. (Everyone now seems to be
on Citalopram and Prozac, so it was very prescient!)

It was quite a minimalist song, quite modular. There's very

little movement in the lyric, so it is a bit futuristic in that regard.

Basically it espouses the idea – which isn't in the book – that if you want things you can't have, that's going to make you unhappy. And once you realize that all life is an illusion and that love is a dream, then it frees you to be happy – a bit of a Buddhist philosophy. I was doing a lot of reading about fairly heavy stuff at the time.

It's quite instrumental – everything's played and then it cuts down to the drums and John actually used to play it without hi-hats. When we did a German music show called *Rock Pop*, to play it he set up his drums and they said, 'Haven't you got a proper kit?' And he said, 'No, this is all I play on it.' They were surprised. It was very stripped down and minimal and angular. So musically it was about as far away from 'Ever Fallen in Love' – with its layers of backing vocals – as you could get.

How was the sleeve design conceived?

For this one I went to see Malcolm at his studio on Tottenham Court Road. He showed me this idea for an image that he'd found of these two kids standing next to a giant carrot – which is somewhat reminiscent of some of the more psychedelic scenes in *Alice in Wonderland*[5].

There's more than one colourway available for this sleeve design?

The way that the sleeves are printed, they're printed three to a sheet – 'three-up', as it's called in the trade. So Malcolm had done a test sheet where there were three different colourways. They were all on a white background but the lettering was different colours – there was an orange one and a blue one and a green one, and he asked which one I'd like. He explained that they were printed three-up, so I said, 'Can't we have all three?'

Which was what we did – it didn't cost any more to print them that way. I thought, 'Throw that into the mix!' The differences were quite subtle and possibly not noticed by many people. We didn't advertise that there were three different colours but I suppose some people will have found out and bought the lot.

Actually a guy called Marshal Peters has an archive of all the band's sleeves – everything that we've ever released, including imports and acetates. It's a fantastic resource. Thank God for completists!

Were you drunk on one of the appearances on *Top of the Pops*?

We were drunk on all of them! It'd be recorded on the Wednesday, the day before it was aired. The charts would come out on the Tuesday morning and the BBC would decide then who they were going to have on the show. We'd get the call and head straight down to London.

We'd spend the whole day at the BBC. You'd get there in the morning and there'd be a couple of camera rehearsals. Between the last camera rehearsal and the actual recording of the show you'd decamp – decant! – to the BBC bar where you'd see all the pissed newspeople and weathermen, of which there were plenty.

On one of the recordings we'd all bought the leather bikers' jackets on Oxford Street (in London – not Oxford Road in Manchester!). So because I didn't know what to do with my hands I stuffed them in the pockets. And when we did the other recording my mum and dad had gone on holiday to the States to visit family – part of the great Scottish diaspora, in Connecticut or Long Island. They brought me back a jacket that was a bit like flock wallpaper – it was a cream-brown and had swirly raised bits in green. Normally when I went on stage I'd take out my wallet so no-one would be wondering what the bulge was when

I was performing. On this occasion – this was in the days before pound coins, remember – there was £8: a five-pound note and three one-pound notes. I took the money and fanned it out and made a kind of pocket-handkerchief arrangement that I stuck in the breast pocket of the jacket. It was like a red rag to a bull as far as certain members of the public were concerned – they saw it as me showing off with my 'Loadsamoney' – my eight quid – like a Harry Enfield character from the Eighties.

The vocal is impossibly high, isn't it?

It is now, yes! It was at the limit of my range. It wasn't something most people could sing along to.

It was used on an advert for the American Association of Retired Persons...

Yes – I think the slogan was: 'Old people love birthdays – that's why they have so many of them.' The AARP is a bit like Saga in the UK – they lobby on behalf of old people. But to them, 'old' starts at 50! And if you do the maths, that's what age Buzzcocks fans will be now.[4]

And it was used in the film *Shaun of the Dead*, with Ash playing it and Chris Martin of Coldplay singing it.

I would've settled for just Ash doing it.

It seemed like another of these pointless covers – they could have just got you to do it.

I think they got Chris Martin to do it because he's a 'name'. Those

things aren't necessarily to do with who can do the best version;

it's more determined by whose fans will buy the soundtrack album, and whose fans will go and watch the film just for the music on the end credits. It's all to do with that and very little to do with the music. There are people whose job it is to choose music for films and typically, when they're choosing the music for a film, they'll tend to get clearance for up to 200 songs – then, when the film's finished and they have to decide what music will go into where, they start the whole horse-trading thing.

The irony in the lyric was missed by some people, wasn't it? For example, Crass parodied it on one of their albums.

Well, it was meant to be pretty much ironic – like saying, 'OK, well here's the answer.' I thought it'd be a song that would be appreciated by the likes of Crass, with its reference to *Brave New World*! But that's the nature of their political comment.

Notes

1 Strawberry was owned by Eric Stewart and Graham Gouldman of 10cc with Peter Tattersall. It operated from a building in Waterloo Road, Stockport, from 1968 until the early Nineties. Paul McCartney and Neil Sedaka are among the 'names' that recorded there. The studio was so-called as a tribute to The Beatles' 'Strawberry Fields Forever'.

2 The etymology of the name 10cc has been variously confirmed and denied by the different founding members of the band but it's said that the name was chosen because 10cc (or 10ml) is the upper range of the volume of the average human ejaculate (imagine two teaspoons' worth).

3 Malcolm Garrett says: 'The image of the carrot was in this crazy kids' book of pictures of children with random large objects. But I didn't like it: I wanted to use a yellow smiley badge. Obviously this was before the second Summer of Love in 1988, when the smiley badge was associated with taking acid – in the late Seventies the smiley badge was just seen as a leftover from the post-hippy era. So Pete said no to my idea and I said no to his! In the end, because we couldn't decide which design to go with, we settled for just the title of the song, in that hand-lettering that gives it a DIY look.'

4 At the time that these interviews were conducted, in 2012 and 2013.

Why Can't I Touch It?[1]

B-side to: 'Everybody's Happy Nowadays'
Songwriters: Steve Diggle, Steve Garvey, John Maher and Pete Shelley
Run-out-groove message: 'Touch what?'

Where and when was it written?

A couple of days before we went into the studio we were
rehearsing – at TJ's, in the room that everyone thinks is Joy
Division's room. It was on Little Peter Street in Manchester – it's
been knocked down now. You know on the opening shot on the
video for 'Love Will Tear Us Apart', where there's the graffitied
door which opens up into the warehouse space? That's the studio
we used to rehearse in, and that's where 'Why Can't I Touch It?'
came about.

I had to get some money out of the bank and as I was
walking back to the studio I came up with the idea of 'Looks so
real, tastes so real and sounds so real'. When I got back to the
studio I mentioned this idea and then we were playing it, we
were jamming – and that's why it's attributed to everyone in the
band. And I just started singing, 'Seems so real, looks so real/
So why can't I touch it?' It's the quintessential question: 'Why?'
There were a lot of mind-altering substances being taken at that
time that also helped with the writing of 'Everybody's Happy
Nowadays'. 'Why Can't I Touch It?' was about grasping the...
you know, that hippy stuff.

What do you remember about recording it?

When we were recording it we had Saturday and Sunday in the studio.[2] We spent the Saturday morning setting up the equipment and sound checking. We recorded 'Everybody's Happy Nowadays' and then we decided to have something to eat. We went to a nice Greek restaurant in Stockport and had lots of wine and ouzo and retsina and went back to the studio in quite a mellow state and laid down the backing track for 'Why Can't I Touch It?' So that gave it...rather than the jerkiness of 'Everybody's Happy', which was spiky and had a bit of an amphetamine rush to it, we'd calmed down so it was a nice, laid-back groove. And we played it a couple of times and Martin took them and then we had it. We'd written it just the day before we recorded it. But by then, you see, we were quite good! We'd had lots of practice and lots of time in the studio as well as playing live, so we were all quite in tune with each other and how we played. The next day we recorded the vocals and a few overdubs and mixed it. That was the speed by then that we were working at.

I heard it has an alternative title.

What's that?

'Why *Won't* You Touch It?'

No, no, no! No. Honestly – where do you hear this stuff? [laughs]

You still play 'Why Can't I Touch It?' from time to time to this day.

I like to do 'Why Can't I Touch It?' at festivals instead of 'Moving Away from the Pulsebeat' because it's got more of a festival feel. 'Pulsebeat' needs to be in a small space because it's more oppressive. If you're on a field with the wind blowing, the drums never sound as meaty as when you're on a stage inside.

Notes

1   'Why Can't I Touch It?' is a favourite of many Buzzcocks fans, including
    many musicians. It speaks of the ineffable, the intangible and the
    unfathomable. Apparently, it's the second-most popular Buzzcocks
    song on Spotify after 'Ever Fallen in Love'. Steve Garvey says: 'It's very
    popular in the US. They say, "Man, what a great bassline: how did you
    come up with that?" It's a great groove song. They often play it on the
    University of Pennsylvania and Princeton University radio stations in its
    7-minute entirety.'

2   John Maher says: 'I know for sure we were present for the mixing
    process. I remember that because I was concerned about a small cock-
    up I made while recording 'Why Can't I Touch It?' (I blame the ouzo). It
    was an out-of-place hit on the snare, but Martin (Rushent) solved it by
    upping the volume. He said it'd make it sound deliberate. He was right!'

Harmony in My Head

Stand-alone single
B-side: 'Something's Gone Wrong Again'
Recorded: 1979, Eden Studios[1], Chiswick, London
Mixed: Marquee Studios[2], Soho, London
Released: 13 July 1979
Songwriter: Steve Diggle
Producer: Martin Rushent
Sleeve designer: Malcolm Garrett

It was the first A-side that Steve wrote and sang on.

Yes. Some people didn't realize at first that it wasn't me singing.
The single review in *Sounds* said, 'Pete Shelley's voice has gone
very gruff'!

I believe there's more than one version of the sleeve?

There ended up being two different sleeves: a red one and a
blue one. Steve had always said he wanted the sleeve to be
red – 'post-box red', I think were his words. So Malcolm Garrett
sent off the artwork to the printers for them to produce the proof
[sample] copy. When it came back it was in blue – the blue
and the red had been reversed. So Malcolm made a note on it
saying they'd got the two colours mixed up. It was sent back to
the printers and the printer changed everything round so it was
red with blue lines on it. They were just about to set the machine
running to print off the sleeves when the guy who'd made the
proof copy saw what they were doing and said, 'No, it's the other
way round – you've got the blue and the red mixed up' – so they
mistakenly changed it back again. So the first pressing of it was
in the blue sleeve, and the next batch came out in the red, as
Steve had wanted it. Consequently the intended colourway is
rarer than the one that was printed by mistake. It's ironic that

the entire debacle of printing the sleeve in the wrong colours is an illustration of 'something going wrong'.

It seems very redolent to me of Seventies Manchester: of shopping on Market Street on a Saturday afternoon – the UCP and Brentford Nylons and the old Piccadilly Records[3].

'Nothing ever happens to people like us/'Cept we miss the bus'. Taken in what is now Manchester's Northern Quarter, 1979.

That's what he was aiming at: that's what it's about. It's Steve's Joycean stream of consciousness.

Were you getting a bit fed up of the whole 'fame' thing by then?

Yes, a bit. I'd become very disillusioned. I mean, your impression is that when you're famous that'll be good because people will be listening to what you're doing, but really I found that the more famous you get certain sections of the audience become more negative. The audience expect to be entertained. By becoming famous, the paradox is that you actually lose the communication with the audience. You find people aren't listening to anything that you're doing or saying; they have their own agenda and they expect you to do what they want, to entertain them. But, as Tarantino said, 'I'm not your monkey – I refuse to dance for you.' And so I really wanted to hit Buzzcocks on the head – it had become too much of a burden. We'd only been big for about two years and we'd done quite a lot during that time, but the nature of fame itself is that it's a savage monster; it isn't your best friend. It isn't on your side and it feeds off you.

You think you're famous because people like what you're doing, so you think that what you do people will like, but it's not like that. It's OK when people are writing nice things about you, or if they're writing bad things when you're fighting against something, but then it becomes really petty and you think, 'What's the point? Why am I doing this?'

It was becoming a pain in the arse, in the same way as it did for The Beatles. They got sick of the touring but for me the touring wasn't the worst thing – it was people's expectations and 'the business', and people's belief that you were part of 'the business' and therefore you should 'play the game' – rather than be honest to yourself and to where you'd come from.

But you didn't get a lot of bad press.

No, but the bits that were there got through and I wasn't as thick-skinned as I thought I was. The bits that got through rankled.

Notes

1   The Sex Pistols also recorded at Eden Studios.

2   Marquee was a recording studio connected to the famous Marquee Club in London's Wardour Street. The Marquee was noted for launching the careers of many big-name bands of the Sixties; however, it also played host to punk and new-wave bands in the late Seventies and early Eighties. Buzzcocks themselves played there on 4 August 1977.

3   Piccadilly Records is now on Oldham Street, the main thoroughfare in Manchester's Northern Quarter. It still specializes in selling vinyl. In the 1970s it was located on Piccadilly Plaza, hence the name, on the same parade of shops as Brentford Nylons. Piccadilly Records moved premises after a management buyout in 1990. It has won many accolades over the years including *Music Week*'s 'Best Independent Record Store' and it is a mecca for the city's music tourists.

Something's Gone Wrong Again

B-side to: 'Harmony in My Head'
Songwriter: Pete Shelley

What's this about, then?

It's a bit of a jokey song. It's a catalogue of things that can go wrong in life – not being able to find socks, cutting yourself when you're having a shave (I'm sure women know about that as well!). 'Look at my watch to tell the time but the hand's come off mine' is a reference to Hylda Baker[1]. Her comedy routine used to go: 'What time is it?' 'It's ten past.' 'Ooh, I must get a little hand put on this watch.' It was one of her running gags. I had a digital watch at the time, though – they were all the rage. So it's not completely autobiographical.

It's all the minor, petty annoyances that are in everyone's daily life.

I once saw Howard completely lose his temper when a bus turned up really late. He was trying to get into town and he was there, screaming at the bus driver and taking his number and everything. So that was the inspiration for 'Nothing ever happens to people like us/'Cept we miss the bus'.

'I turned up early in time for our date/But then you turned up late...' Well, that's often happened to me.

And then the line, 'Need a drink, go to the pub/But the bugger's shut...' The pubs in those days used to open at 11am, close at 3pm and then open again at 5, then shut at half 10. So when we were on tour we couldn't sit in the pub in the afternoon before the gig – we'd hang out in the dressing room, where there was usually stuff to drink, or back at the hotel.

And the line 'Need a smoke, used my last 50p': cigarette machines in those days used to take 50p for 20 cigarettes – that's how long ago it was[2]! I think they're more like 50p each now.

So when did you give up smoking, and why?

Well, I gave up for health reasons really. I finally managed to kick the Nicorette gum in April 2001. I was on the Nicorette for nine and a half years, apart from when I went to the pub – it doesn't really go with lager. Everyone else was smoking so I used to say, 'Go on, give us one, then.' I'm completely clear of it now, though – I never want a cigarette even when I'm drinking.

What can you tell us about the music?

It's inspired by The Stooges – the repeated note on the piano is similar to 'I Wanna be Your Dog'. In fact I bought Iggy Pop a drink to thank him for the fact that I'd 'borrowed' from him. 'An immature artist "borrows"; the mature artist "steals"!' It was in a hotel in London. There was a French band called Téléphone[3] who were produced by Martin Rushent and I used to know the singer and guitarist. Martin and I went to see them when they were supporting Iggy Pop. They were a French rock 'n' roll band – a very rare thing, but quite huge in France. In fact one New Year's they played to a quarter of a million people at the Place de la Concorde, where they used to have the guillotine and where the sister to Cleopatra's Needle is. I was at the bar and there was hardly anybody there. Iggy Pop came up to the bar so I bought him a drink and I said, 'I'll get this, it's my payback for using the ding-ding-ding-ding'. He just took the drink; I don't think he even registered what I'd said.

It's a good, noisy, thrashy song with a bit of passion in it – yelling at all the things that have gone wrong. And there's the guitar solo. I wasn't actually listening to the track when I recorded the guitar solo so it is quite a...Stooges, Velvet Underground-type homage.

Something's Gone Wrong was a compilation of Buzzcocks covers.

Yes, all bands from Seattle. It was an homage.

Many of these seemed like quite pointless covers – they didn't augment anything you'd already done.

The best one is 'Why Can't I Touch It?'. It's got the riff going in the background and it's someone ringing up a radio phone-in and he's asking the presenter, 'Well, it feels so real, and it tastes so real...so why can't I touch it?' And the presenter's getting more and more exasperated and he's saying, 'I don't know what you mean; why *can't* you touch it?' Someone said the presenter was Larry King, but I'm not sure if it was.

'Something's Gone Wrong Again' seems like a quirky choice as the B-side to the US release of 'I Believe' – I mean, not the most obvious one.

It went down quite well in the States. In LA a radio station used to use it in a jingle that they played to introduce the traffic news – so it must've struck a chord. I was told they used it as the ident whenever there was a pile-up on the freeway or traffic jams or something, as they explained why people would be getting home late. Because, of course, in those days there were no mobile phones, so if you were stuck in traffic you couldn't just ring home and ask them to keep your tea warm for you.

Is it popular with people in the States? The things you list in the lyric seem very British and, more specifically, very northern.

It was on *Singles Going Steady*, which was released in America because everywhere in Britain and Europe people had heard the singles but it was 1979 before we went to the States. The first two albums hadn't been released there and none of the singles had, so it was thought that people in the States could be brought up to speed by releasing an album of the singles and B-sides so that they'd know who Buzzcocks were and then they'd go out and buy *A Different Kind of Tension*. More people will know it from *Singles Going Steady* than as the B-side to 'Harmony in My Head'.

Some of the themes are universal – like frying eggs and breaking the yolk. It's that punk idea of how it's not the big things, it's the little annoying things that you really want to yell about, and putting them in a funny, quaint way.

I've always found it quite dark – sinister, almost. Although there's an element of comedy to it, it seems to be about someone teetering on the edge, who could be tipped over by the next minor thing that goes wrong.

Yes – it has got something of the night about it! And it does get rather shouty at the end. But there's always the two sides – approaching even the worst things with a dark humour. We weren't doing comedy records but there was humour in some of what we did. And that makes the telling of some dark things even more real, more human. I mean, you've got to laugh, haven't you?! Or else you'd cry.

Notes

1   Boltonian comedy actress Hylda Baker made a handsome living by exploiting her northern-ness. In 1978 she made an album of tuneless parody covers of current pop songs, *Band on the Trot*, with professional comedy Cockney 'Arfur' Mullard. They appeared on *Top of the Pops* with their cover of 'You're the One That I Want', from the film *Grease*, which reached No. 22 in the UK Singles Chart.

2   It's been written elsewhere that Pete once needed help from John Maher to get cigarettes from a machine, as he wasn't tall enough to reach the coin slot.

3   Téléphone were the biggest-selling French rock band of all time and have sold around 10 million albums to date. Their earlier output was charmingly punky, although (like many other bands of the era) they lost some of their 'je ne sais quoi' when they started straying away from the 3-chord thrash towards the end of their 10-year tenure.

You Say You Don't Love Me

Single
B-side: 'Raison d'être'
Recorded: 1979, Eden Studios, Chiswick, London
Mixed: Genetic Sound, Streatley
Released: 28 September 1979
Songwriter: Pete Shelley
Producer: Martin Rushent
Sleeve designer: Malcolm Garrett

This didn't chart, rather surprisingly.

That's because we didn't go on *Top of the Pops* with it. *Top of the Pops* was everything in those days.

'You Say You Don't Love Me' and the B-side, 'Raison d'être', both appeared on *A Different Kind of Tension*. Had you given up on the idea of putting out non-album singles?

That was the record company's decision. It was released to coincide with the UK release of *A Different Kind of Tension* and also *Singles Going Steady* in the States.

Weren't there some changes at the record company at this time?

United Artists had got taken over by stealth. It became Liberty United. There was a gradual turnover of people and the people we'd known and were used to working with were no longer there.

The bassline is very prominent in this song.

Yes, Steve Garvey was very skilled as a bass player. He could
hear tunes in the basslines, rather than just being like the

Ramones or other punk bands. If you listen to Steve's bass playing and also Tony [Barber]'s it's full of little tunes and melodies – not just root and fifth[1]. He could always sense what a song needed. And, as with all Buzzcocks songs, it's the complete picture which gives the impression of complexity because the songs are a tapestry of all the sections of the orchestra.

It's another striking sleeve design – it seems to presage Eighties graphics.

Yes, it was the dawning of a new decade. This single was on *A Different Kind of Tension* so the design is in keeping with that. And we went for strongly contrasting colours again, as we had on the sleeve of 'Ever Fallen in Love'. *A Different Kind of Tension* was the first album where we printed the lyrics in the sleeve, so Malcolm was interested in the detail of the small type. He had the idea that printing the first proof of the lyrics on the back of the single sleeve, with all of the corrections for the typesetter clearly shown, was akin to showing that the single itself was a first proof for the album.

Had Malcolm heard these songs before he designed the sleeve?

Yes, he would have come to the studio and had a sneak preview.

It's a beautiful lyric that's helped many people over a heartbreak.

Well, it's a situation that everyone's been in, isn't it? First the realization that your feelings might not be reciprocated – but you still live in hope; then the acknowledgement of the other party's lack of interest and your reasoning with yourself that it might not be the idyll you imagined; then finally becoming reconciled with it. It's about the healing process. You think you'll never get over it – and then you do.

It's very clever how you change the meaning in each verse yet keep the structure of the verse the same.

Yes, it's a very economical way of writing songs! You don't have to think up a fresh idea for each verse – you just tweak some of the words and it totally changes the meaning. It's in 'Ever Fallen in Love' and 'Lipstick' as well.

How come 'You Say You Don't Love Me' didn't make it on to _Singles Going Steady_?

It was only released as a single in the UK the same week that _Singles Going Steady_ was released in the States. And I think the quality would've suffered with nine tracks per side on vinyl!

Notes

1 Steve Garvey says: 'I made an effort on that song. [That bassline is] hard – even I have a hard time playing it.'

Raison d'être

B-side to 'You Say You Don't Love Me'
Songwriter: Pete Shelley
Producer: Martin Rushent

Where and when was this written?

It was written in 1973 – it's another Jets of Air song. It was written about the drummer, I think – because he always turned up late. He didn't have blue eyes, though – they were brown. It's not necessarily literal.

Blue eyes are a theme that popped up in some of your solo work – they're mentioned in 'Never Again' and in the track 'Blue Eyes' on *Heaven and the Sea*.

Well, like 'Sixteen', it's just an artistic device. Elton John has used it [in 'Blue Eyes'] and also Bob Dylan in 'A Hard Rain's A Gonna Fall' – so I'm in good company there.

It's not about having a romance with a gentleman, then?

That's one interpretation!

So it's not really a love song at all?

No, not really. But if that's what you want to hear it as...!

I wouldn't've thought there'd be much scope for teenage same-sex shenanigans in 1973 Leigh.

Oh yes, there was – you'd be surprised! Don't forget, I went to an all-boys' grammar school.

Your sexuality is a moveable feast, isn't it? And so is gender. That's one of the peculiarities of writing songs in English – if you were writing in, say, French or Italian, it'd be clear from the endings of the words which gender of person you were addressing, and which gender of person was singing the song – but, as we don't have that in English, a love song in English could have been written by someone of any gender to someone of any gender. There's a layer of ambiguity to English-language love songs which songs in other languages don't have – which may explain the popularity of British pop music all over the world!

How did you envisage it would be played?

Well, like that. This is how Jets of Air would've played it.

Did you play gigs with Jets of Air?

Yes, I used to organize them – in church halls and that kind of thing. We used to charge 10p – in fact, at the last one we played we charged 20p. And that was a lot of money in those days! We used to give them a disco as well – the drummer with the blue-brown eyes supplied the records.

So did you learn French at school?

Yes, but I was always bottom of the class. I was trying to be sophisticated by using the French.

It says, 'Ne sais pas le raison d'être' in your solo song 'Telephone Operator' as well.

It sounded so good I used it twice! I don't actually know what it means. Sometimes when you're writing a lyric the feel that it *might* mean something is more important than what it actually does mean.

You were quite prolific even at this time. How did you start writing songs yourself?

When I was a kid I used to be interested in a lot of Thirties and Forties songs. I used to ask my mum for the lyrics from them and then I'd learn to play them – and from doing that I learned how to write a song. In those kinds of songs the solo isn't a classic rock solo; it's really just picking out something based on the melody, and this is how I write my solos. Generally you can sing my solos! I like to keep it simple – I don't believe in making a rod to beat my own back.

I got into Roxy Music around the summer of 1971, when I was taking my O levels, and that inspired me even further. Songwriting seemed like the natural progression from listening to music. Then later, when I was at Bolton Institute of Technology, there was a little secondhand shop near the college. I went in there one day and they had a wind-up gramophone. It was a 'picnic' model, with a wooden case with the horn enclosed inside it, so it wasn't like a His Master's Voice one, and I bought a lot of old 78s from the Twenties, Thirties and Forties. At the library there was the sheet music for *The Great Gatsby* – it was for piano but it also had the guitar chords. That was a lot of the old classic songs – 'Ain't She Sweet' and things like that. I found I could learn a lot by listening to songs from that era, about the theory of how songs are constructed.

One of the first songs that I wrote was 'Yesterday Night'. It hasn't been recorded; it wasn't that good. It was a bit derivative – of bad songs! But generally I wrote songs that were different from what I was listening to, unlike some other formative songwriters – to write a song that was like someone else's just didn't appeal.

What can you tell us about the guitar solo? It takes up the entire second half of the song.

Well, like my other guitar solos, it's 'crafted' rather than some kind of 'riffing' over a set of chords. This one has a Krautrock feel, as that's what I was listening to at the time.

It's a charming song that's a favourite of many fans.

We rehearsed it for the 'Back to Front' gigs that we did with Howard, John Maher and Steve Garvey in 2012 but we didn't end up putting it in the show. We didn't have a lot of time to prepare for those shows and time during the performance was limited (effectively it was three shows in one). We couldn't possibly have played all the songs we were requested to play! And although we have a hard core of diehard fans who want to hear the later stuff, most people who come to see us want to hear the punkier numbers, so we left it out.

A Different Kind of Tension[1]

Studio album
Recorded: 1979, Eden Studios, Chiswick, London
Mixed: Genetic Sound, Streatley
Released: September 1979
Producer: Martin Rushent
Sleeve designer: Malcolm Garrett
Run-out-groove message: 'The rose on the chocolate box' (Side 1)
and 'The thorn beneath the rose' (Side 2)

Can you explain how the recording was done?

It was in the summer of '79. It was recorded over a couple of weeks. It was mixed at Martin Rushent's place. He had a mixing desk in a cottage in the grounds of his house. At that time he hadn't built the studio that became Genetic. In one of the rooms he had the equipment for the studio and a little room next door was used for doing the overdubs – bits of guitar and vocals and things. But we'd done most of the stuff at Eden.

The way that we decided to record this album was quite different from the way we'd done the others – quite radical. We'd get into the studio sometime in the afternoon and we'd start to play through the tracks that we wanted to do that day. We'd play until we got what we thought was a decent take with the right feel and then Martin would edit the multi-track tape into the bits that we wanted and he'd send those off to a place where they had two 24-track machines and have copies made. It might be a process where we'd get a good verse that we thought was right and that'd be sent off and we'd have 4 or 5 of those made. So the next day we'd get a tape back with the 4 or 5 verses that we'd made along with however many choruses we'd ordered; then piece by piece, section by section, Martin would splice them all together – almost in the same way that now, if you were doing it with computers, you'd copy and paste.

But this was physically copying and pasting, almost like making a collage. Then Steve and I would put on guitars, extra bits and vocals until we got the track as we wanted it. So there was never really a time when all the band were in the studio at the same time without us recording.

It wasn't like the old-fashioned way; it was a bit of a hybrid method, so there'd be a bit more consistency. I mean, no matter how well people play there are parts that work really well and parts that are just passable and Martin wanted to capture the optimal bits so he could make it the best it could be. So the multi-track tape was put together from a lot of edits. You couldn't see them, there were lots of fine ones – there wasn't loads of splicing tape all over the place. But as the tape was going through the machine, at regular intervals, say when it got to the second verse, you'd see the splice go by – so you could see the actual edit[2]. So it was done differently from the other two albums. This led on to the way that Martin worked with Human League and on my solo album *XL1*.

Nowadays a record producer has a load of tricks at his disposal. I mean, if you record a drum track and you aren't satisfied with it you could run a program that moves the drum beats around to where they should be, so they're not just that little bit out. It's only very tiny amounts but it is noticeable. One part might have lots of power and impact and another might... it might sound good, but there are minute flaws. So music isn't made now just by setting up microphones and pressing 'record'; it's processed. It's less organic and more homogenized than it used to be – but that's what people are used to hearing.

How did the album get its name?

A Different Kind of Tension was taken from a review of *Love Bites* by Jon Savage. The sides were named as well – Side 1 was called 'The Rose on the Chocolate Box' and Side 2 was 'The Thorn Beneath the Rose'. That was dreamed up by Jon Savage – or was it Paul Morley? One or the other.

Where were you staying when you were recording this?

Near Baker Street, in a service apartment.

What gigs were you playing at this time?

This is when we had Joy Division supporting us. They had an album coming out so we said, 'Come and tour with us' – because we always preferred to take people we knew on tour.

It must have been a shock when Ian Curtis died.

We'd nurtured them and we'd seen them develop and grow so it was a blow, yes.

Where were you living at that time?

I think I was still living in the house in Gorton with Francis, Carol and Fran.

What guitars did you play on the album?

I was probably back on a Gordon Smith – not the one I played on *Another Music in a Different Kitchen* because that was stolen at Liverpool University. The first one I had was No. 58 but then I got No. 53. I bought it secondhand in A1 in Manchester. I've still got it somewhere.

I had a custom-made one as well that I was using at about this time.

How many guitars do you own?

I don't know. It doesn't interest me at all. Rich [Henry], our guitar technician, stores my guitars for me. When we're going to do a gig he asks me which one I want to use and I'll say, 'A black one' – like women with cars.

For quite a few years now I've been using an Epiphone – it's made by Gibson but it's the cheapest one they do. I think it was £100, new. But it doesn't go out of tune, which is what you need when you're playing fast. I have the tuning checked before we do the encore and it's usually still bang-on. Steve, though, has got guitars that are too expensive to play. He's got that daft Rickenbacker that looks good but won't stay in tune – that's why he only plays it for a couple of songs, and then he has to change over.

I'm not really a guitarist's guitarist. But you use what you feel comfortable using. I'm just looking for a good, solid, working guitar – something you can just put on and then go. 'It's the message, not the medium!'

Where did the idea for the sleeve come from?

I think the design might have been based on some Russian art, some Constructivist thing – they were famed for their geometric poster designs. Malcolm was great at adopting and adapting famous artistic styles. There's many a time when I'm going round a gallery and I'll think, 'Oh, that's where *that* comes from then!' It was different from the idea that the sleeve is just an advert for the band.

Who took the photos?

The one on the front of the sleeve was taken by Jill Furmanovsky on – was it Waterloo Bridge? And we each chose our own photos

Orphans (according to Joe Strummer's assessment of Buzzcocks' sartorial style) left on a doorstep, in what is now Manchester's Northern Quarter, 1979.

Live at Scotfest, 'the family friendly music festival', 1979.

A worried-looking Pete is mobbed by female fans at Scotfest, 1979.

EVERYBODY'S
HAPPY
NOWADAYS

BUZZCOCKS

Sleeve design by Malcolm Garrett, available in
different colourways. Note the hand lettering.

Sleeve design by Malcolm Garrett – a taster
for the graphical style of the ensuing decade.

Buzzcocks live onstage at Club 57, Irving Plaza, New York, 1 September 1979.

Snaps taken by Buzzcocks drummer John Maher give a glimpse of life behind the scenes during the 1979 tour of the States.

The reality of touring – playing for an hour and a half a day and, apart from that, a lot of travelling and waiting around.

Pete caught in a pensive moment at the airport on tour in the States.

The band enjoy a day off at Walt Disney World, Orlando, Florida.

John Maher, self-portrait on a tour bus.

TICKETRON

1201	MATEOS AT THE PALLADIUM	14 ST/3RD AVE
	NEW YORK NEW YORK	DATE/EVENT CODE 1201 11ORCH
CENTER	BUZZCOCKS	8:00P CENTER
$8.50		11ORCH K 113
K	NO CANS/BOTTLES	$8.50 K
11/19	06725461BX0833 4204/4	NO REF/EXCH.
113	8:00P SAT DEC 01 1979	$8.50 113

Yet more waiting around on tour. Some cool dude in the entourage is wearing a 'What Do I Get?' green shirt.

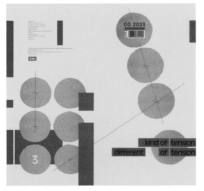

The back was always as important as the front, as on this sleeve design by Malcolm Garrett.

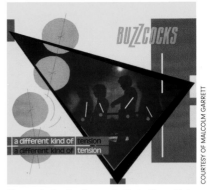

Sleeve design for Buzzcocks' last album. Note the 'triangular cover', mentioned in 'I Believe'.

A collage by Linder, 'Untitled', which portrays woman as an eager-to-please household appliance and man as little more than a libidinous consumer of gadgets.

Copies of the *Secret Public* newsletter along with a membership card and official club badges. There didn't seem to be an issue no. 1. Is this a gap in this fan's collection, an oversight by the Secret Public team or a Situationist prank?

Pete onstage at Manchester's Ritz in 2017. This event was part of the Design Manchester: DM17 festival, 41 years after Buzzcocks began. Poignantly, this was the last gig Pete played in his home city.

Pete Shelley Official Starway replica guitar, no. 80 of 88, produced by Eastwood Guitars in 2007, made to commemorate the legendary, long-serving instrument.

that were to be used on the inner sleeve – Steve's was one that was taken by his partner, Judith.

The sleeve art with its bright colours and jolly geometric shapes is a bit in contrast to what's actually on the record.

We always liked that juxtaposition – the joyous and the 'What the hell is going on?' I like that thing with the music as well, where you have a happy tune and the most depressing, wrist-slitting thoughts behind it.

Were you really going to call it *Don't Worry, It's Only the Third Album*?

We weren't going to call it that; that's just a message that's printed along the spine. The whole thing is full of clues and red herrings and references. Of course you'd only see it if you had it stored vertically with the spine outwards.

On the sleeve notes it even tells you which channel I'm playing through and which one's Steve. I can't remember whose idea that was or what good it was, but you can tell who's playing what. I come out of one speaker and Steve comes out of the other.

Were you not going to tour with *A Different Kind of Tension* at the album's 30-year anniversary, like you did with *Another Music in a Different Kitchen* and *Love Bites*?

Another Music in a Different Kitchen and *Love Bites* took longer to tour the world than expected, and the albums were re-released. But with *A Different Kind of Tension* there wasn't going to be a physical release, so there couldn't really be a tour – it was only available online to download.

Side 1

'Paradise'

Songwriter: Pete Shelley

Do you remember much about writing this?

It was an early song. I wrote 'Paradise' in September 1973, one Saturday morning. I wrote two songs that day – the other one was 'Maxine', which was on one of my solo albums. I had the house to myself as my mum and dad had gone shopping. When they came back at midday I'd already written two songs.

It's simple to play but there are strange chords in it – you have to keep your eye on the ball while you're playing it. The solo is just the E chord being slid up the neck – so it's just a normal, open, three-finger E chord. You keep your hand in the same place and go up a fret, then up another fret, then down...If you were to write down what's going on, it's using simple methods to make something that sounds more intricate than it is.

There was something of The Velvet Underground and Roxy Music in it – they were two of my influences at the time I wrote it. I don't see Bryan Ferry so much as a lounge crooner – I like it when he writes *songs* with an interesting sense of melody. Like 'Editions of You' on Roxy Music's second album, *For Your Pleasure*.

I don't know how it came about but it just works as a really good song; it's a great opener.

What I thought you could use it for – and I'm surprised no-one's approached you – is as a benefit single for a knife-crime charity.

I think the line about the 'knife-fight on Saturday night' was probably inspired by Elton John's 'Saturday night's alright for fighting', because when I heard that it reminded me of Velvet Underground.

So what was it like playing with Steve Garvey and John Maher at the 'Back to Front' shows in 2012?

It was great. I enjoyed it because we were playing with people who wanted to play the music. I mean, the reason they stopped playing with us was only because they had things in their lives that were more important to them than being in a band – not that they'd stopped enjoying the music. John's just as good as he was, and Steve Garvey I've played with a few times over the years[3]. He played on the 'Man and Machines' tour I did for my solo album, *Homosapien*[4] – that was about three months after Buzzcocks split up. He went to live in America but then he was back in the band from when we re-formed in 1989 until Tony Barber joined in 1992. John Maher was with us on the original tour after we re-formed and then he re-joined us after Mike Joyce left and he toured with us in Australia and Japan.

'Sitting Round at Home'

Songwriter: Steve Diggle

What did you think of Steve's songs on this album?

Well, I enjoyed playing them and my contribution to them. I'd always said I wanted Side 2 for this idea I had, this 5-act drama, and Steve had half of Side 1. It seemed fair.

Is this what life's like when you're not on tour, eating your breakfast while you watch the lunchtime news in your pants?

That's what it was like for Steve. You notice that he had on the ITV *News at One*, not the BBC[5]!

'You Say You Don't Love Me'

See page 190.

'You Know You Can't Help It'

Songwriter: Steve Diggle

As a teenager I loved this. It was open and honest and direct and it spoke about love in a way that was humorous and down to earth.

Well, that's Steve: open and honest and direct. His songs are largely autobiographical. You could get to know him well by just listening to his songs on here.

If you look up this lyric online, instead of 'You can't help thinking what she's got', it says, 'You can't help *eating* what she's got'.

That shows that people who post lyrics on the internet need to wash their ears out. It's like that Jimi Hendrix song, isn't it – ''Scuse me while I kiss this guy'. The misheard lyrics are almost better than the originals.

'Mad Mad Judy'

Songwriter: Steve Diggle

Do you know what this is about?

I thought, like everyone else, that it was because his girlfriend was called Judith. I know that *Jude the Obscure* is one of his favourite books, though. You notice it says in the lyric, 'Ain't nothing left in all/The world, 'cept obscurity'?

'Mad Judy' is also a poem by Thomas Hardy. It's possible Steve studied *Jude the Obscure* or the poems of Thomas Hardy when he did his O level in English.

What's that spoken-word bit at the end about?

As a consequence of the way we recorded it we didn't know how many end bits we needed, so Steve just carried on singing at the end of the song so that bit at the end is ad-libbed, just to fill the tape.

He's lost his northern accent a bit since then, hasn't he?

Oh yes, definitely. There's an interview on YouTube with us in Boston in 1979 and he's all northern and 'Ee bah gum'. He's got this transatlantic, rock 'n' roll accent now – like that kind of Keith Richards thing.

We've played 'Mad Mad Judy' in recent years but it was difficult to get the rest of the band to want to play it. Steve would rather play 'the set' as we've been playing it for years than revisit even his own songs.

'Raison d'être'

See page 193.

Side 2

Side 2 is very different from Side 1 – much darker, almost dour. It seemed like a new direction for Buzzcocks.

Side 2 was explaining the journey from the poppy Buzzcocks of 'Promises' into the more angular and trippy phase of

'Everybody's Happy Nowadays'. The first side of the album is poppy and it's only when you get to Side 2 that it gets a bit strange.

It was a semi-concept album – Side 2 was what you could call conceptual anyway. It was a journey – to the point where everything is split apart and competing, contradictory. It's very driving and, I think, Wagnerian. It's quite heavy – stern. I like that challenging aspect of it.

I found Side 2 very difficult to listen to when I was a young teenager – it was painful to me, almost traumatic.

I think it might have been one of those that would have been better with a 'Parental Guidance' sticker on it! It is a bit of a Pandora's box. But that's where my headspace was at the time.

Some reviews at the time commented that *A Different Kind of Tension* was more consistent than the first two albums[6].

But is that more consistent in the playing or in the way the tracks are put together? It's true, Side 2 was put together as one piece. Steve Garvey said we should put Side 2 as Side 1 as it's more consistent, it's an entity. I'd imagined for Side 2 something like what The Beatles did with their album *Abbey Road*. Paul McCartney envisaged the whole last section of Side 2 as being one song – the songs segue into each other, they're a continuum – and that's what I envisaged for *A Different Kind of Tension*.

'I Don't Know What to Do with My Life'

Songwriter: Pete Shelley

When and where was this written?

I seem to remember I wrote it when I was coming home from seeing *Superman* at the cinema, so it would have been 1978 – it was a matinee.

You seem to have written a few of your songs when you've got in from a night out or the cinema.

I don't know if I was particularly inspired by what I'd seen – it may have been that I was living in Gorton and after I got off the bus to go home there was a walk, and I tend to write a lot when I'm walking. You've got a steady rhythm and a tempo, so it's a bit like working to a click. And it lets your mind drift off. When I'm walking I often play little tunes in my head – especially in those days, when there were no iPods or Walkmans.

I can hear the music really vividly in my head, so writing the tunes is no problem. The hard part is working out how to play them!

I did get a Walkman soon after that – I think it was in 1980. The model I had was a Stowaway – they hadn't even come up with the name Walkman at that time. It was about as big as a brick – and it was £100! That was a lot of money in those days. But it was revolutionary as the only alternative for music on the move was to have a ghetto blaster strapped to your shoulder.

It sounds like you were quite confused at the time, quite conflicted.

It was as the song says – 'I Don't Know What to Do with My Life' – but it wasn't necessarily autobiographical. It's about being unrequited, yes – but I'm not suicidal, I'm resigned to it. As it says in the line, 'I think I'm getting more than enough – of love.'

But you *were* loved – you got a lot of love off your fans.

Being adulated isn't quite the same as having someone in your life – and I've never been all that comfortable about it. You worry that the 'you' that fans adore isn't the real you: it's a public projection, 'the face that you keep in a jar by the door'[7]. It can be quite lonely.

'Money'

Songwriter: Pete Shelley

Can you explain what this is about?

As the keen-eared ones will be able to tell, there's no mention of money in the song. I thought, there are loads of songs called 'Money' or about money – like that Beatles' song and Abba's 'Money, Money, Money' – so I thought I'd do a song called 'Money' that isn't about money. Surprisingly no-one's ever asked me why. I like the idea of having a song with a title that doesn't make reference to something in the lyric. In *Alice's Adventures Through the Looking Glass* the White Knight sings her a song called 'Ways and Means' but it doesn't say anything about ways or means in the lyric and the alternative title, the one that you'd expect it to be called, is 'A-Sitting on a Gate'. So I liked this contrariness. Another example is The Monkees' 'Alternate Title', which would otherwise have been called 'Randy Scouse Git' – but the words don't appear in the song.

Is it about having money, about the way that suddenly becoming better off makes you feel?

No, it's not about that at all. It could've been called 'Life is a Zoo', but that'd be too easy. I called it 'Money' just to perplex people.

It seems to be about feeling trapped.

It's about alienation, about the distance between people – about being compartmentalized. That's why it says 'life is a zoo' – we're put in our separate cages and kept apart.

Was this in part inspired by you living in Gorton and being handy for Belle Vue Zoo?

No, I never went to it, believe it or not. I was never tempted. I believe it was grim.

You don't seem to be very motivated by money or the material.

That's not why I wanted to be in a band, no. It's never been the prime directive. And then when you get it, it comes with its own set of problems. I suppose I'm naturally frugal, being brought up in the Fifties and Sixties. You couldn't just borrow money in those days. Most things we had when I was a kid were on hire purchase – and we 'made do and mended'.

I was encouraged to open a bank account as a youngster – I had one with the Trustee Savings Bank. I also had a Post Office account that you bought the savings stamps for. And I was always looking for things to do that didn't cost money – libraries, galleries, museums – or standing in bookshops and reading the books without buying them.

I had a paper round when I was a teenager and so I was earning a little bit of money, and I got my mum and dad to take out a stereo record player on hire purchase. It had a record deck and a built-in cassette recorder. It wasn't a stereogram – that used to be like a piece of furniture – it was on a plinth with a smoked Plexiglas cover. When anyone that I knew had a record that I liked I'd borrow it for the night and tape it – and I ended up with a large collection of music. And there was the secondhand record shop in Leigh that I had an arrangement with, where they'd let me choose an album, take it home and record it and bring it back the same day to get back the price I'd paid for it, minus 50p (an album was probably 3 quid at the time). It meant I could listen to lots of stuff without being incredibly rich – but if it hadn't been for that I probably wouldn't have got as much into music.

I used to buy sheet music as well but after a while I just started making up my own songs.

You read music, then?

Not really. I can work it out as if it were hieroglyphs – but I'm not ready to build a pyramid yet! I can read chord symbols and I can work out what the sheet music means but I'm not a sight-reader. I don't actually write the music – all the songs that we do, we learn the songs, so it's never actually written down. Occasionally when we're learning the songs we write the chord symbols down but sometimes if someone asks me what a particular chord was, I don't know off the top of my head – I'd have to get a guitar and work it out.

I've got a good ear, though. The BBC website had an online music section where you can test your musical ability. It was testing your ability to recognize pitch, sense of rhythm, etc. I got top marks on those, far more than what most people would be expected to get. But then it had questions about how much you enjoy music and I scored less than 50 per cent on that.

Sometimes I feel that I don't really like music! You can become quite critical when you're a musician. I mean, things that you like are usually things no-one else likes. For example, I was the only kid in the village who listened to Velvet Underground and there was only me and Howard I knew of that listened to the Ramones – but nowadays that stuff is so popular that it's become almost tragically unhip to really like them. Punk was something which was universally hated – until everyone thought, 'Wow, this is a good idea' – and it became universally loved! Everyone's on the bandwagon then. And when you're making music, all the music that you do is because of the things that you *don't* like rather than those you do. That's why I don't make music that sounds like Phil Collins or Coldplay! And I mean, the songs I like are already in existence so I don't try to replicate those either.

I suppose I've developed a good ear because I do a lot of music in my head. I remember I was on the bus once when I was first learning to play guitar. I'd been listening to 'Heart of Gold' by Neil Young and I realized I could tell what the chords were just by listening to it (listening to it in my head, I mean – even Walkmans hadn't been invented then). It's not necessarily perfect pitch but it's to do with recognizing the relationships of the notes to each other and the 'feel' of the chord. Each chord has what's almost like a fingerprint. So if you played me a single note I couldn't necessarily identify the note but if you play me a chord I can recognize it. This is good for when I'm playing guitar because I know what chord I'm aiming for, what chord will come next.

Have you kept all that sheet music that you used to buy?

The only sheet music I've still got is the one of The Beatles' *White Album*.

'Hollow Inside'

Songwriter: Pete Shelley

This too is a little disheartening...

The songs were all written at different times but I have this idea that the songs in the order they're in on the album tell a story. It starts off with 'I Don't Know What to Do with My Life', goes into the feelings of alienation with 'Money' and then 'Hollow Inside', with almost a sense of the void – then it's resolved with 'I Believe'.

'Hollow Inside' is about the dissolution of the ego – so it's quite trippy. It was a groovy track and the lyric is quite simple, just with the change of the pronoun altering the sense of the words. Yes, it is bleak – I'm a lot happier now.

I was suffering some existential angst at the time. We'd thought that punk was the most non-commercial form of music – then, after the success of 'Ever Fallen in Love', it put us out of my comfort zone. We'd appear in the gossip columns of newspapers – it wasn't what I'd signed up for.

Then there was a disconnect. Once you become popular, the people who come to see you cease to be special; they're just the ordinary people swept along on the wave of your success and they expect that you're supposed to be entertaining them, rather than just doing what you're doing. There was a similar thing with Beethoven where he broke away and said, 'I am the artist, not your servant.' You can see it in the film *Amadeus* as well, where the nobility treat the musician [Mozart] as though he were a performing chimp or something.

I subscribe more to the romantic notion of the artist, rather than the artist as entertainer. I consider what I do is entertaining, but I don't try and modify what I do to gain adulation.

Between the time we recorded *Love Bites* and *A Different Kind of Tension* I had to be persuaded to stay in the band – I wasn't really enjoying it any more. It was like the fun had gone out of it. It's like in Pink Floyd's *The Wall* where the pop star flips out, or even in that David Essex film *Stardust*, about the pop star who burns out. The whole thing had become unreal – and when the songs become about you and your relation with the industry, that's always a danger sign.

When you're in a band, you can get your hands on a
lot of drugs and you have a lot of time to fill. It's like in that

documentary with Allen Ginsberg and William Burroughs in it[8]. Burroughs comes out with this great line: 'When we were young we used to think that staying up all night and taking drugs was really good. Little did we know.'

You've never found being in a band as tough since then, though, have you? Even though you've toured extensively since you re-formed.

No, no. When you're in your twenties it's a time when you're growing up and you've got all the insecurities and existential dilemmas inherent in that; and so all the problems get compounded. And people keep telling you that you're God, which can be a strain.

Were you suicidal at that time?

Oh, yes. But in my teenage years it was like 'suicidal chic'. You have to remember, for a long time mental illness was considered quite cool – it was considered to be a sign of creativity. Was it Aristotle who said, 'I'd rather be a miserable human being than a happy pig'?

Did you start to feel better as soon as you left the band, or did it take you some time to recover?

When I left it was like a weight off my shoulders. I felt I'd painted myself into a corner. It was good doing my solo work. A lot of the songs I played then I'd written before Buzzcocks, so it wasn't as though I had to carry on being 'Pete Shelley of Buzzcocks' – I could be myself. It was good not to have to do *A Different Kind of Tension II*, or that kind of thing.

'A Different Kind of Tension'

Songwriter: Pete Shelley

This is a song with a lot of complex ideas in it.

I have William Burroughs to thank for this. He did some interviews in *Job*, a literary magazine in the States, in the late Sixties. There's a series of interviews on different subjects such as Scientology[9] and his own drug addiction. But there's one point where he's talking about the reactive mind[10] – basically it's one of these Scientology things. If you want to become involved in Scientology they 'audit' you by rigging you up to what they call an E-meter[11]. It's a lie-detector kind of thing and you're attached to it by holding a tin can in each hand. They're just empty tin cans that have been washed and the labels taken off them. Precision instrumentation, you see! You wear headphones and you get one word or command in one ear and a contradictory word or command in the other ear. The idea is to clear your mind of any memories of stuff which might have happened to us in the past – bearing in mind that we're all immortal Thetans who so many million years ago were thrown into volcanoes and we've all had many lives. It's supposed to drive you loopy, basically – so I wasn't doing the audience much of a favour by subjecting them to it. I used some of the examples Burroughs had mentioned and made up some of my own. If you're listening to it through headphones you get one word in each ear, like L Ron Hubbard, the inventor of Scientology, intended.

So did you play this song live when you were touring with the album? It'd be tricky to replicate on stage.

Oh yes, we did! In order for me and Steve to be able to synchronize reading out the commands we had huge pieces of cardboard that would be flipped over the monitors by one of the road crew – we had no teleprompters or anything – and we'd both read out a word or command. It sounded fairly much as it does on the record.

'I Believe'

Songwriter: Pete Shelley

This is a song that covers a lot of themes.

Some of it is about having conflicting ideas or things that you can believe – but, just because you believe something, doesn't make it so. It's about how we live in a world that we make, that's constructed by our own minds.

Like in 'What Do You Know?' it says, 'You need only believe and you'll believe' – it's about the strange things that humanity has believed in and how, when people believe something, it imbues it with more of a certainty than it perhaps warrants. Like when it says, 'I believe in the workers' revolution/And I believe in the final solution' – it's not that *I* believe in them, but millions of people did.

And the lyric says, 'I believe in the immaculate conception/And I believe in the resurrection' – although I tried to emphasize the 'erection' in 'resurrection'!

A lot of people have read a lot of things into it. Like a woman who brought her daughter along to a gig; I was chatting with her afterwards and then she wrote me a letter saying that where it says, 'I believe in the things I've never had/And I believe in my mum and my dad' had made her think about the fact that her own parents were no longer with her.

And then it says, 'I believe in the web of fate/And I believe I'm going to be late/So I'll be leaving/What I believe in.' You're looking for those plays on words when you're a songwriter, and trying to develop layers of meaning.

Then it says, 'There is no love in this world any more' – now, that means lots of things to different people. It's great to be able to yell it out. I rationalize it. It's about how love's something that's generated in your mind; it doesn't exist. There is no external love – it only exists in people's heads. It's completely a construct.

When I was a teenager I used to think that love was something made up by marketing people to sell women's magazines.

Well, in a way this is in support of that.

But now I know it's not because I know how oxytocin works.

Yes, but that's just another drug, isn't it? Your body producing its own drugs that then work on your mind.

You don't think love exists as a force, then – a power that joins us all together?

I don't think particle physicists have discovered 'the love particle' yet, no! And the observable universe is affected by you observing it – you can't have one without the other. The universe doesn't exist if you don't exist. There is no absolute – everything's relative.

You've read quite a bit about quantum physics...

Well, I'm an avid watcher of *Horizon*[12]! And I loved *Tomorrow's World*[13].

Were you brought up in a faith? In the BBC's *Brass Tacks* debate show about punk that was aired in 1977 you said that you were a Christian.

Not particularly. I did go to a Church of England primary school and so went to church as part of that. And I used to go to the youth club and argue with the vicar about...the same kind of thing you'd argue about with the Jehovah's Witnesses – the philosophical stuff. But then because I went to a Church of England school I know a lot of things that happened in the Bible, which a lot of people who didn't go to a church school wouldn't know (Lot's wife turning to a pillar of salt, or that bit where they're in Sodom and they say, 'Bring the men out here so we may have intercourse with them!'). I see it as a philosophical system – no better and no worse than any other.

You were taking a lot of acid at the time you made this album. Is this what made you start exploring these religious ideas?

Not religious ideas so much – I was interested in the process of how you construct reality. There may be a bit of Buddhism in there.

It's quite a melancholy song.

It's amazing how something that's so bleak and without hope is loved by the people who sing along with it at gigs. It's almost like a defiance – *The Scream*.

What's 'the book with the triangular cover' that's mentioned in the lyric?

The triangle is the cover, in the sleeve design.

So had Malcolm heard the songs before he designed the sleeve for this album?

I don't think so. But I think we knew it was going to incorporate a triangle – it's one of the three 'primitive' shapes designed by the Bauhaus school of modernism and we'd already used the square on *Another Music* and the circle on *Love Bites*. So that's why I sing it in the song – it's referring to the sleeve. Later the sleeves for *Singles Going Steady* and *Many Parts* [a compilation that included all the songs from *Parts 1–3*] follow on with firstly a rectangle and then an oval, as the next primitive shapes in the series.

There's also an echo of a line from 'Mother of Pearl' by Roxy Music. The lyric in that says, 'Career girl cover/Exposed and another/Steps right into view' – it's a similar rhythm to 'Triangular cover concealing another aspect from view'.

So when you play it live and you leave the stage one by one, whose idea was that?

Well, after I'd finished singing there didn't seem to be much point in staying on the stage. And Steve started doing a guitar piece, doing a Jimi Hendrix on the floor, and it just grew from there really.

It's a bit like Haydn's 'Farewell' Symphony[14], isn't it? Is that where you got the idea from, or is it just coincidental?

It's that kind of idea, really. I mean, it's hard to do a fade live! And it gives the audience a chance to sing along.

It was recorded for *Live Legends*, made by Central TV in 1989?

Yes, that was on our reunion tour.

And it was released as a single in the States[15]?

A Different Kind of Tension was the first album to be released in the States, apart from *Singles Going Steady*, so it was to coincide with that.

Was that the only single to be released in the States?

Yes, apart from *Parts 1–3*, which was released as a 12-inch.

It seems like a curious choice for a single, for a market that isn't already familiar with your output – it's not as instantly accessible as some of your other singles.

Well, it was a song that went down really well live, so people obviously liked it. And the idea when you're entering a new market is to get people to hear what you do, not necessarily to sell the most records.

'Radio Nine'

Songwriter: Pete Shelley

Is 'Radio Nine' like that stuff that you and Steve used to record when you got your first tape recorders, kind of experimental stuff?

In 'Radio Nine' you hear 'Everybody's Happy Nowadays' as it would have sounded on transistor radios when everyone listened to Radio Luxembourg at night – the static and the fading in and fading out.

There was a perception at the time of this album that 'Everybody's Happy Nowadays' and 'Why Can't I Touch It?' were a departure from 'Promises' and 'Lipstick', and it was meant to highlight the difference between the poppy Buzzcocks and the more weirded-out Buzzcocks – so the idea was that you were tuning between radio stations. It's analogous to taking a drug trip, so quite psychedelic in that way.

How did you get that effect – the sound like you're tuning in a radio?

We put it through a phaser and we got a radio and switched through the channels. And we called it 'Radio Nine' after The Beatles' 'Revolution Nine' that's on the *White Album*.

Notes

1   Steve Garvey says: '*A Different Kind of Tension* is the most popular album over here – people love that album in the US.'

2   Apparently Martin Rushent had devised a custom-made 'ruler' for measuring the minute sections of tape when he had to make these kinds of edits.

3   Steve Garvey says: '"Back to Front" was a lot of fun, although it was a little nerve-wracking – but then when I got on stage all the nerves went. I wish I could still make a living doing that because compared to what I do now [carpentry, working for a major developer] it's a piece of cake!'

4   Steve Garvey: 'I had to learn all those songs and we had to play along to a tape. It's acceptable now but to me, at the time, it was shocking.'

5   There used to be, and maybe still is, some snobbery about the perceived superiority of BBC to ITV. It's felt in some quarters that BBC programmes are more edifying as they place the emphasis on education and improvement, rather than entertainment, which those who disapprove claim is the focus of ITV's output.

6 Steve Garvey says: '*Tension* wasn't as spontaneous – we took a little more time over the arrangements. I took a bit more time writing interesting basslines. The punk-rock thing was over then, so we had to develop.'

7 Quoting The Beatles' 'Eleanor Rigby'.

8 This is likely to be *Burroughs: The Movie*, made by Howard Brookner in 1983. It is the only documentary to be made with Burroughs' approval and participation.

9 Scientology – a belief system that has been variously described as a 'cult', a 'business' and a 'new religious movement' and may, in fact, be all three.

10 The 'reactive mind' is a concept fundamental to L Ron Hubbard's system of Dianetics, initially intended as a branch of psychiatry and psychological treatment but rejected by orthodox practitioners of those disciplines.

11 This is so-called because it measures electro-dermal activity, variations in skin conductance caused by sweating, which itself can be caused by physiological or psychological stress. The reliability of lie detectors is heavily disputed and the Church of Scientology protects itself with a disclaimer that says that the E-meter is used solely for 'spiritual purposes'.

12 *Horizon* is a documentary programme made by the BBC, the subject of which is generally science or, occasionally, philosophical matters. It was first broadcast in February 1964 and the format has changed little, if at all, since then.

13 The BBC's *Tomorrow's World* ran from 1965 until 2003 and presented the latest developments in science and technology.

14 The symphony was written to be performed by Austrian musicians who were reluctant guests of Haydn's patron, the Hungarian Prince Nikolaus I. In the final *adagio* movement, each musician snuffs out the candle on his music stand and creeps silently away, leaving only the two lead violinists. Apparently, the message was received and the entire retinue returned home the next day. The symphony is still played in this way today.

15 Steve Garvey says: 'We were offered to sign a good deal with Columbia in 1978–9 "over here" – they turned The Clash into superstars and they could've turned us into superstars – but we went with a start-up label, Miles Copeland's IRS. They'd had a lot of success with bands like the Go-Go's but they didn't know what to do with us – they hadn't had the experience.'

Part 1: Are Everything

Stand-alone single
B/w: 'Why She's a Girl from the Chainstore'
Recorded: 1980, Advision Studios, Fitzrovia, London
Mixed: Townhouse Studios[1], Shepherd's Bush, London
Released: August 1980
Songwriter: Pete Shelley
Producer: Martin Hannett
Sleeve designer: Malcolm Garrett

What was the idea behind *Parts 1–3*?

We released *Parts 1–3* after the release of *A Different Kind of Tension*, after we toured America. I thought [detective series] *Kojak* was make-believe until I got to New York, and there's all steam rising up from the manholes and yellow taxi-cabs beeping at each other. The TV programme depicts it quite accurately. I hated it. And I just wasn't enjoying being where I was with the band at the time.

So instead of doing a whole album we thought we'd do a run of singles and then release them as an album. The idea was to release six singles and then put them on an album at the end of it. But unfortunately, Martin Rushent, who produced everything that we did for United Artists, was in the States working on a project, so we ended up going in the studio with Martin Hannett, who'd produced *Spiral Scratch* and also at about this time was producing Joy Division. Any stories you hear about Martin Hannett's escapades in the studio are true! The whole recording was chaotic, to say the least.

So *Parts 1–6* then would have formed the fourth album you were contractually obliged to come up with?

No, we'd hoped that *Singles Going Steady* that had been
released in the States would count as the fourth album.

People bought it and the label made money from it so it was, it was an album.

So you hadn't signed a contract saying that you'd come up with four albums' worth of original material?

The contract didn't say that, no, but they were of the *opinion*... The person at the label who took that opinion later apologized.

Were the sleeve designs for *Parts 1–3* also designed as a set?

They were intended to be released as a set so the designs are linked: 'Part 1' has got one stripe, 'Part 2' has got two and 'Part 3' has got three. And as there's no A-side or B-side either side of the sleeve can be seen as the front or back.

How did you first meet Martin Hannett?

He was our agent in the early days, trading under the name Music Force and operating out of a ramshackle Georgian slum on Oxford Road. It was just a couple of doors down from the *New Manchester Review* [a forerunner of Manchester's culture and listings magazine, *City Life*]. We used to pop down and sit in the office and chat and he'd say he was a record producer and we'd laugh and we hatched the scheme to make our own record.

Had Martin Hannett changed since you recorded *Spiral Scratch*?

Well, he'd had success! *Spiral Scratch* was one of the first production jobs he did – but by the time we were recording *Parts 1–3* he had Joy Division and John Cooper Clarke under his belt, as well as a whole host of other artists on Factory.

When we recorded *Spiral Scratch* my dad had noticed when he visited the studio that, as fast as Martin was moving the sliders and twiddling the knobs, the engineer[2] was changing everything back as soon as he'd turned his back. But by the time we were recording *Parts 1–3* he was used to everything being done his way.

Where and when was it written?

It was written when I was on holiday in Sorrento – I had the idea when I was in the bar of the hotel one day. It's almost like an M C Escher print – there are bits intertwining into other bits, and other bits that remain constant. It's all about how we construct the world; the world is made up of our hopes and fears and dreams. They are limitations on how we perceive the world. It's a continuation of some of the themes on *A Different Kind of Tension*, which you could say is a Buddhist way of looking at things. At the time there were lots of little sheets of blotting paper doing the rounds – including in the studio. So I dropped

PHOTO BY KEVIN CUMMINS

Taskmaster-producer Martin Hannett, taking a cigarette break in the studio, 1980, when such things were allowed.

a tab of acid every day that I worked on 'Are Everything'.
I was 'in the zone', so to speak, on every part of that song –
the recording, the mixing...

Did you find acid helped you to work?

I don't know whether it helped! I remember it being quite chaotic.
We'd go into the studio and we'd be either waiting for the drugs
to arrive, or waiting for them to kick in. Martin Hannett used to
put the tape machine on so it just cycled – it's a wonder the tape
didn't wear out. I used to be off my head, crouched under the
mixing desk. Martin used to monitor very loud and when I got
to the point where I knew where I was I used to go out into the
studio and do it. There's an instrumental bit in the middle. We
had an LA box, which is a box of percussion instruments in it –
maracas and things to bang and shake.

We recorded the basic tracks in Advision in the big room there
and then we did the mixing at Townhouse, which was Ladbroke
Grove-way. We'd start in the afternoon and work all through the
night. In fact one night I got back so late to the hotel that they
thought I'd checked out without telling them and they'd chucked
out all my stuff from my room (I was travelling light and didn't
have much with me). In the Townhouse it was a huge long room
so Martin would set up a microphone at each end of the room
and we did this kind of procession down the room, each of us
playing a different instrument from the LA box. Steve Garvey
wasn't there at that time – he'd gone to the races[3]. I think he
thought, 'This is a bit too weird for me.' We didn't see him until
we got back to Manchester. And at one time John got a fire
extinguisher and gave it a blast. It can be heard on the record
among all these little chimes and rattles and things – it's in the
bit where it breaks down and it's just the bass.

Did the recording take ages, then?

Oh, yes.

It wasn't a very efficient way of working; when you recorded *Spiral Scratch* with Martin Hannett you did it in very little time...

Martin hadn't become more time-efficient as a producer, he'd just got more 'out there'. It was on a par with what would happen on a Frank Zappa or Captain Beefheart recording. Of course it was costing the record company but we weren't on a meter – they were happy to pay for it, however long it took.

He was always fun to work with, though. If you listen to *Parts 1–3* now you might think, 'What the hell's that?' But you thought that about a lot of his stuff – that was part of his genius.

You appeared on a kids' Saturday-morning show, *Fun Factory*, with 'Are Everything'. It seemed like a curious choice of song, not particularly teeny-bop.

Well, we'd never defined ourselves as being teeny-bop. The programme was made by Granada and we were based in Manchester, so that's probably the reason why they asked us. We did a rehearsal on the Friday and then Steve and I went to...the Grapes, was it? A pub near the Opera House. There was a youth theatre that was doing *Oh! What a Lovely War* at Wythenshawe Civic Centre; there were a few guys from that and we got talking to them in the pub all afternoon. When it shut they invited us to go along to the Civic Centre with them. Steve went off somewhere else but I went along to Wythenshawe and ended up partying all night with the members of this youth theatre. We had a strange experience when we were trying to get back from Wythenshawe –

the hotel they were staying in was at Southern Cemetery in Chorlton, about three and a half miles from Wythenshawe. There must have been 30-odd people and we were all walking down the road, trying to get a lift. A bus came and stopped to let people off but then when we tried to get on it the bus driver said, 'Sorry, mate, I've finished for the night.' So they begged and pleaded and in the end he let us on and took us all the way to where we wanted to go, even though it was the end of his shift and it wasn't part of the route. As a thankyou to him, the theatre group ended up singing songs from *Oh! What a Lovely War*. It was surreal – it was a bit like a scene from Cliff's *Summer Holiday*.

Then the next morning we had to go to Granada Studios bright and early for the recording of this kids' programme. I felt a bit the worse for wear – I mean, I'd been drinking since the previous afternoon! And appearing on Saturday-morning kids' TV is not the best cure for a hangover.

Notes

1 Townhouse Studios was built in Shepherd's Bush, West London, in 1978 as part of the Virgin Studios Group. It closed down in 2008. Other acts that recorded there were The Jam, Duran Duran, Bryan Ferry and Oasis.

2 This was Phil Hampson, who had started his professional career playing guitar and writing songs. He says he learned his engineering skills 'on the job' recording demos in a small studio.

3 Steve Garvey says: 'Recording the last few things with Martin Hannett was like a drugfest. I was disgusted; I walked out. I think Steve Diggle played bass on some of those songs.'

4 A satirical musical developed in 1963 by Joan Littlewood, the 'Mother of Modern Theatre', with the help of her company, Theatre Workshop.

Part 1: Why She's a Girl from the Chainstore

B/w: 'Are Everything'
Songwriter: Steve Diggle
Producer: Martin Hannett

There was no A-side and B-side as such to *Parts 1–3*.

Because Steve and I both were writing by that time we thought we'd have a side each, instead of an A-side and a B-side. So I came up with the idea of using symbols to denote the sides, like on the Psi cards that they use to conduct mind-reading tests – the idea is that someone chooses a card and then tries to transmit the symbol to a subject who is sitting in a separate room. There are five Psi symbols but we needed six symbols because there were six songs so we had to make up a sixth one. But I think the record company printed the labels as sides P and Q or R and S or something, which is tantamount to calling the sides A and B, so it defeated the object.

Which symbol was the one you invented?

Oh, I can't remember now. Maybe the triangle?

Where was the accompanying video shot?

There was this bloke who Richard Boon knew in a musicians' collective in Manchester who was making videos – it was cutting edge at the time and so they got roped into making a video of 'Why She's a Girl from the Chainstore'. Linder was playing the part of the Girl from the Chainstore and Steve was ranting through a megaphone – it was filmed at Lewis's[1], the department store. The band had walk-on bits where we'd be browsing round the china department – it was when the store was open. It wasn't guerrilla. Lewis's had agreed to it but I don't think they'd realized what would actually transpire! Although I did hear that because it was an amateur thing it wouldn't get played on TV – something to do with being in a union (not the shop workers, the film people). My mum and dad appear in it in the scene where it says, 'She loved her mother and her father, they never missed her birthday', and my niece played the young Linder. So it wasn't a professional video as such – it was the early days of doing promo videos – but it still looked good.

Is it true that your record company didn't see much commercial appeal in *Parts 1–3*?

After Andrew Lauder left United Artists he introduced us to the new guy, Tim Chacksfield, who's gone on to do great things with the back catalogue. At the time he was another great A&R guy – he'd facilitate our vision and would make it happen within the company. But he left and after that it was downhill all the way, because we didn't have anyone who was championing us.

There was a guy who took over and who was running the United Artists side. I had a meeting with him and he'd heard the demos for *Parts 1–3* and he said he 'didn't hear any hits'. For me at that time that was the last thing I was worried about! And, as I say, it's the record company who sell records and get them into the charts – it's nothing to do with the merit of the record. So it was all falling apart. And because of a technicality in the publishing deal with Virgin, we were supposed to get another advance after we'd done four albums, and we were working on the understanding that we could include *Singles Going Steady* as one of the albums – but they decided they'd be hard-nosed about it and wouldn't give us the advance.

What's this 'Bernstein's barrier'[2] that's mentioned in the lyric?

Ooh, you'll have to ask Steve all about that! I mean, I know, but...

Do you like playing this live? You always look like you're enjoying it.

'Chainstore' is one of Steve's best songs – I always enjoy doing it live. I do incredibly high backing vocals on it, so it's a bit of a challenge these days.

Notes

1   Lewis's was a mostly northern chain of department stores, established in Liverpool in 1856. Manchester Lewis's was housed in a neo-baroque edifice that was purpose built in 1915 and so grand it contained a full-size ballroom that also doubled as an exhibition space. The store never fully recovered after the 1996 IRA bombing of the city but the building remains.

2   Sociologist Basil Bernstein was most active in the Sixties and Seventies, and particularly known for his study of class distinction in language use. He noticed that working-class pupils achieved similar results in maths and arithmetic to their middle-class counterparts but were disadvantaged when it came to language-based subjects. This 'barrier', which first becomes apparent in school, is only one of many that speakers with regional accents can be confronted by throughout their lives.

Part 2: Strange Thing

Stand-alone single
B/w: 'Airwaves Dream'
Recorded: 1980, Advision Studios, Fitzrovia, London
Mixed: Strawberry Studios, Stockport
Released: 13 October 1980
Songwriter: Pete Shelley
Producer: Martin Hannett
Sleeve designer: Malcolm Garrett

Where and when was this one written?

I have no recollection of it. It must have been all that acid I was taking! At the time when you're writing something you don't necessarily go, 'Ooh, I'll remember this forever.' I do with some of the earlier ones but I think it's just chance.

The lyric says, 'Got to control this depression'. So were you quite badly depressed at this time?

Well, I have had bouts of depression, yes – not particularly at that time. But it's about *controlling* the depression – how you can be depressed because of the disconnect between the way the world is and the way you want it to be. Going back to that *A Different Kind of Tension*/Buddhist theme, it's saying that an acceptance of the way things are is better than holding on to your hopes and fears of what you *wish* might be. Perhaps the answer is to change the way you are so you can get through it. So it's very defiant – it's not like a Leonard Cohen depression.

What can you tell us about the music?

Musically it sounds like four guitar chords – I can't remember

whether we recorded four different ones or whether we

alternated it. When we played it live we used to alternate them – I'd play one, Steve would play the other, I'd play the third and he'd play the fourth. It's so each chord will 'hang on' and have its natural decay, rather than being followed immediately by another chord. It was meant to be very oppressive.

And this song is another where the lyrics shift by changing certain words, just changing the pronouns.

Who played the cello on it?

An avant-garde cellist called Georgie Born. She was classically trained; she'd studied at the Royal College of Music. She came to the studio and set up her cello and she asked what we wanted. We said, 'Just make it weird.' I think she may have played with Henry Cow[1] and she'd played with the Penguin Café Orchestra[2] and The Flying Lizards[3]. She's also an academic and anthropologist.

Your solo work _Sky Yen_ came out at about this time too.

Yes. It sold quite a few. I started Groovy Records with Francis Cookson – it was sort of an extension of The Tiller Boys. _Sky Yen_ was recorded in 1974 when I was a student at Bolton Institute of Technology. I'd built a little oscillator – you know, with a soldering iron and that. I had a reel-to-reel tape recorder, one that did stereo, so you could 'bounce' tracks: if you recorded on the left-hand channel you could then play back and record on the right-hand channel and mix the thing you were doing now and what was on the left-hand channel and bounce that back.

So one Saturday I was at home and I'd found out with this little oscillator – don't try this at home, folks! – that if I touched the various components I would become part of the circuit and it'd make even weirder noises than it was intended to do. It was like it was playing *through* me, like cyborg music (it wasn't rigged up to the mains; it was powered by a 9-volt battery). There was a rotary control to do the pitch and you'd get this really weird stuff, like echo, that you get because there's a gap between the record head and the playback head; so when you do the second track, when you play them back both together there's a gap which it jumps across. It was only on a small reel of tape that lasted 20-odd minutes.

At that time in 1974 I had my band Jets of Air but I had ideas for two other bands. An electronic one, which I was going to call Sky – but then the guitarist John Williams pinched that name so I couldn't use it. I had one of those little labelling machines, a Dymo, where you turn the wheel and it prints on the adhesive plastic tape – so I labelled it 'Sky ¥'. I didn't know what the '¥' symbol was but then I later found out that it was the sign for yen – so that's how *Sky Yen* got its name.

Then, at college, I started this electronic-music society. We'd play Walter Carlos (now Wendy Carlos) and any other music that

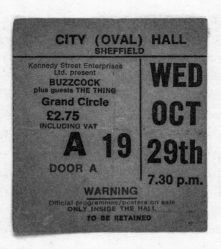

CITY (OVAL) HALL
SHEFFIELD

Kennedy Street Enterprises
Ltd. present
BUZZCOCK
plus guests THE THING
Grand Circle
£2.75
INCLUDING VAT

WED

OCT

A 19

29th

DOOR A

7.30 p.m.

WARNING
Official programmes/posters on sale
ONLY INSIDE THE HALL
TO BE RETAINED

was vaguely electronic, at lunchtimes in the music room. I used to play *Sky Yen* there – to mixed reactions! I used to use it to clear people out at parties. It's like Marmite – you either love it or you hate it. Some people don't even think of it as music but I love it – I can sing along to it! And Groovy also released an album of Francis's called *£3.33*[4], because that's the price we were selling it at. Some of it's played on guitars and it's got drum machines in it. It's experimental, a bit Throbbing Gristle-ish. It isn't easy listening. There are no hit songs on there!

Then there was one we recorded at home on a Portastudio, called *Strange Men in Sheds with Spanners*, but we never got round to releasing it. I thought it'd been lost because Francis lent it to Martin Hannett to listen to and he didn't get it back; and then Martin died, so we could imagine it being thrown into a skip with all his other tapes. I had a cassette recording of it but part of it had been overwritten when someone had accidentally pressed 'play' and 'record' rather than just 'play' so there was a big section of it missing. We managed to find a good copy of it, though, which, when tarted up, as they can do nowadays, sounds great – just as I remember it.

All Groovy Records' output has recently been re-released by Dreg City Records in Chicago – Sally Timms, who I made *Hangahar* with, lives in Chicago and she knew the people who run Dreg.

Notes

1 Henry Cow was an 'experimental' rock group, founded at Cambridge University in 1968. Their music has been described as 'challenging and uncompromising'.

2 Penguin Café Orchestra was an avant-pop band, operating between 1972 and 1997. The idea for the band's ethos came to founder Simon Jeffes as he lay in bed, semi-delirious with food poisoning, after eating 'some bad fish' in the South of France.

3 The Flying Lizards were another 'experimental' band who cashed in on the new-wave phenomenon of the late Seventies. They are best known for their eccentric cover versions of R&B standard 'Money' and Eddie Cochran's 'Summertime Blues', spoken/sung by a bored debutante as the band accompanies her on what sounds like a selection of enamel plates, ancient typewriters and Pete's 'rubber band over a biscuit tin'.

4 £3.33 may seem like a rather eccentric price point but it most likely alludes to the playing speed of a 12-inch vinyl album, which was 33⅓ rpm.

Part 2: Airwaves Dream

Stand-alone single
B/w: 'Are Everything'
Songwriter: Steve Diggle
Producer: Martin Hannett
Run-out-groove message: 'Doris, message in the post'

What's this about, then?

We'd been over to America the year before and there was a big craze at the time for CB radio – '10-4, Big Buddy', or whatever it was. John and Steve both had CB radios. In the song it says, 'Stay off Channel 14', because that was the emergency channel. So it's got all these references to CB. I suppose CB was the radio equivalent of internet chat. Everyone at that time had CB radios – they formed the storylines in soaps and I'm sure people even got married who'd met through CB. It seems to have completely died out now.

When I was at school I had some friends who were radio hams. Do you know that Tony Hancock sketch 'The Radio Ham'? It was like that. They'd have these call signs – some would do it in Morse code – and they'd try and contact people as far away as possible. So part of it was like trainspotting, trying to see how many of these call signs you could get, and how far away. It was on shortwave. They were just chatting really but in order to be an operator you had to take exams because the government didn't want just anybody to start broadcasting. It was a bit of a geeky hobby. In the playground at dinner time you'd have people talking to each other in Morse code to get more proficient at it. There wasn't very much else to do at that time. So for anyone who was technically minded that's what they might do – then a few years later the same guys would have got into early computing and learned programming. I'm sure Steve Jobs would've had a spell of doing shortwave radio!

You were expanding musically at this time – there's brass on this.

Yes, Steve got Henry Lowther, a jazz trumpeter, to play on it. I saw him on TV recently. He'd worked with Bryan Ferry and Van Morrison, among others.

You did the 'Tour by Instalments' to promote *Parts 1–3*.

That's when things started going off the rails a bit for the band. The shows were successful but Steve had this idea that the more successful you are, the less work you do. I think the more successful you are, the *more* work you should do! We had ideological differences. So it ended up with the 'Part 3' tour not happening at all, being cancelled. The rest of the band decided not to do it at a meeting I wasn't invited to. Which led to more disillusion on my part about why I was actually bothering doing it. So the tour was pulled and Alan Wise, the tour promoter, wasn't best pleased, because he was out of pocket.

Part 3: Running Free

B/w: 'What Do You Know?'
Songwriter: Steve Diggle
Producer: Martin Rushent

This one too was recorded by Martin Hannett and produced by Martin Rushent.

He did the same thing that he'd done with 'What Do You Know?' – he took Martin Hannett's tape and finished it off. Essentially it was recorded by Martin Hannett and mixed by Martin Rushent.

It says, 'I've had enough of the day job' – what day jobs had you done before being in the band?

After I finished at college I got a job as a trainee computer operator working for the National Coal Board's computer base near me at Anderton House in Lowton, Leigh (it's no longer there, after the closure of most of the pits in the Eighties). It was one of those big computers like on *Thunderbirds* with the spinning tapes and huge printers and what have you. It used to do all the redundancy cheques and things like that. I used to do a bit of programming but it was mostly setting up jobs for the computer to do. There was me and another guy who started doing the job at the same time – he got put in the computer room, so he was running round changing the big tapes and that, and I was in the back office. The big computer printouts – the company reports and cheques and payslips – would come out

interleaved with carbon paper so you had to put it through a de-collating machine. You had to put all the printouts through the machine so that it would separate off the carbon paper, and we had to operate a guillotine. You had to watch it like a hawk because they wouldn't stop the machine: as one piece was ending they'd just splice on a new stack of paper and if that got stuck in the machine while it was de-collating it'd be ripping everything to shreds and chopping up people's payslips – so it was quite a fraught job. You had to keep your wits about you. There was lots of making cups of tea and that as well but still, it wasn't the best of jobs.

It was continental shifts: five twelve-hour days, followed by a week of four nights. That really didn't suit me all that well. On Tuesday nights they expected you to do overtime because they had to get the payslips to the factories for Thursday, so a few times I annoyed them by saying I couldn't do overtime because I had a rehearsal. (We did rehearse occasionally.) So I went to the doctor and told him I was really depressed. He gave me some tablets that I don't think I ever took because they made my head feel fuzzy. They kept paying me, even though I wasn't going in to work, but I remember getting the letter telling me that they were going to let me go – and coincidentally that was the day before the first Buzzcocks gig.

I had summer jobs – I once worked as the equivalent of a Kwik Fit fitter, doing tyres and exhausts. I got the job from a friend of my dad's. It was OK – whenever it rained we'd have the afternoon off. They'd tell the customers we were booked up then, otherwise you'd be under the car and it'd be dripping on you. I was only there for two weeks but they had me ringing up the suppliers and ordering the parts. And I've always made a good cup of tea, so that helped.

And I had another job where I was a return-to-manufacturer despatch clerk. It was in Bolton at Great Universal Stores, the mail-order catalogue. It was in the department where people send things back when things are either faulty or not the right size and they have to be sent back to the manufacturer. The items that were faulty were sent down to our department. There was one bloke who'd pack the item into a box and seal it up then he'd pass it on to me and I'd label it and take it down to the mail room. I was very keen and eager at first and the two old blokes that worked there told me to slow down, otherwise the foreman would notice we didn't have anything to do and he'd get us unloading fridges. So I learned to write out the labels *v-e-r-y s-l-o-w-l-y*.

I was quite relieved when I was able to give up the job at the National Coal Board. It would have hardly been a job for life anyway, the way things went with coal. Margaret Thatcher put an end to all that!

Part 3: What Do You Know?

Stand-alone single
B/w: 'Running Free'
Recorded: 1980, Advision Studios, Fitzrovia, London, and Pluto
Studios[1], Stockport
Mixed: Genetic Sounds, Streatley
Released: December 1980
Songwriter: Pete Shelley
Producer: Martin Rushent
Sleeve designer: Malcolm Garrett

I notice in your discography that it says 'Part 3' was recorded by Martin Hannett but produced by Martin Rushent.

They were all recorded at the same time but 'Part 3' hadn't been finished and Martin Hannett was unavailable to produce it. I was in the New Hormones office one day and the phone rang and it was Martin Rushent. He said he was building this new studio where he lived in Streatley in Berkshire – he had quite a nice house with a swimming pool and loads of land, and he'd always had a dream of building his own studio. I told him that we'd recorded 'Part 3' with Martin Hannett but he was unavailable to finish it; he was doing something in the States (if you remember when we'd recorded 'Part 1' Martin Hannett had been available and it was Martin Rushent who'd been working in the States). So Martin Rushent said, 'If you can bring the tapes we can have a go at finishing it and getting the single out.'

When he listened to the tape, Martin Rushent thought the demo had far more life to it, so the version that was actually released was not the version that we recorded to be used, it was the demo version.

It sounds quite plush for a demo.

Well, we did do tweaking and stuff. There's a bit before the end with the guitars where it repeats round – that was done with edits. As I said, edits were difficult to do in the days before digital recording, but Martin Rushent was very skilled at doing them. We did the edits, put new vocals on and then Martin Rushent wrote out a part for a brass section, so then we got them in and recorded that[2]. And his studio wasn't even finished at that time. The control room was ready but the studio room wasn't quite built; it wasn't fully soundproofed or anything.

'What Do You Know?' has the sound of one of your solo songs, rather than a Buzzcocks song.

It was made in the same studio where my solo stuff was made, with the same way of working – where it was just me and Martin Rushent in the studio. There was no intention of me starting a solo career at that point – it was just what it sounded like when we were working in that studio and how we put things together. It was a good way of working; I enjoyed working on my own with Martin. I mean, if you're working with a band everyone's got their own opinion on things, but if you're just working with one person and you have a good empathy, a good rapport, you can think of something and they'll come up with a way of complementing it or doing it the way you want but making it even better. It's a great experience working that way. But when you have to convince everyone else of what it is you're supposed to be doing – when you're in a band, it becomes a bit difficult.

So why were the rest of the band not there?

Martin just asked me to come along – we didn't necessarily need the others there to complete it.

I saw you perform this in Manchester in 1999. Did you have a brass section with you? It sounded great. (I was at the back and couldn't see the stage.)

For most of the shows on this tour, PT – Peter Towndrow – who was our guitar technician, played keyboards to simulate the brass. He was a friend of Tony's who used to help out sometimes. But we brought a two-piece brass section with us for the Manchester and London dates. I remember Raf, our manager, had to take the brass players back to London straight after the Manchester show.

What's that bit in the lyric that says, 'I see a boy clad in leather'? It doesn't sound like an image you'd normally get in a Buzzcocks song.

Pete registers his disappointment at the lack of support from EMI in the penultimate *Secret Public*. You can hear his disillusionment and weariness in the uncharacteristically sardonic tone.

He may have been an antichrist kind of figure. It was meant to be prophetic and revelatory.

And what about 'You only perceive what you believe'?

It's another extension of that whole theme of how we perceive and believe things, and how that shapes our world. We all believe what we believe, even if we're wrong! It was a bit like an evangelical-preacher kind of thing – 'I saw the skies open and I heard the word spoken...'

Have you ever taken lessons for your voice? It's extraordinarily powerful on this.

No – I just do all that naturally. But again, it was all done with the help of Martin Rushent. You'd think of ridiculous things to do and he'd help you accomplish it. When it was just me and Martin working together we got on very well – we understood each other.

Notes

1   Pluto Studios, on Manchester's Granby Row, was owned and run by ex-Herman's Hermit, Keith Hopwood. Famously The Smiths' first album was recorded there, as well as The Clash's 1980 single, 'Bankrobber'. Pluto lives on in deepest rural Cheshire and is now perhaps best known for title and theme music, particularly for children's films and TV programmes.

2   Steve Garvey says: 'Martin Rushent rescued "What Do You Know?" by adding the brass.'

I Look Alone

Appeared on *NME* compilation cassette, *C81*
Recorded: 1980, Advision Studios, Fitzrovia, London
Mixed: Genetic Sounds, Streatley
Released: 1981
Songwriter: Pete Shelley
Producer: Martin Rushent

Where and when was it written?

I wrote it on that holiday in Sorrento where I'd written 'Are
Everything'. It was April the 1st 1980. I remember because it was
in the days before credit cards, when you had to take enough cash
with you to last the duration. We ended up running out of money,
so I rang Richard Boon and he was supposed to be sending some
money over, so I was waiting for the postman to arrive as we were
down to our last few lire. As I was waiting the song just came.

It was meant to be 'Part 4'. The other side hadn't been written
yet – I suppose Steve was supposed to write it, as that had been
the pattern with Parts 1 to 3. There was a demo of it and Martin
Rushent and I just pieced it together from that. The handclaps
were done in the half-built studio room at Martin's. We did it and
it sounded great – but then the band split up before it could be
officially released.

It was released on cassette only?

It appeared on the *NME*'s *C81* cassette, released in association
with Rough Trade. You had to collect coupons in the *NME* and
send off for it[1]. It first appeared on vinyl and CD when *Product*
came out in 1989. We played it on the 'Flatpack' tour and the
'30' tour at the end of 2006. It's a song that works well live.

What was happening with the record company at that time? I gather things weren't going all that well.

By that time EMI had taken over United Artists and it was almost as though United Artists had become a filing cabinet of assets that they had and there was no-one that was fighting the cause.

It doesn't matter whose name is above the door of the record company – it's the people who are doing things for you inside that company that matter. And unless you have someone working for you – turning up at the meetings and arguing your case and getting the marketing budget that you need, the release schedule and things like that – then you're helpless.

So how did you get out of your contract with EMI?

When we went in to do the fourth album, Steve Garvey wanted to get a new bass amp, but we couldn't start the recording because we had no money and we had to sell Steve's existing amp before we could buy the new one. Then Martin Rushent found out we were having all these cashflow problems and that's why he suspended the recording at Pluto and suggested I come down to his studio that he was building and start working on new material. We had many meetings with EMI trying to work out a way forward where we could actually afford to operate. We even asked them if they'd like to be involved in the solo project but they were very unco-operative.

We got a second advance and by the time the second album came out we were earning royalties from the first. We left owing them money but that was covered by future royalties that we earned.

Basically we were getting no support from the label – we were just no longer flavour of the month. In the meetings we had with them there'd never be a course of action decided on, or a way to proceed. We were far removed from the people with the budgets who make things happen. It's difficult if there's no funding or interest from the record company. They were willing to carry on paying the recording fees but then nothing seemed to happen when we'd recorded anything; they didn't seem bothered whether we did anything or not. They'd heard the same stuff that Andrew Lauder had heard and been enthusiastic about but they weren't interested in it – so basically I told them to shove it. I was very heated and upset about it at the time but then I thought, 'Right, just one less thing to worry about.'

So that was it really. It was a bit like a 'Get Out of Jail Free' card. I was able to just leave – it was a weight off my shoulders. I felt that I had a career again rather than a millstone round my neck.

So what kick-started your solo career?

When we were having all the money problems in the band, Martin said to me, 'Why don't you come down to this studio I'm building? I've got a drum machine and we can work on some tracks.' So I went down there with just a 12-string guitar[2]. The first track we did was 'Maxine', then 'Homosapien'. They were used in the end as my solo tracks but they were written originally for Buzzcocks. In fact we played 'Homosapien' at Coachella festival in 2012 but there was a bit too much moaning from Steve for it to be a regular occurrence! It was asked for by the guy who runs the festival – he specifically asked for it as a condition of us playing there when our agent booked it. It went down really well – we were voted No. 7 out of the top ten acts over both weekends.

You went on to work very closely with Martin in your solo career. How did you go about formulating the songs? It must
have been different from working with the band.

When I worked with Martin on my solo stuff a lot of the songs were done from the bottom up. For example, the last two tracks on the album *XL1* were 'Twilight' and 'XL1' (named after the serial number of the record). Although I hadn't written the tracks, I had to say what they were going to be called so they could get the artwork together and get the sleeves printed. So we went in the studio one night and I wrote the two songs there and then. I hadn't had them in my head already; the whole thing was put together over just two sessions. I was committed to writing them because they were going to be printed on the track listing – I had no choice! It can be a good way of working, when you're under pressure like that.

It was always quick working with Martin because he'd mix as he went along – he'd be monitoring as if it was a mix, then when he got round to mixing he'd just make it breathe and make it full of life. You could always see where you were – at any point you could listen to it as it actually was. It was exciting working with Martin. We worked well together.

Did you and Martin work alone in the studio – no engineer or technicians?

When it was me and Martin recording at his place it was just the two of us. He did all the technical duties himself: operating the tape, engineering, etc. It created a more intimate way of working where we could bounce ideas off one another.

The last gig for Buzzcocks Mark I was in 1981...

Our last gig of all was in Hamburg in January of that year, the month that 'I Look Alone' came out; our last UK gig though had been the previous December in Bolton, which seemed fitting as that was where it'd all begun[3]. It was our Christmas show and there was quite a party atmosphere.

When we split we never had any idea we'd get back together – but then we realized we'd had something special, something really unique, and we felt we should have another go. When we re-formed, eight years had gone by and we'd all done a lot of growing up by then and had a chance to work on our solo projects – we'd had a chance to get it out of our systems[4].

And you're still going strong, all these years later.

When I was a youngster, back when we signed with United Artists, we could never have envisaged that we'd still be doing it all these years later. I mean, you don't, do you? In those days we thought people who were over 30 were old fogies – we would never have thought we'd be playing guitars in our sixties!

We've had our ups and downs since then but largely it's been good. People still seem to like us, and that's what matters at the end of the day.

Notes

1 Two coupons from the *NME* and £1.50 were all that was needed to secure your copy of the seminal *C81*, 'a free influential music cassette made to celebrate five years of independent music' – which, if you remember, Buzzcocks had kick-started. It might have been more appropriately named *C80*, as the running time was nearer to 80 minutes than 81 – and the tracks will have been recorded in 1980 for release in January 1981.

2 Martin Rushent's son James, a founding member of 21st-century dance-punk band Does It Offend You, Yeah? and a producer in his own right, says of the time when Pete recorded in the Genetic studio: 'I don't remember that much about this period; I was pretty young at the time. Dad used to tell a funny story, though, about Pete falling into a bed of nettles drunk one night and having to spend the whole rest of the day in an ice bath! I remember Pete being around the house as well; he was always a nice and polite guy. I do remember my dad showing everyone the "Telephone Operator" video and being excited about it.'

3 The last UK show for Buzzcocks was at Bolton Sports Hall on 20 December 1980, promoted by Wise Moves – presumably Alan Wise's trading name.

4 Steve Garvey says: 'We were a pretty tight band when we re-formed – we were all older, and more competent musicians.'

Something had obviously 'Gone Wrong' for Pete on this day – he could've done with a new blade but, happily, the machine wasn't broke. *C.*1981.

conclusion

What Do I Get? The Enduring Legacy

And we did, indeed, still like them.

But what came next? After the blistering years described by Pete in our conversations, when the last chord of 'I Look Alone' fell silent, what did he – and Buzzcocks – do next? Was this explosion of sound destined to fade away as the years rolled by, or would it play on into the future?

Thankfully, the answer is emphatically the latter, played on both by Pete and Buzzcocks themselves and in the way that their success shaped the musical landscape to come – in often quite surprising ways.

The band initially re-formed in 1989 with their original lineup, funded in part from royalties Pete earned from Fine Young Cannibals' rendering of 'Ever Fallen in Love'. The band's reunion was received rapturously and their 'Telling Friends' tour of the UK proved that they could still pull the crowds. They obviously still had 'it' – if 'it' is some cracking songs, a dazzling stage presence and a slightly raffish charm.

Unfortunately for Buzzcocks fans, John Maher found he didn't want to neglect his other commitments and resigned after the first UK tour – he'd built a successful business assembling specialist engines for Volkswagen Beetles used in drag racing. He had been only 21 when the band split in 1981 and his time in Buzzcocks was, for him – like other people's years in higher education – part of his ascent into adulthood but not his entire life. Maher was supplanted briefly by Mike Joyce from The Smiths, who then left to join Public Image Ltd for one album – apparently he wanted to 'keep busy' and had felt a need to fill his diary with other obligations when Buzzcocks suggested that they might want a short sabbatical. After three years Steve Garvey, too, decided that he could no longer commit to commuting between the band in London and his family in New York, so he also quit.

Buzzcocks quickly picked themselves up and dusted themselves down, however, and soon recruited drummer Phil Barker and bassist Tony Barber, two Londoners who came as a package – they had already played together in several punk ensembles and provided an exceptionally tight and cohesive rhythm section. They were also mega-fans of the band and knew all the songs not only back to front but also inside out. Pete and Steve were awed by their familiarity with the back catalogue and so snapped them up straight away.

The Shelley, Diggle, Barber and Barker lineup of Buzzcocks was the longest-lived to date. They produced five albums, with Barber as producer on three of these. These works were hailed as the natural successors to the three United Artists albums, with the band reaching a level of maturity and ease with themselves that they had not achieved in their earlier output. They had fans across the globe and toured many times in the US and as far afield as South America, Australia and Japan – audiences that had not had a chance to see the band in their first incarnation.

The Barber-Barker lineup was invited to play with many stellar acts and at many leading venues. In 1994 they were invited to support Nirvana, even then one of the biggest names in music. In 1996 they supported at the much-publicized Sex Pistols' comeback – a huge, landmark show in London's Finsbury Park. And in 2003 they played to an audience of thousands at New York's prestigious Madison Square Garden, supporting grunge trailblazers Pearl Jam.

Throughout the Nineties, Buzzcocks made more media appearances than they ever did in their first flush of fame – their segments on shows as varied as Channel 4's *Big Breakfast* and the late-night comedy show *In Bed with Medinner* demonstrating that their appeal extended beyond an audience of greying, balding ex-punks. This wider popularity saw them appear on countless soundtracks across film, TV and, more recently, video games, with particular highlights being appearances in the films *The Party Animal* and *Ghost World*, and a cover of 'Ever Fallen in Love' in *Shrek 2*. As well as featuring in the hugely popular *Guitar Heroes* video-game franchise, the band also appeared in the Marvel Comics-inspired game *Guardians of the Galaxy: The Telltale Series* with 'Why Can't I Touch It?'[1]. On TV, the bassline from 'Ever Fallen in Love' has been heard many times in the background of UK soap *EastEnders*, as though emanating through the walls of a neighbour's flat, and 'Ever Fallen in Love' also made an unlikely appearance in *The Simpsons*. Eagle-eyed viewers may also have noticed that a poster for a Buzzcocks gig was a permanent fixture on the wall near Central Perk for the duration of *Friends*. Buzzcocks' songs have also been used in numerous ad campaigns all over the world, with Pete Shelley writing a jingle especially for Pepsi in 1996[2].

Also in 1996 came what would turn out to be an enduring moment in the band's popular legacy, as their name was sequestered by comedy music panel game *Never Mind the Buzzcocks*. The show ran for 28 series on BBC and the band found that they instantly become a household name in the UK – although, risibly, less-informed members of the show's audience thought that presenter Mark Lamarr and panellist Phill Jupitus were founding members of punk's Fab Four.

Pete was frequently called upon to be a talking head on any programme discussing the history of punk and also, unexpectedly, appeared on the BBC's *Antiques Roadshow* in 1994.

In 2002 there was a short-lived musical marriage between Shelley and Devoto: the techno-infused *Buzzkunst*, which was a considerable diversion from the guitar-driven three-minute romps for which Buzzcocks are famed. It showcased their expertise with modern musical technology and demonstrated that the two still had a considerable creative chemistry.

The Barber-Barker lineup of Buzzcocks was stable from 1992 until Phil left the band in April 2006, to be followed by Tony in the summer of 2008. Danny Farrant, a versatile multi-instrumentalist who has performed with The Alarm and Spear of Destiny, as well as teaching music and appearing in orchestras and other more traditional ensembles, took over on drums; while Chris Remington, a loyal stalwart of Steve Diggle's solo band and a gifted bassist, completed the new rhythm section. The band continued to tour extensively, even playing in the newly opened-up China. They are a firm favourite at festivals, where they can find themselves playing to tens of thousands.

Buzzcocks shows continue to draw the crowds and to satisfy the critics. In 2009 the band toured with the 'Another Bites' show, where they played their first two albums back to back. And 2012 saw an even more longed-for spectacle – the 'Back to Front' show, which was in three acts: a performance by the Shelley-Diggle-Remington-Farrant team, followed by a set from the 'classic' Garvey-Maher lineup of the band and last, and most extraordinarily, a reunion of Shelley, Devoto, Diggle and Maher to perform the four tracks from *Spiral Scratch*. Despite not having played professionally for years, Maher and Garvey shone and some reviews say they stole the show.

In 2014 Buzzcocks released their ninth studio album, the long-awaited *The Way*. *The Way* was crowdfunded, with fans pledging monies that paid for the recording of the album. Pleasingly Buzzcocks were going back to their

roots – crowdfunding is the 21st-century version of the band's independent, self-financed releasing of their first record, *Spiral Scratch* and, like self-publishing, it guarantees a level of creative freedom that can be compromised when signing to a traditional record label. Although its founding members were approaching their sixties, Buzzcocks were still bucking the system.

When Pete sadly died in December 2018 it seemed momentarily as though the future of Buzzcocks, his brainchild, would be jeopardized – but at the time of writing the band are still touring, continuing valiantly without their co-creator, with Steve Diggle assuming lead vocals on all the songs.

As Buzzcocks' legacy has evolved over the decades, the band's output on United Artists has been reissued in several forms for various audiences. Their first compilation, *Singles Going Steady*, consisted of all the band's A-sides on one side of the 12-inch vinyl with all the B-sides on the other. It was released in the US in 1979 to coincide with the band's tour of America, then was released in 1981 in the UK after the import from the States had sold unexpectedly well in their native country. Hailed by the *NME* as 'the best album Buzzcocks never made' on its UK release, it has sold reliably in its various issues over the years. In 2003 it was ranked among the greats in Rolling Stone's '500 Greatest Albums of All Time'.

Singles Going Steady is revered by both fans and non-fans alike: for non-fans it crystallizes the band's oeuvre, while devotees of the band relish the experience of hearing the eight flawless A-sides, followed by the eight peerless B-sides, back to back. It seems surprising that this format, being so clever yet so obvious, has not been used by more bands over the years. (Maybe there have been few other acts whose singles and B-sides are all so consistently perfect that they stand up to this kind of showcasing.)

As with many legendary acts, compilations have been released offering fans a more complete archive, including the definitive *Product* box set – all the band's output that was recorded for United Artists, plus 'I Look Alone' – and *Inventory*, a divine collector's item of CD miniatures of all the band's singles that were recorded in the United Artists years. In 2020 a box set containing all Buzzcocks' albums and singles post-re-formation, including rarities and previously unreleased tracks, was released by Cherry Red. In a sign of their solidifying status as icons of their genre, the Buzzcocks' rereleases have sold vastly more than any of the band's original oeuvre (excluding *Singles Going Steady*).

The band have won several awards since they re-formed in 1989, perhaps the most notable being the Mojo Inspiration Award that they earned in 2006 in recognition of the countless musicians who cite them as a guiding light.

The Mojo award felt particularly fitting, since their greatest legacy is – unsurprisingly – in their music, and the impact it has had on those who followed their explosive early output.

Many ensuing artistes have been influenced by Buzzcocks. Green Day, one of the bestselling music acts of all time and certainly the most successful act to emerge from any punk genre, are usually cited as the classic example of a band that has attempted to emulate the Manchester quartet's sound, though Mike Dirnt, Green Day's bassist and co-founder, refutes this: he claims to have never heard Buzzcocks before his band was first established in 1987[3]. Bands that have more freely admitted to being inspired by Buzzcocks include REM, The White Stripes and Arcade Fire – although the latter's generous use of orchestral instruments and the lush arrangements of their 'baroque pop' might camouflage the influence of the comparatively spartan 'Orgasm Addict' or *Another Music in a Different Kitchen*.

That many listeners can instantly recognize the essence of Buzzcocks in the work of Joy Division is not surprising, given their shared background and indeed producer. Bernard

Sumner's guitar style, which relied heavily on barre chords and a distinctive kind of distortion, is similar to Buzzcocks' sound and this is most apparent in Joy Division's live recordings from the *Unknown Pleasures* period. Peter Hook's bass work draws heavily on Steve Garvey's style, particularly the lines Garvey plays on 'Walking Distance' (from the album *Love Bites*), while some of Steven Morris's drumming bears a striking similarity to John Maher's – compare the percussion on Joy Division's 'Atrocity Exhibition' to that on Buzzcocks' 'Moving Away from the Pulsebeat'. Although the lyrical themes and mood of Buzzcocks' and Joy Division's songs are very different, a talent the bands share is their versatility – illustrated by the diversity of the songs featured on each of the bands' albums. The two bands are further united by the 'industrial' nature of their sound, often mentioned by critics and other musicians but difficult to define. It has no connection with the industrial-rock sound of Nine Inch Nails and is nothing as obvious as a melancholy or bleakness, inspired by Manchester's factories and cellar dwellings (although you can hear that, too, in Joy Division); it's more akin to the 'angularity' of which Pete speaks, which is due in part to the influence of Krautrock with its subtle hint of darkness and its stark, Teutonic pragmatism.

Pete's vocal style – a peculiar combination of punk venom, rich vibrato, yodels and even yelps, all within an astonishing range – is so unique that it's difficult to bring to mind any other singers who sound quite like Pete or who even cite him as an influence. The 'Oh-ohs', though, a joint invention of Pete and Martin Rushent and a signature of many Buzzcocks' songs, have been used to good effect by The Undertones (for example on 'Listening In', from their eponymous first album) and by Paul Weller, in both his solo songs and those by The Jam – they can be heard as a pleasing embellishment to The Jam's 'When You're Young', which sadly now is little played and seldom mentioned but which made a very respectable No. 17 in the UK charts in August 1979.

Lyrically, Morrissey's themes of abandonment, yearning and disaffection have much in common with the subjects of Pete Shelley's songs ('all that "woe is me" stuff,' as Steve Garvey so succinctly puts it). Given that Morrissey was a music fan in Manchester and only slightly younger than Pete and the two Steves (and, in fact, fractionally older than John Maher), it's not hard to imagine him being influenced by Buzzcocks – who, at the time of punk, were almost certainly the most successful band in the northwestern city.

What's more surprising is that Bruce Springsteen may have been swayed by Buzzcocks' sound and attitude. Reputedly Springsteen spent a lot of time listening to Buzzcocks between the recording of his 1975 breakthrough album *Born to Run* and its 1978 follow-up, *Darkness on the Edge of Town*[4]. *Darkness* was recorded between June '77 and March '78, so Springsteen would have only been familiar with *Spiral Scratch*, 'Orgasm Addict' and possibly 'What Do I Get?'. (*Another Music in a Different Kitchen* was not released until March 1978, meaning that Springsteen would have been unlikely to have heard it while still working on *Darkness*.) The album *Born to Run* was a musical celebration of Americana but *Darkness on the Edge of Town* seems more like an elegy for the same cultural themes. Although the musical influence of punk is difficult to discern in the tracks on *Darkness*, there is indeed a previously unheard ferocity to Springsteen's lyrics on the album, with lines such as, 'Got a head-on collision/Smashin' in my guts' and 'I wanna spit in the face of these/Badlands' being as vitriolic as of any of those heard in British 1977 punk[5].

All four members of Buzzcocks in the 'classic' period were self-taught musicians and this autodidacticism was no doubt a major factor in the formulation of their unique sound. In the first fifty years of pop music, pop was considered to be ephemeral and even a flash in the pan, so anyone who wanted to learn electric guitar, bass guitar or drums would have had to save up to buy the instrument of their choice and master it themselves by playing along to their favourite records. The four Buzzcocks were also all particularly adept musicians, especially when compared to some others in the punk genre (not naming any names, of course).

By his own admission, Steve Diggle taught himself to play guitar by emulating the styles of his Sixties heroes: The Beatles, The Kinks, The Who and the Small Faces. He also borrowed from the stagecraft of The Who's Pete Townshend. The guitar sound that he and Pete Shelley created together – commonly cited by cloth-eared commentators as being *the* defining characteristic of Buzzcocks' style – has been admired and adopted by a plethora of ensuing acts. In fact it has been widely acknowledged as forming the foundation stone for the guitar sound that dominated the indie scene, starting in the Eighties and extending to the present day. (The complex relationship between Pete and Steve Diggle – at its heart fond, yet at other times as fraught as a bad marriage – may have provided both the creative tension and the closeness that allowed the two musicians to develop this method of duetting.)

It's not only Pete's and Steve's guitars that define the famous Buzzcocks sound; the other members of the band contributed equally to the pot. Bassist Steve Garvey had initially been a guitarist but switched to bass after being wooed – and wowed – by the playing of Martin Turner, bassist with folk-rock ensemble Wishbone Ash. Steve had been playing in rock covers and cabaret bands (which would perform the biggest hits of the moment – like a Pickwick Records *Top of the Pops* album come to life) in working men's and social clubs since the age of 14 and, because he'd started out as a guitarist, by his own reckoning his 'chops were good – I was a decent player'. Steve was noted for his exceptionally melodic and even intricate style – which was quite at odds with what some other punk bassists were playing (compare, for example, the bass work of Sid Vicious or Dee

Dee Ramone). Steve remembers how his sound came to be: 'Generally Pete and Steve would just be playing barre chords; they'd be strumming the same thing, so for me it was a little like playing in a 3-piece band. It was a wall of fuzz, of distorted guitars, and within that there's a lot of space, a lot of room to make melodic basslines. I tried not to "pedal": I was looking to add a little countermelody in there, add some interest. I wanted to show a bit of flair – I don't know, maybe I was a show-off! But I just did what felt natural, and nobody stopped me.'

The defining characteristics of Steve's style are his arpeggiated basslines (as can be heard in 'You Say You Don't Love Me') and his frequent use of the upper two strings of the bass – which may be common in jazz and jazz-fusion genres but were largely at odds with the simple, root-and-fifth pattern of bassline favoured by many punk bands. Again, Garvey credits Pete's and Steve's playing style with his development of the 'trebly' sound: 'The two guitars would be playing the same chords and the bass is in the barre chords, so I could play higher up.' Garvey had been influenced by the style of Andy Fraser from Free and he also admired the 'lead' sound produced by Chris Squire, bassist of prog-rock band Yes. Garvey says: 'It's true that I use the upper two strings more than other bassists, and maybe that characterizes my style – but maybe that's because I just wanted to be heard! Andy Fraser would use the upper strings a lot, then he'd switch to the lower strings for the "dynamic" – for contrast, for dramatic effect – and I think I did that a lot too, especially in the faster songs.'

Bruce Thomas of Elvis Costello's Attractions, although a decade older than Garvey, mentions Buzzcocks as an inspiration in his memoir of the Sixties and Seventies music scene, *Rough Notes*. And, of course, Peter Hook of Joy Division and New Order is famed for his exploration of the upper reaches of the bass. (Hooky says that initially this was because the amplifier he used was so trashy that he had to play high 'to be able to hear what [he] was doing' over Bernard Sumner's guitar and that later, when he began playing sequenced, synthesized bass with New Order, the more melodic, more 'lead' style suited the sound of the equipment.) Hooky's bassline in Joy Division's 'Love Will Tear Us Apart', for example, follows the melody so closely – and is played so high up on the instrument – that in orchestral terms it has more similarity with a second-violin part, written as a complement to the first violins, which 'carry the tune', than with the lower-end lines written for double bass or cello that would underpin the harmonic structure of the orchestral arrangement.

Drummer John Maher had mastered his craft in six months and, famously, was only 16 when he auditioned successfully for the band. John was a naturally talented percussionist, exceptionally accurate and yet at the same time also able to 'swing', which some more 'metronomic' drummers are unable to do (including, it's said in some quarters, one who later played briefly with Buzzcocks). A drumming expert notes that a key trait of Maher's style is his characteristic and generous use of the 'hi-hat [cymbal] before the roll'. This stylistic quirk can be heard clearly in Killing Joke's 'Pssyche' and 'Empire Song' and, as KJ were of the post-punk rather than 1977-punk era, it seems fair to assume that Paul Ferguson may have been influenced by the Manchester drummer who was only one year his senior. Killing Joke were also famed for their 'tribal' percussion sound, of which Maher was a maestro.

'Moving Away from the Pulsebeat', from Buzzcocks' debut album *Another Music in a Different Kitchen*, is the showcase for Maher's innovative style and innate skill. Although Pete's lyrics usually form the focal point of his songs, in this 5-minute-20 epic (long by punk standards) the lyric seems to be intentionally underplayed; unusually for Pete, the words make little sense, many of the phrases are hypnotic in their repetitiveness, and they seem to have been chosen for their rhythmic quality rather than for their meaning. One can't help but feel that they were written as a foil deliberately to highlight the magnificence of Maher's drumming. The percussion-only intro and the lengthy drum solo (40 seconds long) make this song one of the most powerful of Buzzcocks' live set, whichever drummer is playing them. The tribal sound was later exploited by Bow Wow Wow (Malcolm McLaren's mentees after the Pistols imploded) and it helped propel the *Kings of the Wild Frontier*-era Adam and the Ants to stratospheric popularity in the early Eighties; however, it's safe to say that 'Moving Away from the Pulsebeat' is one of the earliest recorded examples – if not *the* earliest recorded example – of the tribal beat being used in punk.

John Maher's drumming also had a considerable influence on later sub-genres of punk. The characteristic, rat-ta-*tat*-ta-tat style of percussion on 'You Tear Me Up' (from *Another Music in a Different Kitchen*) was adopted by early British hardcore punks Discharge. Discharge were formed in 1977 in the Potteries, the area around Stoke-on-Trent in England's West Midlands, where clay proliferated and which thus became a centre for the production of ceramics in the early Industrial Revolution (Discharge's own record label was called Clay). The Stoke band rose to prominence in Margaret Thatcher's Britain, from 1979 onwards, when the region's coalfields, as well as many of the pottery manufacturers themselves, were being closed down because they were considered 'unviable'. The mass unemployment these closures caused, along with other, more global concerns, such as nuclear weapons and world hunger, gave Discharge and their ilk genuine cause for outrage, which made the sneering indignation of some of the 1977 punk bands look like little more than art-school posturing. The aggressive, rapid-fire style of drumming was named D-beat after Discharge and went on to inspire an entire genre: crust punk, *kängpunk*

(Swedish for 'boot-punk') and crust-beat, as it is also known, is a globally popular subgenre of punk, with bands who represent the subspecies hailing from countries as disparate as the US, Japan, Brazil, Spain and, of course, Sweden, which is home to some of D-beat's more recent flag-bearers. D-beats are also used in some of the punk/metal crossover genres, of which there are many.

And, of course, there's Pete's own guitar style. Pete claimed at every opportunity that he couldn't call himself 'a guitarist' and he seemed to see the instrument as some kind of necessary evil that songwriters unfortunately need as a tool on which to compose. As a rather 'static' performer he may also have seen the guitar as something to hide behind while on stage – and it's worth noting that if Buzzcocks had've been like The Undertones, needing two guitarists and a singer instead of a dedicated guitarist and a guitarist/lead vocalist, Buzzcocks' pay packet would've had to be split five ways instead of four. But Barry Adamson, who played live with Buzzcocks on those few dates towards the end of 1977 and who later worked on Pete's solo album *XL1*, recognizes that Pete had his own, very distinctive style, and he describes it thus:

'Pete was very clever as a guitarist. The guitar sounds that he used defied convention – the pedals, the mixture of sound, the swirl, they achieved this hypnotic effect. It's a unique combination of aural vision, all those elements melded together so when you hear the music you can visualize the sentiment or the romantic element that he was trying to get across. The initial Buzzcocks, before Howard left, had the rawness of punk but then their sound became more refined later, maybe as a result of the addition of the second guitar. Pete wasn't a "guitarist's guitarist" – he saw his guitar as being a way to make whatever noise was necessary to express what was going on lyrically in the song. As he got more into the songwriting, the guitar became a vehicle with which to plot the song's journey. Of course, what everyone remembers, what every guitarist on the planet knows, is the solo from "Boredom". All the rhythm stops and he plays this "anti-lead" consisting of just two alternating notes – which beautifully conveys the idea in the song, the ennui, the sense of being jaded. You think it's going to finish where it seems there's a natural end, after the number of bars that the body might be expecting...and then he carries it on and makes the point even more. I think that's genius. Orange Juice, in particular, were influenced by Pete's guitar playing, as they make the homage to "Boredom" in their [1983] song "Rip It Up" – they make both the lyrical reference ("You know me, I'm acting dumb...and my favourite song's entitled 'Boredom'...") and the musical reference to the song by pastiching the two-note solo. But that's classic Pete, playing it down – when he's the guy who came up with the guitar part to "Shot by Both Sides", which everyone thinks was down to the genius of Magazine and John McGeoch.'

What greater tribute could there be to someone who didn't even consider himself to *be* a guitarist?

When Pete died in December 2018, tributes came pouring in from bands as disparate as Red Hot Chilli Peppers, Guns N' Roses, Mogwai, REM, Duran Duran and Spandau Ballet (the New Romantics of 1981, it has been conveniently forgotten, were only four years earlier wearing bondage trousers and safety pins). The influence of Buzzcocks has resonated through the musical generations – a generation in music being perhaps ten or twelve years – and now, in the first quarter of the 21st century, can be heard distinctly in pop punk and its sub-types, among other genres. Neon pop punk's Forever the Sickest Kids even have a song called 'Whoa Oh!' which has a suitably rousing, Buzzcockian chorus.

But aside from their inspiration on particular playing styles and artists, Pete Shelley's legacy, both through Buzzcocks and the perhaps surprising impact of his later solo work, was to have wider influence on the musical – and even the social – landscape.

Buzzcocks have been hailed as punk pioneers – and quite rightly so. Yet they were more than 'pioneers' – they were seers, prophets and visionaries. By inviting the Sex Pistols to play in Manchester and by billing themselves as support they precipitated an entire cascade of events that changed the face of popular culture.

Imagine, then, a parallel universe where Pete and Howard *hadn't* invited the Pistols to play those two gigs at the Lesser Free Trade Hall and themselves formed Buzzcocks as a result of witnessing one of the band's earliest shows. Without that catalyst, it's all too easy to see another reality playing out.

Punk, far from becoming a revolutionary genre, a ripping-up of the rulebook of fashion and even a way of life, may have remained a short-lived fad that would have existed only (and quickly burned itself out) in London. Buzzcocks brought punk to the provinces and the provinces to punk.

In the Seventies, the entire music-production machine in the UK operated almost exclusively from London. The A&R men (there were no A&R women in those days) didn't venture far from their home turf and they were remarkably slack at picking up on talent that existed outside the capital. Buzzcocks proved that there were vibrant music scenes and exciting acts beyond the Southeast that were worthy of the labels' attention – and financial backing. Mark E Smith, Morrissey, Peter Hook and Bernard Sumner might not have been inspired to form their own bands. There might have been no Fall, Smiths, Joy Division, New Order or any of the countless ensuing acts that cite those bands as influences.

Tony Wilson might have remained a faintly ridiculous regional TV anchor, presenting stories about a sponsored walk that a local Brownie troop was doing or about cats stuck up trees, rather than becoming the founding father of Factory Records and, after his death, the city's secular patron saint. Without Factory Records there would have been none of the post-punk bands that went on to define Manchester's industrial sound in the early Eighties. Nor, a few years later, would there have been the Happy Mondays – nor, conceivably, any of the other 'Madchester' bands that fused jangly guitars with beats from the burgeoning dance scene. And if there'd been no Factory Records or New Order there might have been no Haçienda, which revolutionized the nightclub and laid down the blueprint for the 'superclub' as we know it today. (Had there been no Haçienda, the nightclub might still be a dive bar in a dingy basement where the sticky carpets smell like stale beer, condensation drips on you from the sweaty ceiling and the toilets are constantly and inexplicably flooded.)

By extension, it's perhaps not unfair to say that the Manchester as we know it today might not have existed – the mini-Manhattan where artisanal coffee shops and vegan cafés that transform into music venues at night rub shoulders with the myriad specialist record shops; the 21st-century metropolis whose sky-scraping chrome-and-glass edifices constantly win awards and break records; and the cultural Mecca where music fans from all over the world come to pay homage to the city where so much of that heart-healing, soul-salving music originated (the Salford Lads' Club, famous for appearing on the sleeve of The Smiths' album *The Queen is Dead*, has a room whose walls are pasted with Post-It notes of scrawled tributes by devotees who have come on a musical hajj from as far afield as Finland, Israel and South Korea).

Or, imagine this. If the Devoto-fronted Buzzcocks hadn't taken the risk of borrowing to fund their own pressing of *Spiral Scratch*, it's possible that the independent-music movement in this country would never have taken off in the way it did. Many punk and post-punk bands followed Buzzcocks' lead and formed labels to put out their own records (with the 'shipping' of those records being assisted by larger organizations that were nevertheless independent from the leading distributors). By 1980 there was a dedicated UK Indie Chart, compiled from sales from privately owned and generally alternative record shops, rather than from the chains such as Woolworths and HMV (Boots the Chemist even sold records at that time in its larger branches). Many underground or niche bands chose to sign to the newly emerging independent record labels, as it meant a degree of creative freedom that the established labels would not, or could not, allow.

Indie became not just a nonconformist method of releasing and distributing records but an entire genre. Initially it strictly meant acts that were forced to self-publish as they didn't fit the commercial mould (for example, the entire late-Eighties and early-Nineties dance scene was centred around specialist independent record labels); in time, though, as the major labels began to develop their own independent offshoots to jump on the indie bandwagon, it simply came to mean guitar bands with an alternative flavour who sounded as though they *might* be signed to an independent label. Britpop in the UK and the grunge scene in the US were populated by bands on independent labels – and without the example of Buzzcocks neither might have come into fruition. Certainly there'd have been no Oasis without Buzzcocks and probably no Blur – and conceivably no Nirvana or White Stripes either.

Buzzcocks were unusual in punk in the way that they handled the subject of human relationships. Apart from a small sample of their output (namely 'Orgasm Addict', 'Oh Shit' and 'You Know You Can't Help It'), the bulk of Buzzcocks' songs were genuine, heartfelt paeans to love (or laments to love lost) – and love, it seems, is the four-letter word that was most reviled by punk. There was an honesty and freshness with which they addressed matters of the heart and they gave us a new vocabulary with which to articulate our 'natural emotions'. (Pete's complex and shifting sexuality and the frankness with which he discussed and wrote about the subject were also unique among the 1977 punk bands.)

Buzzcocks' visual appearance was especially striking during the United Artists years and, with their Mondrian shirts or when they were all dressed nattily in black, their look on stage was only fractionally less fetching than that of The Jam (at that time the smartest men in rock). Their image was wholesome and winsome, vastly at odds with some of the other protagonists in punk – it was a stark contrast, for example, to John Lydon's rotten teeth, acne and permanent sinusitis or to Sid Vicious's repugnant self-harm habit. They were the family-friendly face of punk and their frequent appearances on *Top of the Pops* captivated not just the music-loving youth but also their little brothers and sisters and even their mums and grans. So toothsome was Steve Garvey considered to be to teenage girls that he even appeared (more than once) on the cover of *My Guy*, a lurid penny-dreadful that was light on pop content but bulging with photo-stories, problem pages and tips on how to apply eyeliner and do snogging (on the front cover Garvey is pictured with a pouting and lip-glossed female model who looks, worryingly, as though she is about to tear off his shirt with her teeth). Because of their neat appearance and unaggressive stance, it's possible that the Mancunian glamour boys attracted people to punk (particularly girls) who would otherwise have been scared off – or even repulsed – by the genre.

Buzzcocks' record sleeves added to their polished presentation. They were cutting edge at the time, eye-catching yet elegant. And looking at them now it would be hard to date them; they are design classics. Buzzcocks set a precedent as picture sleeves became the norm for most punk and certainly post-punk

7-inches (before that the singles of even the biggest acts had usually appeared in plain paper outers). And Buzzcocks' sleeve art, with its clean lines, geometric shapes and vibrant colours, informed the graphic design of the Eighties. This is partly because the band's image-maker, Malcolm Garrett, went on to design seminal sleeves of the ensuing decade (for example, for Culture Club, Heaven 17 and Duran Duran), but also because he was an early and evangelizing user of computer-aided design – so those graphic designers who adopted the digital technology after him are very likely to have been influenced by his work.

Another influential element of the wider Buzzcocks world is Secret Public, a project that started life as a fan club and fanzine but has blossomed into a thriving online fan community that still exists today[6]. It took its cue from Situationist International, a global fraternity of artists, academics and other intellectuals, whose philosophical system incorporated elements of Surrealism and extreme left-wing politics and saw them carry out 'Situationist pranks' to make their subversive points. Secret Public was named after a publication by radical American theorist Ken Knabb – *The Bureau of Public Secrets*. There was one issue of a glossy, high-quality magazine-style *Secret Public* that included collages made by Jon Savage and Linder, which were of fine-art standard – they were as visually appealing, and made as valid a social commentary, as those of revered pop artist Richard Hamilton (1922–2011), though with more reference to sex, sexuality and gender roles. Linder went on to become an internationally renowned visual artist, having exhibited her feminist photographs, photo-montages and other works on paper at prestigious British galleries, as well as their equivalents in Hanover, Paris and New York. The idea for one of her more fanciful and politically mordant creations, the 'meat dress', was magpied (either intentionally or coincidentally) by Lady Gaga in 2010. Linder had a respectable career as a post-punk musician herself with her own act, Ludus, which was signed to Buzzcocks' New Hormones label. Jon Savage, meanwhile, became one of the country's most respected commentators on punk and post-punk, writing for titles such as the *Observer* newspaper, the *Face* and *Mojo* magazines and the left-leaning cultural-political *New Statesman*, while his brick-thick treatise on punk, *England's Dreaming*, is a must-have of the middle-aged person's bookshelf.

The eponymous newsletter of the fan club, meanwhile, featured all the usual content you'd expect in a fan club newsletter, including upcoming tour dates, lyrics, and interviews with and photos of the band – usually ultrahigh-contrast photocopied images that slotted easily into the 'punky' aesthetic – and contributions from fans. But, true to its punk roots, *Secret Public* was groundbreaking in many ways.

The Secret Public fan club communication attempted to dismantle the 'fourth wall' that separates performers from their audience – and bands from their fans. Pete, in particular, strove to get to know his fans and make himself accessible to them, while the other creatives involved in assembling the 'zine (notably Richard Boon), as well as Pete, were keen to 'demystify' the pop-band phenomenon.

A striking example of this is the publication of the band's accounts from their first complete year of trading when signed to United Artists, August 1977 to August 1978. The band's total expenditure was itemized and, when deducted from their income, readers could see that only £3,108 was left over – obviously worth considerably more in the Seventies than in the present day but, on the other hand, not very much for four professional musicians and their manager to live off for a year. The accounts were prefaced with the sly qualifier, 'This is, of course, private and confidential...' and concluded with the blunt assertion, 'When everyone's making the kind of money a lot of people think is being made, we'll probably not tell you.'[7]

MATTER

We could get going on one thing on some people's minds, including mine, the bands'
our accountants', bank managers' and presumably Pete Silverton's. Yes, "where does
the money go?". For what it's worth (not that much, yet) here's a summary of
Buzzcocks' first year of (professional) trade (August 77 – 78). This is, of course,
private and confidential.
INCOME totals £71560.00 (incl. 2 years' advances, radio and TV fees, gigs)

EXPENDITURE – £68452.00 (see below)

SURPLUS – £ 3108.00 (carried over to Year 2)

Expenditure

Management £5628 (3 people's wages, office, legal fees etc.)
Transport £9238 (hire, petrol etc.)
Crew   £3873 (differing numbers of people + wages)
Supports £2272 (i.e. subsidising support acts)
P.A. system £9788 (hire + purchase, always a problem)
Accommodation £7353 (hotels on tour, recording, etc.)
Stage   £2119 (equipment maintenance, lights, etc.)
Sundries £5490 (daily expenses, initiation costs)
Miscellaneous £2057 (Musicians Union subs, insurance, rehearsal)
Capital Buys £11683 (guitars, drums, amps + all)
VAT   £1894
Group   £7057 (roughly £30 per week, depending)

Total £68,452 (if my additions OK)

Excess Income – £3108

Not much at the end of the day, especially when it's already committed to being
spent tomorrow and the next day. When everyone's making the kind of money a lot of
people think is being made, we'll probably not tell you.
Anyway, all of that prose and accounting, is, I feel, hardly the sort of thing
one would expect a fanclub to be about. Well, if its inclusion is surprising, all
well and good – because surprise is an element we're looking for.
Apart from lethargy alternating with having no spare time contributing to the delay
of this bulletin, another factor was the lack of surprise we found in your response.
Not that we expected to be swamped with material or anything, just that to compile
this took a lot of time, editing, if you like, and packaging what we did receive.
Still, we're happy now, maybe you are.
On to regular fanclub areas...

pic: bridget 0243
154 Secondstone Rd.
Bethnall Green
London E2.

LOVE BATTERY

The inclusion of Buzzcocks' accounts in an early issue of *Secret Public*. They were
already baring their souls – and even their finances – to the fans.

To demonstrate his dedication to the idea of inclusion,
Pete would insist that any fans who wrote in asking for a mention
would get the recognition that they wanted. In what would have
been 1979 or 1980, Scared Stiffs had written to Pete, telling
him about their embryonic punk ensemble and requesting a
shout-out in Secret Public. They'd sent in their own fanzine –

photocopied and produced to a relatively high standard – which, along with their homemade yet convincing publicity material, gave the impression that Scared Stiffs were a group of ambitious teenagers. Little did any of the Secret Public team know that the 'band' consisted of a nine-year-old Buzzcocks enthusiast from a sedate spa town in the West Midlands on guitar and his eleven-year-old cousin on drums – a prototype White Stripes or Royal Blood. The songs were produced in the younger boy's bedroom using a system of two handheld tape recorders so that backing vocals and additional guitar could be overdubbed on to the original recording of guitar, vocals and drums. The cousins had written one original song, 'Inside the Hit Factory', which was taken from a headline that accompanied a Pete Shelley interview in *Sounds*. What seems amazing, given the youth of the two boys, is that they'd fully appreciated, understood, assimilated and repurposed many of Buzzcocks' own ideas – shunning the use of the word 'the' in the band's title and giving themselves not outrageous but quotidian pseudonyms, like Pete Shelley and Howard Devoto (the youngsters billed themselves as 'Pete and Steve Magee'). Although Scared Stiffs' admiration of Buzzcocks and their desire to be mentioned in Secret Public were genuine, their 'band' and the accompanying promotional material seem like a supreme Situationist prank. By turning some of Buzzcocks' own artistic conceits upside down and inside out and then serving them back to them gift-wrapped, they'd somehow out-Situationed the Situationists[8].

It wouldn't be unfair to say that some of the ideas behind the iconic styling of Factory Records and the label's famously maverick ethic may have been 'borrowed' from concepts first formulated by Pete, Howard, Malcolm Garrett, Jon Savage, Linder and Richard Boon. Of course Buzzcocks and their coterie knew Factory boss Tony Wilson and were on friendly terms with him. Factory was extraordinarily progressive in the way it treated its artists, never shackling them down and allowing them the creative freedom offered by few labels at the time. Factory was the most independent of independent labels, and it's hard to imagine that its unorthodox way of doing business was not inspired by the blueprint that had been laid down by New Hormones and the release of *Spiral Scratch*.

The Factory quirk of allocating all of its output and some of its chattels a catalogue number – including a poster that was produced too late to be of any use in promoting the event for which it was created (FAC1), the lawsuit filed against Factory by Martin Hannett when their working relationship broke down (FAC61), the Haçienda nightclub (FAC51), the Haçienda cat (FAC191) and even Tony Wilson's coffin after his tragically premature death in 2007 (FAC501) – was surely inspired by the UP serial numbers that were an unconventional element

An official document, sent by United Artists to record shops in advance of new single releases. It's in the company's corporate colours, brown ink on cream paper.

of Malcolm Garrett's designs for Buzzcocks' singles and album sleeves. And the sans-serif typefaces, vivid hues and bold blocks and stripes favoured by Factory were also strikingly similar to those first used on Buzzcocks records and promotional material. (Peter Saville, Factory's designer and one of the label's co-founders, attended Manchester Polytechnic at the same time as Buzzcocks' graphics guru – they even went to the same grammar school – and Saville has openly acknowledged the fact that he was influenced and even encouraged in his early endeavours by Malcolm Garrett.)

Situationism was a considerable inspiration for many of Wilson's ideas for Factory, as it had been for Buzzcocks' Secret Public and the formation of New Hormones – the Haçienda nightclub was named after a phrase in *Formulary for a New Urbanism*, a Situationist work on the subject of psycho-geography, a study of how urban environments might affect the emotions and behaviour of the individual citizen. It would be unfair to the Cambridge-educated Wilson to assume that he'd only learned Situationist concepts secondhand from Boon, Savage et al – but it's a gratifying coincidence that the philosophy that informed some of Buzzcocks' creative principles also inspired the ethos of the greatest and most iconic brand to emerge from – in fact to jump-start – the entire independent record-label movement.

Although Buzzcocks' influence on other guitar bands has been widely acknowledged, Pete Shelley's own effect on electronic music has been somewhat less discussed – along with the contribution of his solo output to the breaking down of social barriers of sexuality and gender.

Pete's first single, 'Homosapien', and the album of the same name, were illustrious examples of the electronic music that came to epitomize the early Eighties. The single was released in 1981, the year that synth-pop 'broke' in Britain; it was the year that Depeche Mode, Soft Cell, ABC, Duran Duran and the Foxx-less, Midge Ure-fronted Ultravox all had their breakthrough records.

Long-time Buzzcocks producer Martin Rushent had been alerted to the potential of synthesizers by a quirk of fate: he had taken an office nextdoor to the Blitz club in Covent Garden and became acquainted with Steve Strange and Rusty Egan, host and DJ respectively of the club's flagship night and also founding members of New Romantic poster-boys Visage. Rushent had received funding from Radar Records, an offshoot of Warner fronted by Andrew Lauder, the A&R man who had signed Buzzcocks, and Martin Davis, also formerly of United Artists (handily Rushent's office was on the top floor of 60 Parker Street, which also housed the offices of Radar Records⁹). With the funding, Rushent equipped his studio with the latest equipment from Roland, including the MC8 MicroComposer (an early sequencer) and System 700 and Jupiter-4 (analogue synthesizers), plus the Synclavier and Fairlight CMI (early digital synthesizers, capable of sampling). Rushent 'sat in' on the recording sessions of Visage's self-titled debut album, though Midge Ure and the band are credited with the actual production (Barry Adamson and John McGeoch, bassist and guitarist with Howard Devoto's Magazine, played on some of the tracks). Rusty Egan, Visage's drummer, says that when the Visage musicians turned up at Rushent's Genetic Sound with their various items of electronic equipment but no drum kit, the veteran producer was amazed – he had 'never seen this type of recording'. He quickly became acquainted with the new technology, though, and was fully au fait with it when the recording of *Homosapien* started in February 1981.

Initially the songs on the album *Homosapien* had been intended as demos for Buzzcocks' songs. They were sent for consideration to Virgin as well as Island, who agreed to sign

Pete as a solo artist. Simon Draper, one of the founders of Virgin and responsible for the label's marketing and A&R, had heard the tapes and was particularly impressed by the drum effects that Rushent had achieved – he thought they could add some 'punch' to The Human League's latest offerings, the demos of which he felt were lacking a certain something. Later that year Rushent produced Human League's third album, *Dare*, which spawned the award-winning and epoch-making single, 'Don't You Want Me', at Genetic. Some of the electronic musical equipment that Pete had bought in 1980 was used during the making of the album, including the Linn LM-1 drum machine, and tricks and techniques that Rushent had developed when working with Pete will have been used in the recording. *Dare* was considered such a masterpiece of production that Rushent received the 1982 Brit Award as Best Producer in recognition of his contribution to the triple-platinum-selling disc – but he had honed the sequencing and programming skills that Human League's Phil Oakey (allegedly) reluctantly came to admire only earlier that same year, when recording *Homosapien*.

Barry Adamson played bass on Pete's second solo album, *XL1* (released in 1983), and he describes the creative process between him, Martin Rushent and Pete thus: 'Martin Rushent was really "out there" – he tried to bring an almost experimental leaning to the production. Take a song like "Telephone Operator" – Pete would just strum it on the guitar and the three of us would turn it into an electronic semi-masterpiece. Martin Rushent had a way about him, as evidenced with the other bands that he had hits with, and so applying that technique to Pete made for a really interesting result. The Fairlight was used on *XL1* – a digital/analogue sampler/synthesizer, a very special machine. It was temperamental but you could get sounds on there that you couldn't otherwise get – it would turn basic arrangements into something from somewhere else. Of course, Pete could write a song standing on his head but Martin Rushent could get them sounding a certain way that was very different from Buzzcocks.'

Pete's debut solo single was considered such a paradigm of the new genre that Neil Tennant, the then assistant editor of teeny-bop music mag *Smash Hits*, used it as a template for the music that he was aspiring to create. He and keyboardist Chris Lowe attempted to reverse-engineer the single 'Homosapien', experimenting with the marriage of synthesizers and guitars, until they achieved the sound that Tennant had envisaged in his mind's ear. Pet Shop Boys went on to sell well in excess of 100 million records and have earned accolades such as the Brit Award for Outstanding Contribution to Music and the *NME*'s 'Godlike Genius' Award. Pete Shelley was personally friendly with the pair and in the mid-Eighties they shared the same producer: the prolific and versatile Stephen Hague produced Pete Shelley's third album, *Heaven and the Sea*, as well as Pet Shop Boys' first two albums, *Please* and *Actually* (Martin Rushent had retired from the music business temporarily to devote time to raising his family and this is why he didn't produce Pete's final solo offering).

Vestiges of *Homosapien* can be discerned even in the electronic dance music of today: Aphex Twin and The Chemical Brothers are enthusiastic champions of the old analogue Roland System 700, while Orbital, Moby and Future Sound of London have all recorded using the original Roland Jupiter-8 (the 1981 successor to the Jupiter-4). The Linn LM-1 had its limitations and the physical hardware has been rendered obsolete by superior products; however, its signature sounds live on in the form of easily downloadable samples and plug-ins (additional software components for digital audio workstations), with the computerized handclap being an instantly recognizable, telltale feature of the Eighties drum machine.

But beyond the musical influence of the single 'Homosapien', it's also fascinating to note the social role played by the song:

an explicitly gay love serenade that was a dance-floor smash, although it never made it into the UK Singles Chart.

The single 'Homosapien' reached No. 4 and No. 6 respectively in the Australian and Canadian charts and No. 14 in the specialist US dance charts (the 12-inch version may have sold better than the 7-inch, as the longer 'dub' mixes better lend themselves to 'getting into the groove' when under the influence of drugs, particularly MDMA, which was already gaining popularity on the Western world's club scene). In the two Commonwealth nations it was probably bought by members of the gay community and revellers who frequented the countries' cosmopolitan nightclubs, rather than by the punk or younger listenership that had bought Buzzcocks records. The song's popularity would have been boosted by radio airplay on the more adventurous college and independent stations, which was also taken into account when compiling the charts in those countries.

In the UK, however, the picture was different – the single was banned from being played on the BBC and is one of the few songs to have never benefited from such a ban. Although Pete spoke with some levity about the ban, judging by the performance of 'Homosapien' in other territories, it would have made a respectable impression in the UK Singles Chart had it not been for the prohibition; the BBC, even today, is the main influence on the success or otherwise of singles in the country.

The ban now seems unjustifiably draconian and nonsensical – there is no overt mention of sex or sexuality in the song and certainly no obscenity or words that could be considered offensive. With our 21st-century mores and more accommodating attitudes, we view the BBC's historical antagonism towards homosexuality as grossly reactionary and outrageously hypocritical. In 1981 the flouncing, limp-wristed Gloria in the BBC's Second World War sitcom *It Ain't Half Hot Mum* and the mincing, simpering Mr Humphries in the channel's department-store comedy series *Are You Being Served?*, with his catchphrase suggesting sexual availability ('I'm free...!'), were considered to be figures of harmless fun and appropriate for viewing by all the family. Yet a beautiful, heartfelt musical tribute sung by one man to another was deemed so loathsome it couldn't be given airtime even after the 9pm watershed – while the continuous, unambiguous and base jokes about Mrs Slocombe's 'pussy' in *Are You Being Served?*, aired in the early evening, were also judged to be wholesome family fare. The BBC and the people who staff it now are considerably more enlightened than they were in the Eighties – in fact the BBC is a paragon of liberalism and no doubt the broadcaster's current censors would perceive the banning of a record, solely on the fact that it was a paean to non-hetero passion, as abhorrent – and totally at odds with Lord Reith's vision of 'universality' for the corporation.

'Homosapien' sums up the prevailing attitudes at the time with the line, 'And the world is so wrong that I hope that we'll be strong enough...' It has become, albeit unintentionally, an anthem of gay pride and solidarity, although it makes no direct reference to homosexuality and is in no way strident, tub-thumping or even expressly political. Quite simply the poetry of the lyric and the absolute sincerity of the sentiment make their own case in the defence of same-sex love.

As has been discussed in the body of this book, Pete was a committed technophile and a user of the earliest computers – something that his solo career allowed him to explore even further. When his album *XL1* was released in 1983, the code for the ZX Spectrum home computer that was included with it was considered so ahead of its time that it got a write-up not only in many music and computer magazines but also in the American publication *Newsweek* and the prestigious UK-based *New Scientist*. The visuals created by this program can now be seen on YouTube. Not only is it a pleasing artefact in itself, it also forms a valuable historical document of early computer graphics and nascent home computer programming.

Pete was not just a proponent of the emergent hardware and software; he was also a pioneer of the internet. He had created a website of his own lyrics as early as 1994, a time when few of us had even *heard* of the internet, let alone could imagine what it was or what it could do – the web was only in common use by academic and government institutions, and there weren't even many businesses that had a web presence or were routinely using email at this time. The domain name buzzcocks.com was registered in 1995 and the earliest incarnation of the site was created in 1996 by John P Lennon, who was a student at a university and thus had access to the internet.

Buzzcocks.com was a trailblazing example of a particularly well-designed, informative and easily navigable website. A message board/mailing list was set up so that fans could receive news about the band and also communicate with each other and there was also a 'swap shop' where fans could post about buying, selling or trading memorabilia[10].

Pete's vision for the internet, for what it could be, has now come into fruition. Nearly everyone has or can get access to the web, right across the globe. It's a forum where individuals with even the most minority interests can connect and communicate. And it's a place where people can create and, more importantly, share their creations – YouTube, for example, is a godsend for amateur musicians and wannabe performers, who can be heard and watched by people all over the world without having to battle to get signed to a record label or to go to the trouble of financing, pressing and distributing their own vinyl record. The internet embodies the DIY ethos that engendered *Spiral Scratch*.

Pete was also a big fan of giving stuff away – he never sought to monetize the web. He was more excited about the enrichment it could provide in cultural terms, and this dream of his, too, has been realized, with a lot of content on the internet available for free and even cultural consumables that you have to pay for being considerably cheaper than their analogue equivalents – individual songs can be bought online for what a 7-inch single cost in the early Eighties.

Pete *loved* the internet – he loved how it connected people, as well as what it could do for Buzzcocks; and his love of the web, as well as his love of tech in general, is one of the things that defined him. The 'network of networks', which had already been hypothesized and which he may have been fantasizing about when he was working at the National Coal Board in the mid-Seventies, helped keep him in contact with his fans, apart from anything else, and this was one of his greatest pleasures.

In the months after Pete died, many commentators likened Buzzcocks to a latter-day Beatles. Buzzcocks, like The Beatles, were a four-piece combo with two guitarists, two chief songwriters and two frontmen who shared lead-singer duties. Like The Beatles, they had a very fetching visual image – but in Buzzcocks' case this was complemented by the classy and dateless design of their record sleeves, which make some of The Beatles' ones look a little unsophisticated by comparison (and very much of their time). Like that of The Beatles, Buzzcocks' music has provided inspiration for many young aspiring musicians and songwriters – but Buzzcocks also demonstrated that you can 'do it yourself', at least at the start of your career, and by releasing their own debut independently they were among the first 'democratizers' of popular music.

Like those of The Beatles, Buzzcocks' songs embody three-minute pop-perfection with irresistibly singalong hooks, heavenly harmonies and unforgettable riffs, often delivered with a generous helping of dry northern drollery. And as with the Scouse Fab Four, the Punk Fab Four's songs define an era and yet simultaneously they are timeless – in fact, one might argue, they are *more* timeless than those of The Beatles, as they contain fewer lyrical references that can be dated and no faddish instrumentation such as sitars or tablas. Furthermore, the majority of Buzzcocks' songs are written as though by someone of unspecified gender and sexuality, to or about a subject of indeterminate gender and sexuality – and in this way Buzzcocks' songs are more universal and inclusive than The Beatles' songs, which are all written exclusively from the heterosexual-male perspective.

What, then, was Buzzcocks' legacy?

They created superlative songs that brought joy and solace to millions and they changed the cultural landscape for good – and for the good.

That's it.

The blue plaque, awarded by Wigan Council in 2020, on Pete's childhood home in Pennington, Leigh.

Notes

1 This unassuming B-side has been a firm favourite of music supervisors across all media in the first decades of the 21st century.

2 At 30 seconds long, it apparently sounds 'more like Buzzcocks than Buzzcocks'. It's hoped that one day it will surface as a modern-day bootleg on YouTube.

3 Given the popularity of Buzzcocks in the US and among punks worldwide, it seems highly unlikely that Dirnt would never have heard 'Ever Fallen in Love' or 'Orgasm Addict'. Maybe what he means is that he'd never actively *listened* to Buzzcocks' records.

4 'I loved those early Buzzcocks records, all The Clash records, the singles. Because you couldn't get the records you had to try to go and get the singles,' Springsteen told Elvis Costello on TV's *Spectacle* show in 2009.

5 The blue-collar Freehold, New Jersey, where Springsteen grew up, with its commerce and industry that had flourished in the 19th century, but were in rapid decline during Springsteen's youth, and the town's heritage of African-American Civil Rights and other political activism, had many similarities to the working-class Britain of the mid- to late 1970s – and, more pertinently, to Manchester at that time, as England's textile-manufacturing titan made the painful transition from industrial to post-industrial city.

6 Pete himself used to 'lurk' on the Secret Public message board, reading all the fans' posts but rarely contributing. Could there be a higher recommendation for a fan site?

7 It's probably true to say that Buzzcocks *never* made the kind of money a lot of people thought they did. The handful of fans at each gig in the band's later years who'd ask the merch-seller if they could have a free T-shirt – presumably because they thought that Pete Shelley, like Virgin's Richard Branson, owned his own Caribbean island and that Steve Diggle flew the band and the crew to the show in his own airliner, like Bruce Dickinson of Iron Maiden – would have been surprised had they seen the guys buying their Ginsters' pasties at the motorway services on the way to the show and stowing any leftover jars of Marmite or peanut butter from the dressing-room refreshments in their backpacks at the end of the night.

8 As an adult, that nine-year-old recording artiste and producer ended up working in the entertainment industry and, in his professional capacity, realized his dream of actually working with Buzzcocks – but he never told Pete the secret backstory to Scared Stiffs.

9 Malcolm Garrett says: 'I shared this space (along with my drawing board) with Martin Rushent. It had earlier been the studio of Barney Bubbles, the in-house graphic designer for Stiff Records. The entrance to No. 60 was adjacent to the fire exit at the back of Blitz, the main entrance of which was the opposite side of the building in Great Queen Street.'

10 This was actually Tony Barber's idea, and the service thrived until it was eventually superseded by eBay as the global auction site became more popular.

A mature Pete captured in Sedgefield, County Durham, in 2017.

PLAYTHING NO 2

3P

Whenever someone talks about the NEW WAVE they mean the 'new

wave' of music & musicians that have emerged & influenced the
scene in the last two years. The only new wave is in music.
It has succeeded & failed. Succeeded with a reapraisal of the
ideas, aims, & philosophies of a new set of musicians and of
audiences. It failed by our lack to separate the wheat from
the chaf and thinking that one battle wins the war.
The succees is due to action - the failiure due to apathy.
One wave does not make much headway headway up the beach.
If the tide is to turn then one wave must be followed by
another and so on until the six cliffs start to crumble.
This is just the new wave of the turning tide. The next wave
will start from where this one has finnished. So don't slacken
off now, but slip into a higher gear. There still is a lot more
we can do.
     The NEW WAVE is not just about music. It is a challenge to
Consider every thing you do,think, and feel. For some it has
meant a change in fashion and in life style. But most of the
fashion has become cliched and most of the groups have even now
become boring old farts future tax exiles and full of crap such
as saying " I don't want to hear about politics, I just want to
have a good time. It's only rock & roll." But it's not only
rock & roll! If it was then what is all the fuss about it?
Politics is people & people is YOU
I'm not on about party politics not the NF or The Tories. I'm
talking about PERSONAL politics. The way that you react to the
people around you. The ways that you love them, fuck them, hate it
them, slate them. Things like love, jealousy, hate, anger, sex ...
How often do you do some thing to some one & not know why you
did it?
     The NEW WAVE is like a spring clean. You were prepared to throw
out the rubbish in your wardrobe and your record collection.
So why not chuck out all the prides & predu prejudices clutter-
ing up your personality????
     Just think about how you react with other people.
     I'll write more when I think of what to say.

This is all I could think
of. Keep the new wave
NEW. *Pete Shelley*

Pete's own sporadically produced 'zine *Plaything*, 1978.

Index

Acknowledgements

Kid; Howard Lycett and Pete's family; John Maher; Steve Garvey; Barry Adamson; Rusty Egan; Richard Boon; Linder Sterling; Steve White; Seb Matthes and Wigan Council Archives Service for use of photos; Abigail Ward at Manchester Digital Music Archive; Dan Mothers for musical consultancy; Kevin Mann for drumming consultancy; John P Lennon and Joey Headen; Elsa and Ed Stringfellow; Sandra Coxhill; Michael Pollard; Paul Lally, Krishna Stott and the Pete Shelley Memorial Campaign; Kevin Pocklington at The North Literary Agency; Joe, Leanne, Jonathan and the team at Octopus; Tony Barber and all Buzzcocks past and present.

Thanks also to all the Buzzcocks fans who contributed in one way or another to this book.

Special thanks to Francis Dale for Buzzcocks consultancy and photos and Peter Hough (always 'Carlos' to me) for general consultancy and wise counsel.